Alice Morrison was born in Edinburgh, but grew up in Africa before studying Arabic and Turkish at Edinburgh University. After a career in journalism, working for the BBC and as CEO of Vision+Media, Alice then cycled from Cairo to Cape Town and entered the Marathon Des Sables. She moved to Morocco in 2014 and presented her first TV series, *From Morocco to Timbuktu*, on BBC Two in May 2017.

ALICE MORRISON

Adventures in Morocco

FROM THE SOUKS TO THE SAHARA

SIMON &
SCHUSTER

London · New York · Sydney · Toronto · New Delhi

A CBS COMPANY

First published in Great Britain by Simon & Schuster UK Ltd, 2019
This edition published in Great Britain by Simon & Schuster UK Ltd, 2020
A CBS COMPANY

1 3 5 7 9 10 8 6 4 2

Simon & Schuster UK Ltd
1st Floor
222 Gray's Inn Road
London WC1X 8HB

www.simonandschuster.co.uk
www.simonandschuster.com.au
www.simonandschuster.co.in

Simon & Schuster Australia, Sydney
Simon & Schuster India, New Delhi

A CIP catalogue record for this book
is available from the British Library.

Paperback ISBN: 978-1-4711-7427-8
eBook ISBN: 978-1-4711-7426-1

Typeset in Bembo by M Rules
Printed and bound by CPI Group (UK) Ltd, Croydon, CR0 4YY

This book is dedicated to my beloved parents, Jim and Fredi Morrison, and to my friend Charlie Shepherd.

Contents

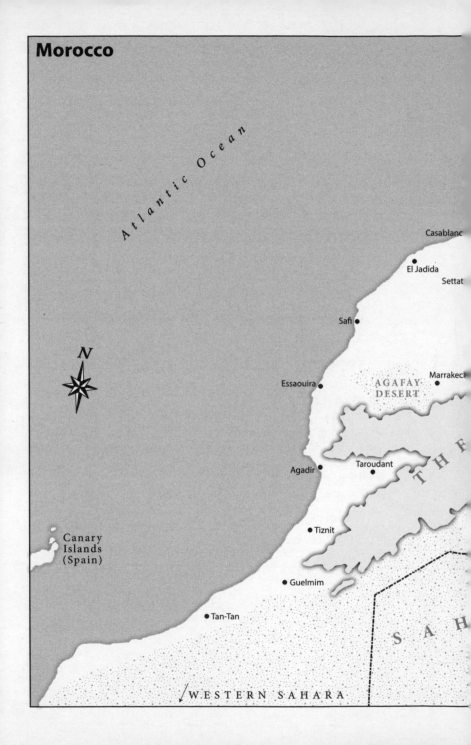

Morocco

Atlantic Ocean

Casablanc

El Jadida

Settat

Safi

AGAFAY
DESERT

Marrakec

Essaouira

T H F

Agadir

Taroudant

N

Tiznit

Canary
Islands
(Spain)

Guelmim

Tan-Tan

S A H

WESTERN SAHARA

ACKNOWLEDGEMENTS

It is so lovely to have a space to be able to thank people. First on the list is Ian Marshall, my publisher at Simon & Schuster, for being so supportive and encouraging and making me laugh too. Thanks, also, to Rachel Conway at Georgina Capel Associates for all of her work on my behalf – can't wait for China! Thank you to Fran Jessop for her careful editing, and I apologise for my reckless use of the comma. Thank you to Tanya Woolf and Robbie Morrison who, by reading and editing my previous books, helped me get to this one. Mrs Godden was my English teacher at school and I still think of her advice – thank you Mrs Godden. My deepest gratitude to all the people in Morocco who have made my life here so rich – and full of colour and joy – and who have given me an enduring love for this magical country. I am so grateful. *Shukran lakum!* Finally, it was Charlie Shepherd of Epic Morocco who got me to sign up for the Marathon des Sables, helped me find my feet in Marrakech and offered me unstinting friendship. We have had many adventures together and I hope for many more.

PROLOGUE

'Oh no,' said my mum when I told her the title of my book, 'you can't call it that, people will think it's a porn novel.' Many apologies to any of you who have picked up this book hoping for lots of sex, you are about to be sadly disappointed, although I am going to start with virgins and a libidinous king. *One Thousand and One Nights* is one of the most famous works of Middle Eastern literature. It tells of King Shahryar, who, devastated at finding out his wife had been unfaithful, vowed to marry a virgin every night, killing her at dawn to avoid a recurrence. Eventually, he'd worked his way through all the virgins in the land until the only one left was the vizier's daughter, Scheherazade. A clever girl, she spun him a tale each night, leaving the cliffhanger for dawn so he would spare her. 'Ali Baba and the Forty Thieves', 'Aladdin and the Enchanted Lamp' and Sindbad all came from these stories.

As a child, living in Dubai, we had *One Thousand and One Nights* on audio cassette (remember those?) read by actors with velvet voices and interspersed with Rimsky-Korsakov's score. We sometimes listened camping on the beach at Ras Al Khaimah with the air still hot from the day's desert sun and the stars bright above us in the blackened sky.

When I started writing this book, I had lived in Morocco for just over 1001 nights and accumulated as many stories about this wonderful country, so it seemed an appropriate title, also fitting the diversity of the peoples and places I am taking you to on this journey. From the vibrant spice markets of Marrakech to the winding medieval alleys of Fez, over the high, snowy passes of the Atlas Mountains and into the heart of the Sahara desert – the ultimate wilderness – I want to share the glory of the different environments and landscapes that have been my home for the past 1001 days and – of course – nights.

These are my stories, so you will find a lot of me in them, or at least Morocco as seen and understood through my eyes. I have included the history I have encountered along the way, although it is definitely my interpretation of it as it applies to what I see and not an academic analysis – any errors are my own. I've written about some of the big adventures I have had in Morocco, they are things that not everyone will get to do, but they are exciting and got me to places that are not always easy to reach.

I also want to introduce you to my Ali Babas, Aladdins and Sindbads as well as Fatimas, Laylas and Khadijahs, because it is the people of Morocco that have made it such a magical experience. I have been welcomed and taken into the heart of families everywhere I have been and allowed to share their lives a little. Too much sugar-laden mint tea and Friday couscous may have made me fat, but the stories have been worth it.

Finally, I want to pass on some of my most useful tips for visiting Morocco itself and a Muslim and African culture. It is knowledge that has come from funny, fabulous, difficult and sometimes bewildering experiences.

For you, the reader, I hope that you laugh a lot and learn some new things; that you find some handy tips if you want to come for a holiday or to live; and, most of all, that my love for this soul-enriching country rubs off on you a little. Who knows, you may even be inspired to come and visit if you haven't already.

Once upon a time . . .

1

MARRAKECH

It is the smell that hits you first; a heady mixture of horse pee, charcoal smoke and perfume from a thousand warm bodies. Then it is the noise, the rhythm of drums and castanets, shouts of 'orange juice, orange juice, orange juice', the bells from the horse-drawn carriages and the shrieks of excited children as they watch street boys launch neon stingers high into the air. Hollywood couldn't make up Jemaa El Fna, the main square of Marrakech: it is Africa, the Orient, magical and mythical but at the same time very, very real. It is also the centre of the city and the country that I had arrived in, expecting to stay for four months, but which has grabbed me and won't let go. It's four years and counting.

When I left the mists of England's Peak District on 2 January 2014 with just one suitcase and the scribbled-down address of my new flatshare in Semlalia, my overwhelming thought was, *What on earth are you doing, you insane woman?*

Why are you blowing up your very nice life once again? I had been persuaded to sign up to run the Marathon des Sables, the toughest footrace on earth, six marathons in six days across the Sahara, and I was coming to Morocco to train for it. I was actually going to do this crazy thing.

Charlie Shepherd – friend, founder of adventure company Epic Morocco, expert on all things Moroccan, running and cycling – has a lot to answer for. 'Go on,' he had said the summer before, catching me at a weak moment when he had just made me cycle up a very large hill, 'I'm going to do it, sign up with me. You can do it. You are good at endurance. If you can cycle from Cairo to Cape Town, you can run across the Sahara. It isn't going to be that hard.'

'But I can't run,' I said, which I felt was an important point, given that we were talking about a 156-mile race across sand in temperatures of over 50°C.

'No problem,' said Charlie. 'You have a good head, which is the main thing.' At this stage, with hindsight, I know that I should have looked at his physique – wiry, athletic, fit – and then mine – none of the above – and said no. But he is a very persuasive person and I found myself believing him. Next thing I knew I was signed up and panting up hill and down dale in the rain and mud round my home in Hayfield with my running partner, Naomi, and Billy the Running Dog.

As it turned out, that was excellent training, but I wanted to give myself the best possible chance of completing the race (alive) and so I took the decision to rent out my house, pack up my cat, and take myself off to Morocco to run in the sun. It helped that I could do my job – writing, social media and media training – from anywhere, and it also helped that I had studied Arabic at university and had lived around Africa and the Middle East. I was looking forward to using my rusty language again and being in all the warmth and hospitality of an Islamic culture.

Three hours and twenty minutes from Manchester airport and I was taxiing into a different world. From the plane, I could see the snow-capped peaks of the Atlas Mountains giving way to the red plains around Marrakech, dotted with spots of green oases and little adobe-built villages. Then, the twenty-first century starts to intrude as you fly over swimming pools and golf courses, banking up for your first sight of the medina, the old walled town, and the famous red rose clay of the city.

Marrakech is not the capital of Morocco, but for me it really is its heart. It is called many things, including the Rose City and the Daughter of the Desert, and it positively oozes romance. It sits on the fringes of the Agafay desert and you can taste that desert in the air, but at the same time, on a clear day, you can see the blue Atlas Mountains in the distance, tipped with snow. It is called the Rose City because it is obligatory to paint your house to match the ancient mud-built houses of the medina. The clay, which originally came from the surrounding plains and mountains, is a rosy-coloured terracotta. Now, of course, most people build in concrete because it is so much cheaper, but the rose-paint rule means that the city still retains its character.

It could equally be called the Rose City, though, for the number of roses growing along the boulevards and in the gardens. A happy meeting of an excellent climate and rich soil means that roses flourish here and are crammed into every tiny corner of soil, dominating the green spaces of the boulevards. They are tended by mainly female gardeners, who you will see early in the morning, bent double, weeding and pruning, bundled up in layers of clothes to keep the cold, and then the sun, out. The first time I passed a group of them I thought something really odd was going on, as they all seemed to be talking to themselves. I wondered if maybe they were taking part in some kind of community scheme for people with mental difficulties and was silently congratulating the Moroccan government on its forward-looking mental health programmes, until I realised that they all had mobile phones tucked into their headscarves.

The medina is a warren of alleyways and tunnels, punctuated by ancient wooden doors, behind which are hidden many-roomed riads, homes built around courtyards, often housing fully grown palm trees and laced with neon-bright bougainvillea. Each riad is different. One thing they all have in common, though, is that you can't believe that something so lovely lies behind an often-unprepossessing door in a dingy alley. Before I arrived in Marrakech, I had imagined myself living in one in the centre of the ancient city. This dream was fuelled by the first place I ever stayed in in Marrakech and which remains one of my favourites. It is called Riad Samsara and is owned by a long-time Swiss resident of Morocco, Jacqueline Brandt.

Riad Samsara is at the far end of the medina, near Bab Taghazout. Finding it is typically difficult. The instructions go something like this: 'You will see a large parking space with sausage sellers. Here, go through the Bab [Bab means gate] and you will pass the mosque on your right. Keep going under the arch past the vegetables and the doughnut stalls.' (Obviously, it is very difficult to pass a hot doughnut stall where they cook those golden rings in front of you and then dip them in sugar without stopping to buy either one of the huge wagon-wheel ones, or a punnet of little, fragrant nuggets. I wonder if this is one of the reasons I like Riad Samsara so much?) 'Carry on and then take the second alleyway on the right and continue until you see the big door on the right. If you get lost just ask anyone for Chez Jacqueline.' The first time I went, I did a lot of asking and eventually paid a little boy 10 dirhams (80p) just to show me where it was and wheel my wheelie bag. My top tip for finding your way round the medina is not to stress about finding things but just to ask and, if necessary, tip someone 10–20 dirhams to guide you.

Stepping through that door was like stepping through the looking glass. It opens out to an ornately tiled courtyard with a marble fountain in the middle, strewn with rose petals. Outside is a cacophony of noise, but inside all you can hear is the song of the birds nesting in the orange trees of the courtyard. Pink bougainvillea and scented jasmine crawl up the walls to the carved wooden balconies that overreach the courtyard. Each room is different, but the grandest is the Hibiscus room. The double bed is so big that I can lie across it without reaching the edges and, if I get bored, I can always repose on the red velvet sofa and look at the art-filled walls. Jacqueline is a collector and has artefacts and antiques in every corner, a family of leather giraffes on a stone-built fireplace, a group of clay musicians on a painted bedside table. But it is the bathroom that really wows you. Burgundy marble on a massive scale and a bath so big you can actually swim in it.

My experience at Riad Samsara notwithstanding, I had decided that for living purposes I wanted the open spaces and easier life of the New Town. Medina life is a very specific thing. You have to be ready to share all you do with your neighbours, who will take a keen interest in your comings and goings. Much of it is only accessible by foot, which makes going in and coming out a thought, and your weekly food shop an impossibility. And, finally, little motorbikes or scooters, called motos here, are a ubiquitous menace, not just a nuisance. They race through the narrowest of streets at 100 miles an hour and if you don't get out of the way, they will mow you down. I have seen a woman in her seventies with big bags of shopping knocked sideways by two spotty teenagers. She ended up turtle-like on her back, her pantalooned legs waving in the air, surrounded by escaping tomatoes and courgettes. I, and everyone else, rushed to help her, save the vegetables, and castigate the spotty youths. Although they were not nearly apologetic enough, in my opinion.

Motos were the final nail in my coffin with regards to any medina aspirations I may have had and so I put up a message on the Expats in Marrakech Facebook page asking for a flatshare in the new town. My call was answered and the universe sent me Alex Stein, a young American woman who was setting up a charitable arm of a large agricultural company in the south but whose base was in Marrakech. Her three-bedroomed flat with a garden was in Sakia El Hamra, Semlalia.

I was to be very happy in the flat but that first night was grim. Alex wasn't there so I arrived in the dark to a chilly, echoing, bare flat. January is cold in Marrakech, where the houses are not designed for winter, and I was very happy that I had packed my hot-water bottle. Alex had bought me a bed and a duvet and pillows, so I was set for the night. But as I switched off my solitary, glaring light bulb and clambered under the covers, I wondered again what on earth I was doing.

The next day things got better. Charlie arrived with a bike for me so I could get around the city, I ate breakfast in the garden in the sunshine, including a mandarin picked from our mandarin tree, and Alex arrived.

'Hellooooo,' was followed by taptapping boot steps as she swirled into the flat dressed in a fantastically cool khaki cape with epaulettes, chunky military-style boots, masses of curly hair and a bright smile. Leaving my home and my friends and family had been a big step, but the minute I met Alex I knew that with her and Charlie I was going to be fine. I also knew that, between the pair of them, I had my very own Google of Morocco advice. First on my list was to furnish my room so that I felt a little less like I was living in Stalag 17. 'Bab El Khamis is what you need for any furniture. It's the local flea market,' said Alex. 'Then the medina for all your other stuff.'

Whether you are a shopaholic or a shopaphobic, shopping in Morocco is an experience not to be missed. Don't worry if you hate shopping at home, doing it here bears no resemblance. Shopping is actually a fantastic way to meet and interact with Moroccans and to learn some basic truths about Moroccan culture and society. But beware, you need to go into it well-rested, well-fed, well-hydrated and with comfortable shoes on – so far, so like a 10-kilometre run – and pace yourself, definitely pace yourself.

There is a Moroccan saying: 'You have the watch, we have the time.' Coming from a Western culture, I am used to doing everything as efficiently as possible and can feel myself starting to mentally huff if I feel I am wasting time. I've tried to explain this to various Moroccan friends and they think it is hilarious. 'What are you saving all that time for?' they ask. Good question, really. Here, time is to be spent, not hoarded.

That first day of shopping was an education. I set off with

a long list of things I needed and strode across Jemaa El Fna, not stopping to look at the snake charmers or monkey wranglers, briskly answering, 'Not today, thank you,' to a young Senegalese man who asked, 'Madame, would you like some big, African cock?', and denying myself the pleasure of a freshly squeezed orange juice from one of the fruit stalls.

Two rugs were the first thing on the list. I picked a likely-looking emporium and delighted the man who accosted me with the inevitable, 'Come in to my shop, just looking, no buying, very cheap' by going in. Aladdin's cave spread out before me, with thousands of hand-woven carpets stacked along the walls, arranged by colour and by type. I felt momentarily daunted. Where should I start? I had no need to worry; Lahcen was at my service. My first lesson in spending time was about to be learnt. Greetings, even to a complete stranger, are likely to be protracted.

Lahcen: 'Good morning.'
Me: 'Good morning.'
Lahcen: 'How are you?'
Me: 'I am fine, how are you?'
Lahcen: 'I am fine, how is the family?'
Me: 'Good, good, thanks be to God. How about you? How's the family?
Lahcen: 'Great, and your health?'
Me: 'It's good. And you? How is your health? Are you well?'
Lahcen: 'Thanks be to God.'
Me: 'Thanks be to God.'

This ritual of greeting is ubiquitous, and once you get the hang of it, it actually makes you feel very connected to people. There is a pleasure in exchanging good wishes before you even start thinking about transactions. It's a world away from the self-service tills at Sainsbury's.

Lahcen and I got down to the serious business of looking at rugs. I was instructed to sit on a cushioned stool as his assistant started bringing down carpets of every size and colour. Each one would be rolled out at my feet with a flourish. I half expected a hidden Cleopatra to roll out of the end. I also felt a bit like Cleopatra as I waved my hand, banishing anything that was too big, too orange or too expensive-looking.

Tea was offered and my immediate, British, reaction was to say, 'No, thank you.' But, I stopped myself and said yes instead. This was the right choice. The assistant went off to get the tea from the tea shop and was soon back with a hot pot, handfuls of fresh mint and mounds of sugar. I had had thoughts of trying to keep my sugar intake down, but mint tea without it is extremely bitter, so I just didn't look as Lahcen ladled it into the pot. If you don't see it, surely the calories don't count. All three of us settled down for a glass and a chat – after all, we didn't want to exhaust ourselves with non-stop rug selection; there was plenty of time.

We talked about life in general, how business was going, and if there were lots of tourists about. I was to learn that no matter when or where I ask about business, I get the same answer, which bears a strong resemblance to when you ask the plumber at home if the problem with the U-bend is going to be easy to fix. First, there is a sharp intake of breath, sometimes a bit of a whistle through the teeth. This is followed by some sorrowful head shaking and a deep *hmmmmm* sound. Then, you get the answer – from the Moroccan shop owner that is, not the plumber, 'Well, it is not bad, thanks be to God, but it is not like it was. No, it is light for this time of year, not like it was in the past. Then, ahh, then . . . it was good. Tourists everywhere and they spent money. Now, they come but they don't spend money.' I would not want to cast doubt on Lahcen's veracity, but he was wearing a very large gold ring and had all the appearance of a prosperous and happy man.

Back to the rugs. I had selected two and they had been stretched out temptingly in the middle of the room. One nice antique one, thick cream wool with multi-coloured diamonds woven down the middle, and one cheap-as-chips pink one adorned with camels, crosses and triangles. Time to get bargaining. Lots of people tell me that they hate bargaining in the medina and that they wish prices were fixed and ask me how much they should bargain down to. I always quote Charlie on this, as he gave me some very good advice when I first arrived: 'Pay what you think it is worth and then be happy with your purchase.' For me, bargaining is a big part of the fun. Sadly, I am not very good at it because I always want the salesman to earn enough profit. I have a vivid memory of going to Imlil in the mountains for a day with my university friends Tanya and Sandra, and watching Sandra with mingled pride, admiration and horror as she beat the price of a red and white pouffe down to almost nothing, leaving the shopkeeper broken, but in awe. To this day, when I go past that shop the owner asks me how my friend is.

Lahcen: 'Ahh you have chosen two very good rugs, very good quality.'
Me: 'Thank you, they are both beautiful. So, tell me, what is the price?'
Lahcen: 'Because you speak Arabic and you live in Marrakech, I will only take a small profit and charge you a local price.'

Me: 'Thank you. You are so kind. What would that price be?'

Lahcen: 'Only 2,300 dirhams for both.'

Me [Noting that the line of 'giving me a good price because I speak Arabic' is a definite fib and with eyes widened in shock, some of it faked]**:** '2,300 dirhams? No, this is not possible. No, no, no.'

Lahcen: 'By God, by God, this is a good price. But what do you want to pay, my sister?'

At this stage, both of us settle back onto our stools and dig in for the long haul. More tea is drunk. Discussions take on the lengthy timescale of Middle East peace negotiations, at the end of which I have got him down to 1,150 Dhs, of which 1,000 is for the nice rug. The cheap one really is cheap.

As he wraps up my purchases, Lahcen tells me, 'You are hard! You are like a Berber woman,' and I learn that Berbers have the reputation of being tight, or as I, a proud Scot, like to put it – good with money. A whole morning had passed, and I was only one item into my shopping list. Time for me to readjust my expectations of how long it would take me to furnish my room, or indeed accomplish anything in Morocco.

Because I had come to Marrakech to train for the Marathon des Sables, a lot of my experiences have been had while out running. I am a very bad runner. I am not built for it and I seem to have an innate lazy gene that resists every attempt to attain athletic excellence. Also, I have a fatal weakness for cake. Even though I hate getting out of bed and those first few minutes on my feet, I don't think I have ever been on a run that hasn't given me something new to look at or think about.

My runs were greatly improved when Linda Lyons, a keen runner, popped into my life. A fellow Scot, she owns Riad

Linda in the medina and splits her time between Edinburgh and Marrakech. She contacted me through Facebook and a great running partnership was born. We are a very odd couple, sadly reminiscent of Stan and Ollie as she is tiny and delicate and I am not.

Our morning route is always full of adventure. We start in front of the Koutoubia Mosque, Marrakech's most famous landmark, just after sunrise to avoid the heat. It is the tallest building in the city at 77 metres, as it is forbidden to build anything higher. It was built by the Almohads in the 1100s after they captured the city from their arch-enemies, the Almoravids. Things did not go exactly to plan, however, and there was a builders' panic halfway through construction when they realised that the mihrab, which is the prayer niche that shows you which way Mecca is so that you can pray in the right direction, was not actually pointing at Mecca. It was five degrees off. Heads rolled and changes were made, but the Almohads also decided to build a second mosque, identical in every respect and detail, except for the mihrab, which would be oriented towards Mecca. When the second mosque was finished, the mihrab was actually ten degrees off. Go figure!

When I started running in Morocco I was concerned about wearing sports clothes and how I would be received as a strange foreign woman lumbering around the streets. But I didn't need to worry.

'Your health!' shouts the guy from the first motorbike that passes.

'Bravo!' shouts the next one.

'Good work!' shouts the third.

Our route takes us round the back of the mosque and into the Hivernage through the sculpture garden that was built for the big environmental conference, COP22. I love the big globe made of bicycle wheels that looks like a giant Moroccan lamp, and we always like to titter as we pass the naked bottom of Atlas (you don't see many naked bottoms here). Then it is on, past the National Theatre and on to Boulevard Mohammed VI. In spring, the fumes from the traffic give way to the heady scent of orange blossom from the trees that shade the route. The first time it happened to me, I couldn't believe my nose. It was like running into paradise. The blossoms are not wasted. Pickers come in small groups and shake them down onto mats they spread underneath the trees. They earn just 25 dirhams (£2) per kilo. The blooms are then pressed down into oils for use in perfumes, soaps and cosmetic products.

If we are feeling strong, Linda and I take on the 'extra bit' which leaves the pavement and takes us along a trail through the olive trees after passing the camel-ride man opposite the Menara mall. This juxtaposition typifies Morocco. On the right, the Menara mall is stuffed with designer shops and fronted by pavement cafés. At night, the fountain is flooded with different-coloured neon lights and a DJ plays, much to the delight of the kids, who love running across it, or just watching the multi-coloured jets. On the left, the camel man sits in his striped wool djellaba with his three camels: two adults and a still-suckling baby. He is there to provide camel rides for tourists both foreign and Moroccan. At the time of day we pass, the camels are having breakfast, munching away contentedly, and, of course, we are always invited for tea.

Under the olive trees, if we are lucky, we catch a glimpse of the army exercising their fine Arab horses, dodging through the trees at a gallop. They stop for us and let us pat the horses' steaming, velvety muzzles. We also meet a nice Belgian man with his dog. Dogs are not really liked by Moroccans. This is, of course, partly due to the fear of being bitten and the threat of rabies, but it also goes right back to the Prophet Mohammed. It is written that he didn't like dogs – cats yes, dogs no. I know this because my friend Martin and I had to read a whole treatise on the subject by a ninth-century Iraqi writer called Al Jahiz when we studied Arabic at university. A page-turner it is not.

We're on the penultimate stretch of our run when we come across Coach. A slim, upright man in his late fifties or early sixties, he is always there, standing by his bicycle waiting for his clients. He gives us a quick session with the weighted bar, stretching and lifting and generally creaking, before we go on to the final sprint back through the rose gardens at the back of the Koutoubia, up past the busloads of tourists having their photos taken with the water sellers.

The water sellers are easily spotted. They wear bright red robes and big, tasselled hats. They carry ornamental goatskin bags that used to be full of water to be bought by thirsty travellers for a dirham. They make much more now in the photographic business, and there is a little gang of five or six of them who are always there behind the mosque. We know them well, and sometimes exchange euros or pound coins that tourists have given them for dirhams. They are a short, cheerful bunch. One of them is the cat and dog man. Every morning, he brings a big bag of entrails and assorted heads for the stray animals in the garden. We know if he hasn't arrived yet because there is always a group of fat cats and plump puppies waiting patiently for him on the edge of the fountain.

Our end is in sight, the juice cart. Depending on the season, it will be laden with oranges, mandarins or pomegranates. Regardless of the season, it is always decorated with Moroccan flags and a large picture of the king. The cart owner is tall and burly with a twirly moustache topping a large grin. He always wears a cream djellaba and a red fez, adding a leather jacket in the winter. That glass of fresh juice, pressed in front of us, makes every kilometre worthwhile.

Of course, it is not done in a rush; there is a ceremonious aspect involved. First the greetings are exchanged, with earnest enquiries for the health of our respective families and many congratulations on our running. Then, the finest pomegranates are selected and slashed in half with a large knife. Two glasses are polished to within an inch of their lives and the pressing commences. The halves are put into the big metal press, the handle is pulled down and the ruby-red juice trickles out. When the glasses are full, our host hands them over with the traditional toast, '*Bisaha ou raha*', which literally means, 'In health and rest'. Linda and I drink with many, genuine, expressions of admiration. We hand over our 15 Dhs (£1.20), say a long and fond farewell and off we go.

Linda heads back to her riad, which is just five minutes from the square. The Marrakech medina is impossible to navigate, but the good thing about it is that all roads lead to Jemaa El Fna, so you can actually never get that lost because someone will always point you towards 'the big square'.

Early on, I decided that the old saying 'When you are tired of London you are tired of life' applies doubly to Jemaa El Fna. It pulsates with life and you can spend hours there, exploring or just sitting and having a coffee. For centuries it has been the focal point of the city, after being founded in the middle of the twelfth century. It used to be where the trading caravans came in to offload their goods and rest themselves and their animals. It hasn't changed much. It is a large, sprawling space, probably more octagon than square, with gardens and the Koutoubia mosque at one end, and arched entrances all around the edges leading you into the secrets of the medina.

If you walk in from the Koutoubia past all the horse-drawn carriages in the centre, there is a spine of orange juice stalls. In front of them are the monkey wranglers and three different sets of snake charmers. A myriad of traders have their goods laid out on the ground. There are the Senegalese, who are showing off butterfly-wing pictures and wooden carved figures, the veiled widows offering henna tattoos, and the sweet-looking old man who has a sinister collection of human teeth which he can glue into a makeshift set of dentures for you. On the left is the area for food stalls, which sets up at sunset for a night of trade. At the far end is the tourist police station, which is useful if you have fallen prey to one of the pickpockets that routinely patrol the streets. Opposite the police station is the entrance into one of the main thoroughfares into the medina, which takes you past the clothes souk. Past the orange juice stalls on your right is the Café de France, down the side of which is a great shopping street, Rue Zitouni (Olive Street), and opposite Café de France is the olive souk, where every kind of olive is piled up in great green and black mounds, with the smell of garlic and the sneeze of chilli emanating strongly from them.

The name Jemaa El Fna is given many interpretations by Marrakchis. Every person I ask has a different story, which rather fits the multi-faceted mayhem of the square itself. The reason for this flexibility in naming goes back to the nature of Arabic itself. In Arabic, every word is based on a root of three letters, which is then given additional letters to add meaning. For example, DRS means to study, DaRRaSa means to teach, MuDDaRRiS means teacher. You get the drift. The root of Jemaa is JMA, which means to gather, and is the basis of the words for mosque, society and gathering. So far, so good. It is FNA that is open to interpretation. In many earnest and impassioned hours of discussion I have been given all the following theories:

It means the gathering of the dead because at one point it was the area where people were executed if they transgressed.
It means the gathering place in the open courtyard.
It means the place for artists, specifically the storytellers.
It means the place of a thousand lanterns.
It means . . .

Café de France always features any time I go to the square. It is a resplendent colonial-style building over several floors, guarded by immaculate waiters in black who are masters at ignoring your signals. Downstairs are a set of clean toilets overseen by a formidable harridan, who barks at any unfortunate visitor who doesn't realise that there is a fee of 2 Dhs to be paid, for which you are given toilet paper. The best position in the café is downstairs on the terrace at the back nearest the glass. You should always sit French-style, that is on the same side of the table as your companion, so that you can both look out onto all the square's comings and goings. A creamy *nuss-nuss*, half-half, which is half coffee and half milk, or an industrial-strength espresso are my drinks of choice. I have managed to ingratiate myself with the maître d' there with one of my little Moroccan jokes. The bottled water is called Sidi Ali, so when I first went and ordered a coffee I asked for a glass of Sidi Robinet on the side (*robinet* means tap in French). This was met with gales of laughter and much metaphorical back-slapping and I was in.

There is a troupe of acrobats who work that patch. Short, lithe and impossibly strong, they are dressed in red pantaloons and yellow waistcoats. There are usually four of them. You'll hear their shouts and their claps as they start their routines. At a run, number one jumps up in the air and does a double backwards somersault, landing with a hey and a cheer. Number two cartwheels past the terrace. Number three stands with his legs akimbo as number four jumps up onto his shoulders and then his hands in a human ladder. Then they all come together to make a finale pyramid. When that entertainment ends, I content myself with snooping on the other clientele. It is a mixture of tourists and, mainly young, Moroccan men. There is the group of hipsters who come every day at 4 p.m. to talk about their film and art projects, easily spottable with their trademark ear plugs, beards and dreadlocks. There are also the tourist stalkers with a bright eye out for the foreign girls, and then the regulars who are there for a coffee, a cigarette and a read of the paper.

Not everything in the square offers such innocent pleasures. The treatment of the animals can be difficult to watch. I don't like snakes at all, but I don't think that naturally quiet, solitary beings should be kept in the light and noise of the square for our amusement. One day as I was heading for an early coffee, I saw two squirrels being emptied out of a bag by the snake charmer and put in a cage next to the snakes. I reacted before I thought.

Me: 'What are you doing? That is so cruel. These animals should not be here. They like the quiet and the shade. This is horrible for tourists. We don't like this.'
Snake Charmer: 'Mind your own business. You are not from here. This is not your country. It is nothing to do with you what I do. This is my work.'

Me: 'Yes, but we are all created by God. You shouldn't treat animals in this way.'
Snake Charmer: 'And you, your country? You kill children in Syria. You kill children in Iraq. You kill the Palestinians. You are murderers. You are Zionists. You say you care about animals. What about people? Get out of here. Get out.'

I was shaken by his words and also upset that I had done nothing positive. I hadn't saved the animals from being treated so badly, and in fact I had made the situation worse by angering the man in charge of them. I did what everyone does when they need advice and called my mum. Her advice was hard to hear but excellent. She told me that he was right. Morocco isn't my country and that I really don't have any right to complain. The treatment of these creatures may be horrible, but it is out of my control. If I don't like it, or can't bear it, then I have to leave. It was a sobering reminder that, however much I love Morocco, which I do, I am an outsider.

Daytime is fascinating in Jemaa El Fna, but it is night-time when it really comes alive. The square is always seething with people out for an evening's entertainment, starting with supper at one of the food stalls. When you enter the food alley, brace yourself: you are about to be given the hard sell. Young guys waving menus block you at every turn, trying to tempt you to their particular stall. Locals all have their favourites and you will hear the cognoscenti saying things like, 'I only ever eat fried fish at no. 14', or, 'The best aubergines are at no. 32.' That is as may be, but I have never been able to differentiate, so I usually just give in to the best sales patter. The long tables are communal, which means a chance to chat with your neighbours and get recommendations on the best dishes. I like to choose four or five to share and always make sure to try something I haven't had before. Juicy chicken skewers with tomato and garlicky aubergine, and, of course, chips are my standard.

In winter, though, I like the snails. There is a line of snail stalls between the orange juice sellers and the food stalls. Some have stools that you can perch on, but most are standing-room only. The snails are little ones in mottled shells and are served with a hot, spicy soup. They do taste good, although I will admit to a slightly off-putting texture, and I never look too closely because I don't want to see any little snail eyes looking back at me.

For entertainment, there is a lot to choose from. If you tire of listening to the singers in their red tasselled caps singing the old slave songs, *gnaoua*, then you can always try your hand at fishing for Fanta bottles, which looks really easy but is not. That long fishing line won't settle on the bottle, no matter how hard you try. I know because I have whiled away quite a few long evenings and invested many dirhams in failure. The thing that draws the biggest crowd, however, is the storytellers.

Storytelling is an art that has been going on for centuries and is often passed down from father to son. You will see a circle of people, standing or sitting on temporary benches, listening with rapt attention as the storyteller holds them in his thrall. Sometimes he will have a couple of people with him playing drums and traditional guitars to add to the dramatic tension. I can't always understand everything that is being said, especially if I join halfway through the story, but the experience of being a part of this most basic and oldest form of human entertainment is always irresistible and I *ooh* and *ahh* with the best of them.

They are minstrels and we are the court. There are some set stories that get told time and again of great heroes, greedy merchants and beautiful maidens and there are also the oral histories that remember the days of the immense caravans crossing the Sahara, bringing unimaginable wealth from the mines of Africa and transporting millions of slaves to their doom. Sitting under the light of the lanterns, surrounded by the smell of the cooking fires, the noise of the crowd fades away and all I can hear is the hypnotic voice of the storyteller as he describes a caravan going through the desert and the privations that the people and the animals suffered. He talks of the Africans chained together: men, women and children crying as they walked into slavery. He tells us that when the caravan got to the next well and it was dry, the camel drivers, merchants and slaves realised that death was waiting. All of us in the crowd sigh and one man calls out, 'God help them!' He describes the next two days when the sun beat down relentlessly on the glaring sand and people were left to die alone as they were conquered by thirst.

Then, just when we can't take much more, he shouts out that they have found a well and it has water. People and animals drank and rested and thanked God for their salvation and the crowd cheers, thanks God and stuffs dirhams into the hat he circulates. As the circle breaks up, we all say goodbye to each other fondly, shaking our heads in relief and laughing at ourselves now the tension has been released. It is as if we were on that caravan together. That is the skill of a real storyteller.

Marrakech is not all about the lure of history, though – it has its modern seductions too. It is a party town, and there are other things to enjoy aside from the innocent pleasures of eating an ice cream with your family in the square. The population of the city is around one million and there are an estimated 30,000 prostitutes working the streets. This is something that is not really talked about in Morocco and a film that came out in 2015, *Much Loved*, which portrayed the life of prostitutes in the country, caused a furore.

The first time I came across this side of Marrakech was, weirdly, in a major Western coffee shop in Gueliz, the centre of the New Town. I was feeling homesick and wanted a treat, so went in for an Americano and a blueberry muffin with Alex. I didn't think too much about the young, beautiful, skimpily dressed girls who were hanging out there until she told me what was going on. 'Alice, we are the only women in here who are not prostitutes.' Then, of course, it was obvious. No normal Moroccan woman would wear a crop top and shorts that show their butt cheeks. It didn't make any sense to me that this was going on in a coffee shop, but I was being naïve. It is a place where lots of foreigners and richer Moroccans congregate, and they are bound to have money as a coffee there costs double what it would in a street café.

A conversation that I had had with a pleasant young Asian guy from Burnley on a flight back to Manchester came back to me. I'd asked him about his holiday and if he had enjoyed it and he said he had and that he had met some really nice Moroccan girls. At the time, I was a bit surprised as it isn't usual for Moroccan girls to go out with strangers, but now the penny dropped. When I asked around a bit more, I was told that there was a lot of sex tourism. Sometimes it was overt, with money changing hands, and sometimes it was more delicately done, with gifts being given rather than cash. There is also plenty of (male) gay tourism, usually between much older European men and younger Moroccans.

It's not just sex tourism though. Morocco is a country where sex before marriage is still absolutely not the norm and most girls are virgins when they marry. It is no longer usual for everyone to get married at sixteen, and in an age when marriage costs more and prospective in-laws want the groom to have a house, a car and a fridge, many men are not getting married until their thirties or even forties. So, what do they do for sex? This is a question that it is quite hard to ask a guy, but I chose my prey and my timing carefully. I was on day two of a long hiking trip in the Atlas Mountains with a good friend who is also a guide and was in his late thirties at the time. I preambled a bit but finally got to it. Initially, he gave me a startled horse look with nostrils flared and eyes wildly looking for escape, but we still had a few days to go and there was no way out for him, so he answered.

'Well, Alice,' he said. 'You know it is difficult here as women have to be really careful of their reputation. Everyone talks and even if they are innocent, if they suspect a girl, it can be very bad for her and she won't get married. Even for a man it isn't good if people think he is having sex with a lot of women. It is considered shameful.'

I was a bit surprised by that bit as it is different to the West, where there is a culture of boasting about weekend conquests. I still hadn't had my question properly answered, though, and I pressed again and asked him what he did as he wasn't married. I did wonder if he was still a virgin.

'No!' he said. 'Of course, we can do everything but "real sex" with a Moroccan girl sometimes, but only if we are serious. Also, I have met some very nice foreign girls who are very kind.'

And there it is, one of the fundamental differences between our cultures. For us, women and men have sexual freedom and we can do what we like with whom we like. A romance with a Moroccan man would be something to be enjoyed and treasured. But, in Morocco, the moral code is entirely different. It can lead to a lot of misunderstandings and heartbreak.

'What about prostitutes?' I asked, thinking that this was going to be a straight 'no', but I was wrong.

'Yes, sometimes. When we have a party, a group of us will get together and they will be there and we will party together.'

One of the things that I discovered very quickly in Marrakech is how cold it is in the winter. The temperatures in the city are extreme. In the summer, my thermostat often reached 48°C and I thought I would explode, but in the winter the marble-floored open houses seemed to trap the cold and I spent a lot of time muffled in layers and layers of fleece in our chilly flat in Sakia El Hamra. By now, Alex had moved up to Rabat with her boyfriend, Mike, and I had two new flatmates, also clever and fun young American women, Liv and Serena.

Before I moved to Morocco, I had worried about sharing a flat. I knew that if I wanted to pursue my dream of becoming an Adventurer I was going to have to really scale back my spending. Sharing a flat was a necessity, but I hadn't shared for nearly twenty years and I wasn't sure that I still had the flexibility to do it. I'd got used to the luxury of my own space and was not looking forward to a return to what felt like a student lifestyle. It is strange how often in life the things that you dread are the things that turn out to be the best, and this was a case in point.

We had a ball. I learnt lots of new things about America and our celebrations grew to include Thanksgiving as well as Christmas. We'd go out running together, cook together and in the summer do daily trips down to Gueliz to eat goat's-yoghurt ice cream in Softy Sweet and watch the immaculate Frenchmen pass by carrying their little lapdogs. Liv and Serena spent lots of time telling me, in the nicest possible way, that I was a total dinosaur and had to clean up my political correctness act. My vocabulary expanded to include words such as 'cisgender' and 'heteronormativity', and I was given a stern talking to about my tendency towards privilege. I joke, but it was a genuine education and I loved my time with these bright, open-minded women. Of course, with a house of three women, clothes and fashion played their part, and in the winter we were all about the acrylic pyjamas.

If you have visited Morocco between November and March, you cannot have failed to notice the women proudly strutting their stuff in the streets in their pyjamas or fleecy robes. My favourite ever was a lady riding her moto, dressed in a lurid acrylic djellaba with leggings underneath, a flowered headscarf and, perched on top, a black velvet, old-fashioned riding hat. That's what I call style.

On this particular Saturday, Liv, Serena and I decided it was time to take to the streets in our very own offerings and do a tour of the city. Serena, who is six feet tall and looks like a young Elizabeth Taylor, chose a violent turquoise tunic, with cut-out tigerskin print cat heads on it and black leggings. Liv wore a red flower in her long auburn hair to match her red fleecy pyjama bottoms, and on top she sported a mixed leopard-print and polka-dotted creation. I had gone for a sophisticated look with a fluffy scarlet and white checked ensemble, which had a large bunny rabbit wearing heart-shaped glasses on the front and cavorting baby bunnies round the bottom of the legs and sleeves. Lipstick on, hair brushed, we hit the town.

First of all, we went into Starbucks for a coffee. '*Bisaha* (your health),' giggled the girl as she served us and gave us a thumbs up. Then we caught a taxi down to the square. The taxi driver was openly approving. 'Ahhh,' he said. 'You are wearing Moroccan clothes. Very good. You look very, very beautiful. You have chosen very fashionable and pretty outfits. Bravo. And they are practical. Bravo. Very, very nice.' We were definitely riding high on the approval scales as we posed outside the Koutoubia and then in the middle of the square for pictures and our adoring public. '*Zwina* (beautiful)' was called out on every side with no hint of irony. We had cracked the dress code.

To cap off our day, we decided to hire a caleche to ride home in. The caleche is the racing-green, open-topped carriage drawn by two matched horses that you see being used for trips around the city. The best ones are approved by Spana, a local animal welfare charity, and the horses are usually well cared for as they command high prices. If I was going to be reborn as a four-legged animal in Marrakech, I would definitely be praying to come back as a caleche horse.

When we approached the stand near the square, there was nearly a riot as the drivers fought for our business. All the rules of who gets the customers first were thrown to the wind as the drivers contemplated the pyjama-clad beauties that stood before them. We got a really good price, too. The ride took us up the main road from the old medina to the New Town past outdoor cafés, busy shopping streets and tree-lined boulevards. We waved, queen-like, to the crowds who, literally, cheered us as we trotted towards home. We had put on our pyjamas in the morning with a sense of irony, but that had not been reflected in the reactions we got. If you ever want an ego boost or to be warmed by a 100 per cent approval rating, you know what to do.

I don't know if there are many other people in the world who would say that one of the best days of their lives was spent up to their thighs in pigeon shit. If you meet any, ask them to get in touch as I feel we would share some kind of connection. My pigeon shit fetish stems from a day I spent working in a tannery in Marrakech. You can't come to Marrakech and not buy some leather. It is ubiquitous: vividly coloured slippers wink at you from shops stuffed to the brim and there are leather bags, belts and pouffes in abundance. Leather is a big export for Morocco and the quality is considered excellent. You should always have a good sniff of what you are buying, though, to make sure it has been cured properly, and also check that the dye is well fixed and you aren't going to end up with a bright blue patch on your T-shirt from where your new bag has rubbed.

That leather comes from the ancient tanneries, which lie in the leather quarter of the city, and I had organised to spend the day there for the BBC Two series, *Morocco to Timbuktu: An Arabian Adventure*. This had come about because I had been lucky enough to be introduced to Harry Bell from Tern TV in Glasgow and we had agreed that we would love to do a big adventure in Morocco for a TV series. He had done all the hard work and persuaded the BBC that this was a great idea and they really should entrust it to a totally untried and untested presenter, me, and so *Morocco to Timbuktu* was born.

The premise was to follow the old salt routes which stretched from Tangier in the very north of the country, across the Atlas Mountains, through the Sahara desert and on to the famed city of Timbuktu in Mali. These routes had been travelled for centuries by merchants trading salt, gold, slaves and ostrich feathers in the days when a kilo of salt was worth as much as a kilo of gold, as immortalised by the storytellers in the square.

It did turn out to be a fantastic adventure, but I certainly wouldn't have expected my day in the tanneries to be one of the high spots. Part of the remit was to show the goods that had been traded, and how they were manufactured all those centuries ago, hence our jaunt to just outside Bab Debbagh. We'd set off early in the morning and it was still and misty. The workers were straggling in and a group of them had stopped off to have a bowl of salty porridge being cooked in an alley. There was a group of half a dozen folk, sitting on their tiny stools over steaming bowls as the lady in charge ladled in big dollops of the hot oats. A bowl costs around 30p, and I may be biased because I'm genetically predisposed to like porridge, but it is pretty delicious.

I was met at the entrance to the tannery by Naguib and Mohammed, who were going to show me how everything worked. Naguib and I hit it off immediately. He was tall and strong with a real twinkle and had worked in the tannery for forty-eight years. As a schoolboy he used to come here after school and in the holidays. I had always thought that it would be a terrible job as it is hard work and you spend most of your day immersed in vats of chemicals, which smell vile, but Naguib was really proud of his craft and put me right.

'Our grandfathers, our ancestors and before them and before them worked here. It goes back to a distant history. It feeds our children, gives us everything,' he told me. The tannery claims to be 1,000 years old and the methods being used to cure the hides remain much the same. At the height of the trade, the finest leather commanded very high prices as it was used for books which were a highly sought-after luxury. There is a story told with much awe about the time one merchant splurged on 250 books when he arrived in Marrakech from west Africa, which would have cost a fortune. Now, I assume, it would be a super-yacht or a couple of Porsches.

I'd been told to wear old, disposable clothes for the day and I had on leggings and a trusty fleece. Naguib tenderly wrapped my feet in plastic bags and then helped me pull on the long rubber waders that I would need for the vats. I also had cloth gloves followed by rubber gauntlets to protect my hands.

The whole tanning process is complex and has many different stages. They all seemed to involve some kind of slightly gross activity, though. To start off with, we salted the skins and then pulled the hair off with our hands and rinsed. Great handfuls of it came out every time I moved my hand along the skin until the hide was bare. There was still the occasional globule of flesh which hadn't been properly removed when the animal was skinned.

The next stage was to get into one of the vats to start trampling the hides. I haven't mentioned the smell yet. The stench of sulphur and pigeon shit in a tannery, in fact in the whole leather quarter, is overwhelming. You can't take a breath without drawing it into your lungs. The closer you get to the vats, the worse it gets. I am not sure it would be possible to ever get used to it. The vats were filled with a murky grey, watery sludge. When I asked Naguib what it was, he said water, pigeon shit, quicklime and poison. I wasn't sure what to be more worried about – the shit or the poison – but I was thoroughly enjoying myself and leapt in gamely after Naguib and Mohammed. This was a tactical error. I had not considered one factor: they were both over six feet tall and I am not. They were in there up to the top of their waders and I was in there with grey pigeon shit water running over the top of my waders, down my thighs and into my boots. My waders were filling up fast. Argh! I flailed around torn between horror and hilarity.

'Naguib, Naguib, get me out of here!' I yelled. Thank goodness for upper body strength. The pair of them hauled me out of the tub, squelchy and pongy. They thought it was exquisitely funny.

There was no rest for the wicked, though, and we went onto a shallower tub, filled with the same delightful mixture. There we stomped around in a circle, creating a whirlpool. The combination of the hides winding around your legs and the current we had created made it hard, physical work. I tried to imagine doing it in the heat of the summer when Marrakech hits 48°C, or doing it if I were fasting for Ramadan and couldn't even have a drink of water.

My thighs were burning when we went on to the rinsing tub, where we had to rinse the hides again. This involved a very intricate technique. You had to swish them through the water, capturing the air to make a kind of balloon. Of course, Mohammed and Naguib made it look really easy, swishing away rhythmically, but when I tried, I just couldn't get my hide to balloon. Mohammed tried to teach me: two thumbs on the hide, swish it through the water, turn it inside out and then scrape off the fatty residue and hair. I was useless, but did manage to amuse myself by sticking my finger through what had been my little goat's bumhole. The men were focused on their task and, TV cameras or no TV cameras, had their hides to get through, so used me as a junior labourer, telling me to drag out the wet hides and pile them up or to carry them over to the next vat. I started to feel like part of the team, and enjoyed the mindless, physical process of it, just doing what I was told.

One of the very last stages sounded romantic. Naguib told me that the hides are soaked in mimosa to strengthen them and start to neutralise the smell. I will never think of that sweet-smelling flower in the same way – the mimosa vat did not smell anything like my Jo Malone scented candle, that is for sure.

I think it was the camaraderie that made that day so enjoyable. I also got to learn lots of new things and to stomp about in vats of dirty water, which is something we don't do enough as adults, but my enduring memory was of being accepted and put to work by Naguib and laughing our way through wader disasters and being sucked into a whirlpool of pigeon shit. As I left, Naguib's last words were, 'Don't forget to come to work tomorrow. Eight o'clock.'

The men of Marrakech are definitely romantics. No, 'Phwoar, get your tits out,' as you pass by a building site here. It is '*Ya Ghazelle* – Oh! Gazelle!', or, '*Vous êtes ravissante* – You are ravishing!' Maybe it is due to the warm summer breezes, the roses that are planted everywhere, or the division of the sexes that makes everything just that little bit more exciting . . . but whatever it is, this is a very typical exchange.

Me and the **taxi driver** (any taxi driver regardless of age or number of teeth remaining)
Me: 'Peace be upon you.'
TD: 'And upon you.'
Me: 'How are you?'
TD: 'Not bad, how are you? How is everything?'
Me: 'Thanks be to God. How are you doing?'

TD: 'Blessings of God be upon you, how are YOU doing?'

Me: 'Thanks be to God, Lord of all the Worlds.' (I have branched out from the greetings norm and slipped in a little bit of an extra here with 'Lord of all the Worlds', which I know will earn me many brownie points.)

TD: 'You speak Arabic very well. Are you Lebanese? Egyptian?'

Me: 'Thank you for these compliments. No, I am Scottish. I learnt Arabic at university.'

TD: 'Ahh Scotland, you are Swedish. Very, very cold there. It snows all the time not like here in Morocco.'

Me: 'Yes, it does.' (Sometimes I explain where Scotland is but usually I just accept our move into Scandinavia. I am sure I have Viking blood in me so it is not that much of a stretch.)

TD: 'Are you Muslim?'

Me: 'No, I am Christian.'

TD [with great disappointment and some anxiety for my soul]: 'Oh, but why are you not Muslim? You have read the Quran and the Hadith and the Sira. Islam is the seal of religions. You must become a Muslim. Will you become a Muslim?'

Me: 'May God bless you, we are all People of The Book, the Sons of Adam.' (This is a good response for ALL occasions and questions of any kind and doesn't involve me having to apostatise.)

TD: 'Are you married?'

Me: 'No.'

TD: 'WHAT??!!' (This is always a dangerous moment, as the taxi driver swivels round fully to face me, with a total disregard for road safety, and looks at me with a mixture of astonishment, pity and opportunity.)

TD: 'But why are you not married? You are a GAZELLE! You are beautiful.'

Me: 'Well, thank you very much for the compliment. That is very kind of you.'

TD: 'Are you a virgin?'

Me [without hesitation and with a total disregard for the truth of a youth pleasantly misspent]: 'Of course I am! I am not married!' (I usually try to look outraged and virtuous simultaneously.)

TD: 'I will marry you.' (Said very decisively and in a tone that suggests no further discussion is needed.)

Me: 'Thank you.' (Nervous laugh.)

TD: 'No, no, no. You must be married. I will marry you. Here, take my phone number. My name is Ali. We should get married. I have a taxi.'

I know that the taxi should sway it for me and that I am a cultural monster for not actually wanting to be married, but the fact that Ali only has one top tooth, which is hanging on by a thread, means, I fear, we will not make a match, flattered as I am. By now we have arrived at my destination. Ali makes me put his phone number into my iPhone under his watchful eye, makes me promise to call him and we part the best of friends.

Marrakech is all about the bustle, the encounter and the jostle of modern and ancient squeezed together in one place, but just hours away lies a place where neither modern nor ancient mean anything. There, nature is king, and it is a form of nature that I doubt will ever be beaten into submission by humans. I'm talking, of course, of the Sahara desert.

2

THE DESERT

Dunes shining gold under a pink dawn stretch out as far as you can see. The air is completely still. The cold of the night is giving in to the warmth of the sun as it breathes life back into the sand. The night breezes have swept the sand clean of camel footprints, but you can track where the desert foxes have trotted and see the light imprint of the birds where they have briefly landed. The world is fresh and new again and so are you. This is the seduction of the desert.

In a way, it is hard to understand why the desert holds such a fascination for so many of us. After all, it is just endless miles of sand, a very hostile place with seemingly not much in it. When you spend any time there, however, it is that very simplicity that becomes the attraction. There is the sand and there is the sun. Blue and yellow. Life is whittled down to its basics. You have to have enough water and food and it is a good idea to be wearing clothes that protect you from the sun, yet can also keep you warm when that sun disappears. That is about it; everything else becomes a bit of an irrelevance, just stuff that is going to get sandy, and that you will have to carry.

All that space and emptiness gives you room to breathe and to imagine. It allows you to focus on small things and get enormous pleasure from them. Dung beetles become more exciting than a Formula One racing track. Did you know that a dung beetle can pull a piece of dung 1,141 times its own weight? That is like me pulling six double-decker buses. The universal yellow of the sand transforms under your eyes to a hundred shades between white and crimson. It is quiet, so you listen. It is empty, so you look. It is difficult, so you try.

There are two main areas of desert in Morocco: the Agafay, which you can reach in half an hour from Marrakech; and the Sahara, which is a long drive south. Sahara just means 'desert' in Arabic, and it is in the Sahara that you find the big dunes and golden sands that you picture when you hear the word 'desert'. The Sahara is only the third biggest desert in the world, but it is the hottest, with an average temperature of 40°C. And even though it only gets the bronze medal for size in the desert world championships, it still covers an area roughly the size of the United States or China: 9.2 million square kilometres (3.6 million square miles). It is also bordered by three oceans: the Mediterranean to the north, the Atlantic to the west and the Red Sea to the east. Political borders divide it now, but for centuries it was the heart of the Amazigh (Berber) nation and nomads roamed freely from west Africa to Sudan, Morocco and Egypt.

It wasn't always dry, and in many areas you can discover rock carvings and paintings from prehistoric settlements showing abundant wildlife and depicting a long-lost hunter-gatherer society. It also has a surprisingly varied geography. The majority of the desert is comprised of rocky plateaus flanking stone and gravel plains, salt flats and dried-out river beds, where thorny bushes and acacia trees are dotted round tiny patches of water. You will also find the Apple of Sodom (*calotropis procera*), surely the most evocatively named plant in the world. It is a tall plant with fleshy leaves and large green globes. These are hollow, but the flesh contains a toxic milky sap that is extremely bitter and turns into a gluey coating resistant to soap – don't pick one! If you do open one, they are a bit like a puff ball inside and explode with a *pooff*. There is a thin, silky fibre running through the plant, which was used as wicks for guns by the desert Arabs. It is also believed to have been used to weave the robes of the Jewish High Priests. It gains its historical notoriety, though, from the infamous 'Death in the Pot' story told in the Bible: 2 Kings 4:38–41.

Elisha the prophet returned to Gilgal, where there was a famine. A group of wise men came to meet him and he told his servant to prepare a stew for them. There wasn't any food because of the famine but the servant obviously wanted to please his master, so he went off into the fields and scavenged. He must have been chuffed when he came across the juicy-looking Apple of Sodoms and gathered up as many as he could. He cut them into bite-sized morsels and put them into the stew. However, his cooking was not met with the delight he was hoping for. When the men started to eat it, they shouted out: 'Man of God, there is death in the pot!' Fortunately, Elisha was a quick-thinking prophet and also a man with some God-given powers. He threw flour into the pot, requested his servant serve it up again, and, lo and behold, the poison was gone and all that was left was a tasty (I may be embellishing here) stew.

Most people don't visit the Sahara for the scrubby plains, however; they want to spend time in the Ergs. The Ergs is the name given to the large areas, or seas, of sand which you can reach from the towns of M'hamid and Merzouga. The two largest in Morocco are Erg Chigaga and Erg Chebbi. These sand seas are home to the pristine sand of the dunes, some of which can reach heights of over 180 metres (590 feet). They are constantly changing shape due to the winds that sweep across them. They can also be formed by the very occasional rain that falls. It averages between 100 millimetres (4 inches) and 250 millimetres (10 inches) per year. To contrast that with my home in the Peak District, annual rainfall there is 1,329 millimetres, or 52 inches.

When you come to Morocco, a night or two spent in the desert is a must-do. Take a camel to a luxury camp and sit listening to the Berber drums while looking up at the Milky Way, warmed by the campfire, a glass of wine in hand after your four-course dinner with chocolate mousse for desert.

How lovely it sounds, but my experiences of the Sahara have been very different. The Sahara and I had form before I ever set foot in Morocco. As a young, just-graduated teacher who thought that she was indestructible, I had hitchhiked round it in Egypt. Thumbing lifts on motorbikes and military transports and happily bedding down next to army conscripts for hours at a time as we waited for the next truck to come through a checkpoint. As a late-forties former CEO who thought she was indestructible, I had cycled across it on rutted sandy roads through the Sudan, which played havoc with my nether regions and tested me on an anvil of nearly unendurable heat. As a fifty-year-old putative Adventurer, I was to run 250 kilometres (156 miles) across it for the Marathon des Sables (MdS), the toughest footrace on earth. The race that had brought me to Morocco.

'Why oh why oh why', you may ask (I certainly did), 'did you do that?' As I mentioned earlier, I signed up because Charlie was doing it and I am easily led. That spur-of-the-moment, what-the-heck decision was to lead me along a long and unpredictable path of adventure, discovery and pain – lots of pain. It was also to allow me seven days really in the desert, feeling every part of it and experiencing it in a way that was truly a privilege, and a curse.

I have visited the desert in Morocco many times since, but it is this experience that really allowed me to understand it in a visceral way. I literally felt it. The physical aspects of being in such a harsh environment; the camaraderie of battling through the Sahara together; the constant focus on water; learning to accept the extreme heat; and, of course, the tales round the campfire. Although running 156 miles through the sand for fun is very much a Western concept, I felt as though I was experiencing a tiny measure of what it is actually like to live in the desert or to cross it on foot and by caravan.

So my story about the Marathon des Sables is not really a story about running or even about endurance; it is a story about the desert itself and the way that this vast, empty space wheedles its way into your soul. Spend just one night under the stars surrounded by the deep silence of the dunes, then get up to see the first rays of the sun wash the sand, still gentle, and you will be hooked. The total harshness and unforgiving nature of the landscape somehow strips you back to your simplest self. The worries of day-to-day life and the burdens of all the material ties you have fade away or are burnt away in the face of the unrelenting sun and the never-ending sand. In the desert, there is nothing else.

The Marathon des Sables is the original 'toughest footrace on earth'. Arguably, as the sport of ultra-running has flourished, with runners looking for ever more extreme races, it may no longer hold that crown. I would probably pass it on to the Barkley Marathons, which is a 100-miler with a sixty-hour time limit. This race is so impossibly difficult that it only has a 1 per cent finish rate. Fifty-five per cent of the time, no one succeeds at all. All those who fail are bugled in with the 'Last Post' when they finally find their way to the line.

MdS, though, was quite tough enough for me, thank you very much. It takes place every year in April in the Sahara desert of Morocco. Every year, the route is slightly different and a closely guarded secret till the start line, which satisfyingly allows the finishers from each year to categorically assert that their year was the most difficult. My year *was* the most difficult. It is a six-stage, seven-day run. It starts in the dunes near Merzouga and loops round close to the Algerian border, with the final stage taking you to a dusty outpost in Tarbaart, from where it is a three-hour drive back to Ouarzazate and the luxurious embrace of the Berber Palace hotel. The distances are: Day 1: 34 km; Day 2: 41 km; Day 3: 37.5 km; Day 4: 81.5 km; Day 6: 42.2 km; Day 7 (charity stage): 7 km. You did read that correctly, Day 4 is a double marathon. But if you can keep soldiering through it, you have the prospect of a longer rest before Day 6. The race officially ends on Day 6 when the medals are given out, but you still have to complete the next day, the charity stage, although you are not timed.

The race is semi self-supported. What this means is that you have to carry all your food and equipment for the week on your back. The organisation supplies communal eight-man tents and water at every check point. You have to bring the rest, and you have to balance what you want to bring against the weight of carrying it while you are attempting to run up and over dunes in high temperatures for a long way.

From the day I signed up for the race in the summer of 2013 until the day I stood on the start line in April 2014 next to Charlie, listening to 'Highway to Hell' blaring out from the loudspeakers, my waking thought had been, *Oh no, I'm running the MdS, I need to train, diet, pack, panic* ... And my last thought before I went to sleep had been the same. I spent nine months in a state of fear at the thought of what lay ahead of me and the enormity of the task this non-running runner had taken on.

Without Charlie I definitely would not have done it. We would go out to the Agafay desert to run through the *oued* (dried river valley) for five hours in the sun. We did the Nomad's ultra together (60 kilometres) for practice. Well, I say together – Charlie is much faster than me and did it about three hours quicker. He won the true friend badge as he stayed on and came down the course to meet me and encourage me to the end, even though he must have been exhausted himself. We could obsess endlessly to each other about training programmes and race plans (mine was easy – finish). We did Pilates twice a week to get our core strength up, often closely resembling tortoises being tortured. We met once a week for lunch – fish for me, carbs for Charlie. We had hundreds of long phone calls comparing our kit, how much each thing weighed and how to keep the weight down. I really have Charlie to thank for making me hyper-aware of each single gram. Really, though, he made the whole thing fun, and we had unforgettable adventures along the way.

When race time finally arrived, Charlie and Saaid, who was driving us down, arrived nice and early to collect me from home. I had spent the whole of the previous day packing my kit and trying to get the weight down to a minimum. I had cut the stem off my toothbrush (9 grams) and decanted all my dried food from their foil bags (25 grams each) into plastic bags (2 grams each). It was strawberry season, so I had bought a couple of kilos to eat in the car, mindful that there was going to be no fresh fruit where we were heading. Strawberries are one of the joys of spring in Morocco and grow to the size of a small plum. You can get a kilo for 10 dirhams (80p).

The drive down to Ouarzazate takes you over the Tichka pass and the High Atlas Mountains, at that time of year all clad in spring green with a few remaining spots of snow, and down to the gold of the sands. We were in high spirits, lots of nervous laughter and comparing of kit and how much weight we had managed to save. We stopped off past the Tizi n' Tichka for a coffee at the best café in the mountains, Asanfou. I think it has an Italian coffee machine because, even though it is in the middle of nowhere, it really does serve the most delicious brew. Their dog had just had a litter of puppies and we had the extra pleasure of five little bundles of fluff gambolling around us and playing tug of war with our trainers' laces.

In Ouarzazate we detoured to the airport to pick up another runner, Christophe Lesaux. He was one of the elites, a French runner hoping for a top-ten place and needing a lift out to camp. When I saw him my heart sank. I was a giantess beside him. He was tiny and waif-like with corkscrew blonde hair. I felt like a hairy mammoth sitting next to a gazelle. Were we really both going to run the same race?

We stopped for lunch at Tinihir, a small town en route. Tinihir has that Wild West feel to it: a wide main street lined with run-down shops, which should have tumbleweed rolling through on the dry wind. We ordered the ever-delicious roadside staple of chicken and chips with onion, tomato and green pepper salad dressed with lemon and garlic. As we were sitting there, a poor-looking man stumbled down the pavement and threw up in front of us, then staggered on. 'Glue sniffer,' said Charlie. 'You get a lot of them. It's cheaper than alcohol.'

Like every country, Morocco has its share of addicts and the homeless, far fewer than the UK, but none the less shocking. Months later in Marrakech, my flatmate and I were in Jemaa El Fna at around 8 p.m. We had gone down to join the crowd and watch *Gladiator* on the big screen as part of the Marrakech Film Festival. I was just getting over the shock of Russell Crowe speaking in French, '*Je m'appelle Maximus Decimus Meridius, commandant des armées du Nord, général des légions de Félix, fidèle serviteur du véritable empereur, Marc Aurèle. Père à un fils assassiné, mari à une femme assassinée. Et j'aurai ma vengeance, dans cette vie ou dans la suivante,*' when we noticed that two young kids beside us had plastic bags over their faces and were sniffing away. They couldn't have been more than eight years old and were obviously street children. Liv is a truly good person and would not look the other way, so we tried to get help. I asked the men beside me to do something, but they brusquely said 'no' and moved on, so Liv went to get the police. They came and talked gently to the boys, took the glue and walked off with them. It was a kind of solution, but only for one night.

The closer we got to where the MdS camp was, the more nervous I felt. I tried to distract myself by seeing if I could eat a really big strawberry whole and by talking to Christophe about his ultra-running lifestyle. The former worked but left a big mess, and the latter just made me feel worse. He told us that MdS was '*un petit répos, les vacances*' for him, as it was a stage race, so he would get to sleep at night rather than a run-through when you have to do a super-long distance in one go. We had been driving along the *piste* (dirt road) for an hour or so when Charlie said, 'There it is.' In the distance was a thin black line. Our tents stretching out in a massive semicircle ready for the 1,100 brave souls who were taking on the desert that year. My stomach roiled in a stormy fashion.

Saying goodbye to Saaid, I felt like I was losing my last hope for redemption. Even though I had been working towards this for months, I wasn't ready. We had arrived before the buses bringing in the runners from the airport so we had our choice of tents. We had been told beforehand that we had to share with fellow Brits as the tents were divided up by nationality. We, however, wanted to share with Moroccans because we live here. There were a couple of problems with this as we soon found out. MdS is really expensive and very few Moroccans can afford to do it, either in terms of money or time, so those who can tend to be the elites who are quasi-professional runners. One look at the tense forms resting with their legs up in the tent to preserve energy was enough, and we turned tail and headed off to the British section, choosing the tent right at the end of one of the three semicircles. We reckoned it would always be easy to find, was like a semi in that it only had another tent on one side, and was close to the edge of camp if we needed to wander off for a wee. It also had the advantage of being Tent 101.

Each tent was a traditional black Berber goat-hair affair with two sides down and a front and back that could be rolled up. In the middle was a sturdy pole made of poplar and there were more poles in the corners. On the ground was a well-worn carpet that shielded us from the sand and pebbles. Each tent held eight people, lying sardine-like with kit stashed at heads or feet. As I was to find out later when I spent time with a nomad family in the Jebel Saghro, the tent was exactly like those used by the Bedouin. Charlie and I both opted to be at the very edge of the tent on either side, as that way we would have a bit of privacy and someone next to us on only one side. The negative was that this was probably the hottest spot and a bit claustrophobic.

We had gone outside to check out the camp and were chatting away to some other early arrivals when we looked back and saw a man getting naked in our tent. Not only that, but he appeared to have feathers on his head. This was going to be a very interesting desert experience, I decided. Bob, the fireman, was our first tent mate and the feathers were from his parrot, who had died, and of whom he had been very fond. We also had Bruce, a very fit triathlete-type originally from South Africa but living on a boat in Hong Kong, with whom I would share my nightly rooibos teabag (2 grams); Neil, a Scot living in Hong Kong, who had run the Gobi Desert Ultra, so had experience, and who gaffer-taped his nipples with a big black X to stop them chafing; Bill, ex-army, japester and all round good egg with the silliest balloon-like gaiters that caused much mirth; and finally Ali, a pilot and romantic who had just got engaged and was very much in love. He also suffered from terrible nose bleeds and later in the race I was to swap him some Wemmi Wipes for some sun cream so he could stuff them up his nose to stem the flow. We had a body space free but, even with a vivid imagination, I couldn't picture how we would have fitted another person in.

The first day and a half were spent in camp acclimatising, having our kit checked, doing a little stretch run and being told all the rules and regulations. The entertainment was provided by one of the organisers demonstrating how to use the toilets. Of course, when we were out running we had the whole desert to enjoy, but put 1,100 runners and a couple of hundred staff into one camp overnight, and there needs to be a system. Cue the brown plastic bag and the plastic toilets. Dotted on the outskirts of the camp were a number of tallish, narrow tents. Inside them were the toilets and outside them was a big black bin. Our demonstrator climbed up on top of the Land Rover, grabbed the loudspeaker and looked out over the crowd. 'You will be given one of these bags every night,' he promised. 'When you feel the urge, take it with you to the white tents. There you will find a toilet. Lift up the seat, put the bag around the rim, and put down the lid. Then . . .' His actions spoke louder than words and we enjoyed the theatre as he read a paper and spent some time contemplating the universe. 'Afterwards, you take the bag, tie it and put it in the bin.' Wild applause from the crowd.

There was also something special for the ladies: 'We have some tents near the toilets where the women can go to change and wash,' he told us, optimistically. Bearing in mind we only had our drinking water ration, nobody was going to be having any showers, but since only 10 per cent of the runners are women, it was a nice thought to have somewhere we could go and wipe ourselves down.

In actual fact, I found a better use for the ladies' tents. At night there were security guards on the perimeter of the camp so you couldn't get out of sight if you wanted a wee, which was a real problem. Penis envy? Yes, indeed, so much easier. Cunningly, I had devised a system whereby I would go to the loo properly out on the course, where it was easy to find a private spot of sand, and save my bag for my before-bed wee. Then, I would avoid the loo tent queues, nip into the ladies' tent, wrap the bag round myself and hey presto. I had perfected the art of weeing into a brown plastic bag, standing up. A very useful skill, but perhaps not one for the CV.

Race day dawned and I could feel the adrenalin fizzing through my body. This was it, the reason I had come to Morocco in the first place. I was standing on the start line in the desert next to Charlie, surrounded by 1,000 other runners, all ready to take on this enormous challenge, with the sun above and the race helicopter stirring up a sandstorm. Patrick, the race organiser, made his morning speech in poetic French, and had it translated into very prosaic English. Then we were off, under the arch and away to the dunes.

The first couple of kilometres were on the flat and I spent it just trying to keep my nerves and breathing under control and reach something resembling a comfortable pace. Then we hit the sand dunes and the fun really started. Sand dunes are hard to run up, as you will know if you have ever tried it. I had actually taken a twelve-hour bus ride from Marrakech down to Zagora three weeks before the race so I could get myself used to the feeling. It was one of the best things I could have done, as it took away all fear of the unknown and helped me enjoy the dunes rather than dread them. I had developed a technique of springing up on tip toe, bent forwards and then plunging down on my heels as lightly as I could to save energy. One of my fellow runners, Nicola, nicknamed me the camel spider, which I was rather proud of.

In the desert, everything is vivid and clear. There are no greys or ambiguous shading. The sun is hot, the sky is blue, the sand is gold. Everything is simple. In a race, too, everything is simple: you have to get to the end as fast as you can and in as good a shape as you can. There is something intensely, and bizarrely, relaxing in that. We live lives that are full of variety, choices, decisions and responsibilities, and it can be exhausting. That first day, midway through the morning, I came to a high point. All I could see in front of me was an infinite Erg, an infinite expanse of sand with the dunes rolling ahead. Right along them were scattered the runners, tiny in the distance. They looked like ants scurrying along a sandy floor. The sun had bleached the colour out of the land and the sky to make them both silver and there was a heat haze shimmering towards the Algerian border. All I could hear was the sound of my heart beating in my ears and my breathing. I felt perfectly alive.

That feeling was gradually beaten out of me as the day progressed. I had liked the dunes but I was definitely a lot less keen on the salt flats. Throughout the week, whatever the course for that day, I always seemed to hit a salt flat at around 3 p.m. and be on it till around 5 p.m. This is the hottest part of the day in the desert, when the sun not only crushes you from above but reflects all its stored heat back at you from below. You become the sweaty spam in a sun sandwich. Salt flats are traditionally used to break the land-speed record – think Andy Green in his ThrustSSC across the Black Rock Desert in the USA, going at 713 miles an hour. Now, put that thought right out of your head. My speed dwindled to nothing every time I hit one. The worst thing was when I could see one coming up in the distance and knew that the torture would soon begin. It was crazy. Here was a flat, hard-packed surface that I should be able to trot across comfortably, and wanted to cross as quickly as possible, but, no, the head and legs conspired to make me walk those cracked acres.

I learnt that everything in the desert is salty. At the start of the race you are given salt tablets to try to help avoid dehydration and I religiously took one every half-hour. That salt boost definitely worked to my advantage and kept me healthy through the week, but the side effects were that I sweated out huge quantities of the stuff. By the end of the day, I could actually scrape a layer of it off my face with a fingernail and my black shorts were stained white. My eyes were red from the sweat running into them and my sunglasses had a film of fine white streaks.

Oh, the pleasure when you see the finishing line for the day ahead of you and therefore the prospect of getting off your feet. I think it is the same for any long journey across the desert, granted running it is a bit extreme, but any distance travelled in these conditions makes you grateful for the sight of your camp. Sultan Tea was one of the race's sponsors, and they had a stall right after the line where they would call you over for a cup of hot, sweet mint tea. When you have been drinking unpleasantly sun-heated water all day to try to quench a never-ending thirst, there is nothing, ever, that can compare to that tea. Typically, the man in the kiosk, beaming and congratulating you on arriving, took care to make sure that there was some ceremony involved. Even though he was only pouring it into a little plastic cup, he'd lift the teapot about half a metre from the cup and pour from a height so that a good froth would form on the top of the tea. When I asked why Moroccans pour like that I was told, 'It is to connect the heavens with the earth.'

I needed a little bit of heaven. I had had a fantastic first day, but my body was still shocked by what I had put it through. Back to the tent to get horizontal, raise my legs and just stop moving and rest. I was the last man back and was cheered in. Morale was high and we swapped tales of our magnificent efforts on the dunes, compared food and water notes and generally enjoyed the warmth of the shared endeavour. Charlie had had a storming day and, as always, looked like he had just got back from a light game of tennis. Mr Cool.

The camp was our home and I loved it, but it was a strange place. Over 1,000 people divided up into seven- or eight-person tents, arranged in an open-ended circle. The tents were black and made of goat and camel hair, so looked a little like black sails from a distance. In between, colourful Lycra-clad runners would be hobbling slowly from place to place on painful feet. In fact, the camp could easily have doubled for a post-apocalypse zombie camp.

Over the next few days, we all developed a strong routine in the tent. When you are doing something so difficult and so focused, I find it really helps to have an order and structure. It gives you something to cling on to when you are dealing with a lot of uncertainty of the 'Am I going to get through this alive?' variety. And it is something to look forward to when you are out on the route.

Mine was unvarying after the race. I would get back to the tent and find out how everyone had got on, then take off my backpack and shoes and my running clothes and use a bit of water to soak a Wemmi Wipe (2 grams). This is a tiny pellet of fabric about the size of a cough sweet which expands out into a strong tissue, and I would wash my face, feet and undercarriage with it and then use it for loo roll later. Cleanish, I would put on my nightclothes. I had only brought one set of running clothes and one set of night because of the weight and I had one spare pair of socks for emergencies.

My running clothes were a sports bra, long-sleeved top, buff, cap, compression shorts, calf sleeves and two pairs of socks – Injinjis of finest merino with toes and light hiking-style Bridgedales to go over them. My shoes were Hokas, which had a thick sole to keep me away from the hot sand, and I got them two sizes bigger to accommodate foot swelling and (as I was to find out) bandages. For night-time I had an ordinary bra, a synthetic puff jacket to keep me warm (the night temperature dropped low and my body temperature tended to fall quickly when I stopped), compression tights and flip flops. Getting changed in a communal area was always a bit of a palaver. I would use my side position at the tent so I could at least turn away from the guys. Bruce had the most delicate method, however: 'Time for you to take a look at that view outside the tent, Alice,' was my cue to avert my gaze.

As soon as I had my night clothes on and my sleeping bag and mat rolled out, I would make up my daily recovery drink. Food, like everything else, was rationed. The race organisers decree you carry a minimum of 2,300 calories, which they check when they inspect your kit to make sure you have all the mandatory safety items, and I had worked out exactly what I would need for each day to reach that amount: Extreme Adventure porridge, 1 Clif bar, 1 Bounce bar, 6 x dates, 6 x salted cashews, 1 x Rego recovery drink, 2 x rooibos teabags, 4 x Nuun electrolyte tablets (I'd mixed up the flavours so I would get a surprise every day), 1 x Extreme Adventure hot meal in the evening.

After the drink, it was time for foot care. It will come as

no surprise to learn that the biggest threat to runners in the desert, apart from dehydration, is destroyed feet. The combination of marathon or double marathon distances, sand and extreme heat wreak veritable havoc. With grim humour, the MdS organisers named their medical tent Doc Trotters, and I was a daily visitor. You'd hobble up, wash your feet in disinfectant, put on the little plastic blue booties they give you and then wait to go in. As the race progressed it all got more and more barbaric. Sometimes you heard screams coming from inside and grown men would come out tight-lipped, green-gilled and red-eyed. When inside you would lie flat and put your feet in some poor medic's lap. They would prick and take the pus and fluid out of any blisters, using a scalpel for any truly terrible examples, and then bandage you up and let you go. I was to find that my toe socks were fantastic for keeping the bandages on, which was a big bonus, and I have started wearing them for hiking too if I am likely to incur foot damage.

No rest for the wicked. Time to get dinner on. Our water rations were actually reasonably generous and part of them was used to cook my Extreme Adventure dehydrated meals and have my two cups of rooibos tea a day. I had a little Esbit stove, which is a tiny three-legged contraption that I could pile half a fuel cube on and that was enough to boil 500 ml of water in my titanium mug. Half of that would go into my food, which I had tipped into a cut-off plastic mineral water bottle, and the other half was for my tea, my absolute luxury, shared with South African Bruce. Dinner was pretty good. I had chosen different types of meal: chilli, curry and spicy pasta. The shepherd's pie had failed the taste test in training. I craved things with a bit of zing in them. For breakfast, because I love porridge, I had only brought strawberry porridge. Rookie error! By the end of the week, I couldn't face it and was having to hold my nose while I gulped it down. Your taste buds change in the heat and you want savoury not sweet. Dates are probably the only exception.

I like to be prepared, so I would then make sure that I had everything I needed in place for the night and as much done as I could for the day ahead. By now it was dark and there was time for a little bit of inter-tent socialising. Charlie and I would go over to the Moroccan tent to see how the elite boys were doing and exchange *Salaam Alaykums*. One evening a nice Belgian man in a crocodile suit came to visit. There was also one chap who wandered around in bright yellow hot pants with handprints on the bum cheeks – always raised a smile. The beautiful thing about a race like the Marathon des Sables is that you get to share it with people of all nationalities, abilities, backgrounds and personality types.

I think it must be like the caravans of old when they crossed the desert – it is so tough that you suspend your judgements of your fellow creatures and bond with them through the endeavour. I don't speak Japanese but I made friends in the Japanese tent and went to visit them every evening to talk about our day through sign language and much nodding and smiling.

The highlight of every evening was when the messages from home came through. Family and friends can email the organisation and every day they print out the messages and bring you the sheets. We'd all go silent as we read and absorbed the love and encouragement coming to us from people so far away, forgetting our feet and our fatigue, and taking heart for the next stage.

Bed. Well, sleeping mat, blow-up pillow and sleeping bag to be precise. Both triumph and tragedy were involved when it came to my sleeping arrangements. The real triumph was my £3.99 blow-up pillow with fleecy cover – a massive 120 g but worth it. My eye-wateringly expensive and very light Marmot sleeping bag was also on the side of triumph. The tragedy was my, also expensive and very light, sleeping mat. It was very comfortable, but it rustled, and I mean loudspeaker rustling. Every time I moved it sounded like I was treading crisp packets underfoot with gay abandon. This was a disaster in a tent full of exhausted runners lying cheek to jowl. The boys were all far too nice to complain, but I knew that my popularity level was dropping fast and the effort of trying to keep absolutely still was not worth it. Day two I ditched the mat and just slept on the rug. Another lesson from the desert: you don't need as much stuff as you think you do.

I actually slept incredibly well. The desert air and the physical tiredness knocked me out and morning came too soon. It was always a rush. Loo, clothes, cook breakfast, repack bag, check all is in the right place to be accessible. The tents were dismantled every day by a Berber tent crew who came around in flatbed trucks and who were totally immune to any form of bargaining over timescale. It is the one time in Morocco that I have found things operating to a strict deadline. At 7.30 that tent was coming down, whether you and your kit were in it or not. On the first day, sure of my charm and expecting the usual adulation when I trotted out my few words of Tashlaheet (Berber), I had a rude awakening. Far from giving into my wheedling to give us a few more minutes, I was virtually bundled into the truck with the tent and had to scramble to grab my kit and get out of the way. The lesson was well learnt and after that I respected the rules and the timings. Clearly, the desert brings its own discipline.

The first three days of running went by in a blur of dunes, salt flats and rocky patches. I discovered something about myself and a great new pleasure in life. The self-discovery was that I am really not as nice as I think I am, and it was illustrated by the new pleasure. Water is rationed in the MdS and you get a set amount at each checkpoint and at night. If, for any reason, you ask for more, you incur a time penalty. If you get dehydrated and needed a saline drip, that counted as extra water and incurred a time penalty. My new pleasure? I discovered that I felt a guilty joy every time I trotted past a fit young guy on a drip. Of course I was sorry for him, but it did make me feel that I was doing okay. Human nature is a terrible thing.

One day we passed a village, a hamlet really, near a ruined fortress. About ten houses were scattered in loose formation. The houses were typical for the Sahara, mud-built, with thick walls to protect against the heat and cold and lying low to the ground. All the local kids had come out to watch the runners pass. We made a very strange sight, running past in our fancy trainers and stained and smelly Lycra. Two little girls adopted me and walked with me for a couple of kilometres, clasping my hands and chattering away. They wanted sweeties, but didn't hold it against me that I had none to give them and proudly showed me the bounty that they had collected from some of the other runners. I did wonder how much they would enjoy a high-protein, high-calorie Bounce bar. I also wondered what life was like right out here in the sands, remote from everything that constitutes the modern age.

It seems a strange way to experience the desert, running across it, but it felt to me that I was getting to connect with it in a very real way. Although I was doing something very modern, I believe that the effort involved and the physical nature of it was giving me a glimpse of what it might be like to live this life travelling across the sand as the Sahrawi people have done for centuries. The heat, the terrain, water, food, nightly shelter and your comrades become the only things that matter. You have an end goal in mind, a destination, and all you have to do is reach it. There is no outside interference, no noise from elsewhere. You only use your body and your senses. Your busy mind gets to take a break. You don't really need it. In the quiet, you notice everything and live in the environment, in the moment. Thinking ahead too far is a handicap and you actively stop your mind from going ahead of your legs.

81.5 kilometres. The Long Day had come. The farthest I had ever run was 60 kilometres, which I had thought at the time was pretty extraordinary and which had completely exhausted me. The prospect of adding on another 20 kilometres and factoring in the Sahara desert and a couple of big ascents was daunting. But, it had to be done. Tent 101 had spent the night before discussing various strategies. We had a day and a half to complete the stage, so there was always the option to sleep for a couple of hours at one of the checkpoints if we got too tired. Charlie and I had talked about this before we left and decided that we wanted to keep going and get it done.

Among my messages that night was one from Scott Jameson, who I don't know in real life, but had run the race in 2013 and worn my bib number. It's a tradition to email the person who wears the same number the following year. His words were to come back to me in the coming hours: 'Well done, Alice. Keep up the good work you are making good time. You're heading into the long stage, so listen to your body and rest when you need to and keep the water flowing.

If you decide to go through the night, good luck and never question your ability to finish as that's where eternal Glory awaits you . . . PS How's the toilet roll situation going? People will be starting to run out soon, so watch them panic. It's good for morale! Hee Hee. Speak soon.'

The start line was even more buzzy than usual. There was always the same set-up. A big inflatable white arch in front of us with an electric sensor running underneath that would record our start time from our tags as we crossed. Two 50-metre-long, white, sausage-like barriers lay on each side to funnel us through. Surreally, just beyond this on the right was a huge inflatable teapot advertising Sultan tea to remind us, cruelly, of our finishing line drink. Beside that was the organisation's truck, which doubled us the plat-form for Patrick to make his daily speech and lead us in a rendition of 'Happy Birthday' for the lucky celebrants. We were always standing there for at least half an hour, so some people would squeeze through the barriers for a last-minute pee. Others would be sitting down with their backpacks off, saving as much energy as possible, but most would be chatting to their friends, looking forward to the day and taking selfies. We sounded like an enormous swarm of bees. Through the arch, the red race helicopter was waiting for take-off and when its blades started turning, we knew it was time. Together we'd chant the countdown: 10, 9, 8 . . . then we were off.

As always, those first couple of kilometres were tough for me. My nerves raised my heartrate and, combined with the initial exertion, made it hard for me to get into a breathing rhythm. It is always a jostle at the beginning, too, as the faster runners speed past you and even the slower ones, that you know you will catch later, cruise ahead. The worst thing psychologically is when you are trotting along and a speed walker overtakes you. That is crushing.

Not only was this the longest day, it also had the most ascent, and our first big obstacle was the largest hill we had to climb all week, Jebel Zireg. We approached it across a long, flat plain so could see it coming for ages, which did nothing for the nerves. There was only one path up it through the rocks and there were ropes fixed at the top for safety where it got really steep and narrow. This meant that the runners were in a queuing system. I stressed all along the plain that I wouldn't be quick enough going up and would slow down the people behind me. I really needn't have worried. Another lesson from the Sahara: don't worry. There were 1,000 runners to get up there and it was like the M25 on a Friday afternoon – gridlocked.

Some hardy souls tried to avoid it by going off piste, but the mountain was very unstable and they caused mini avalanches of rocks to rain down on the rest of us and had to stop. Very rude words were exchanged. There was also a pristine sand dune beside us which one intrepid runner tackled. It looked like a hideous struggle as the steepness and soft sand meant he kept sliding backwards. He was alone. Climbing up the path involved actual climbing as there were some big boulders to negotiate. There was one moment, when I was standing in line about 50 metres from the summit, and it was so high, the helicopter was flying below me. I could see for miles right across to the last checkpoint before the hill and the black line of runners making their way towards us. Standing on a mountain in the Sahara desert, queen of all I surveyed.

On the Long Day, the top fifty runners start a couple of hours after the rest of us. This means that the elites will all run past you at some stage and you will get to see them race.

The first of the elites caught me in a series of hillocky dunes, like beach dunes, not long after the hill. I stopped to watch them pass. It was like watching a different, and superior, species. These were men in their element, running with aching grace and seemingly without effort. The desert breeding of the Moroccan contingent showed, and they led the pack. Small and slight in camp, you would pass them in the street without looking twice. But here in the desert their bodies were perfect for the environment and the challenge and they looked magnificent. Ragged cheers followed them from the ordinary mortals. I spotted Christophe with his curly, blond hair and yelled good luck. 'Alice, Alice. How are you? Good luck, *bon courage*,' he replied and blew me kisses as he passed.

My plan for the stage was, as always: keep going and survive it. I trotted where I could and walked when I couldn't. As a result, I kept passing and being passed by a couple of British blokes who were going at a fast walk. They told me I should save energy and keep up a more even pace, and maybe they were right, but I think you have to trust your instincts, and so I trotted on.

The sun was getting low as I faced the next big dune and the light cast shadows that highlighted every ripple on the sand. Dusk in the desert. The heat of the day had gone and the air had softened. When the heat goes, it must be the same sensation as if you have been banging your head against a wall for hours and then stop. The relief is immediate and intense. By the time I reached the top, the sun had set gloriously in red and orange and the light had gone, with just the tips of other dunes showing in the shadows, everything in total silence, all sounds muffled by the sand. I plunged down, heels dug in, trusting my legs and giving in to the darkness and the feeling of being alone on a sea of sand.

The hours of darkness had started and this was going to be a test. The night was clear and the moon was about two-thirds full. Our route was marked by neon glow tubes, like the ones that you see at music festivals. I soon found out that my head torch was not really up to it, so I switched it off and tried to navigate by moonlight and from glow tube to glow tube. It's freaky running in the dark. You have to let go of your fear and just do it. The terrain was flat and sandy so quite safe to run on. Sometimes headlights from one of the patrolling organiser's cars would dazzle me and I'd hear a shout of 'Are you ok?' 'Yes, fine,' I'd answer and keep going. I lost track of time and wasn't really concentrating when (cue comedy music) I ran head first smack into a mini dune and knocked myself backwards onto my bottom. Dazed and confused, I immediately did that thing of scrambling up and looking round to see if anyone had spotted me. Should have gone to Specsavers. I needed to change my tactics, especially as the glow tubes were beginning to lose brightness, and I was finding it harder and harder to find my way without a decent torch.

I speeded up and managed to catch up with Lynn Calder from Aberdeen, who was walking at a cracking pace. We walked 20 kilometres together, talking all the way, and I am still grateful to her for keeping me going faster than I would have gone on my own, even though it hurt at the time, and I spent quite a few kilometres wishing she would slow down. She had decided to take a break at the next checkpoint, but after a failed effort to mix my liquid cereal into my water bottle using a page from my road book as a funnel, I continued alone again. This was a pretty low point. The romance of the desert had worn off and the pain in my legs was the loudest thing I could hear. I employed all my usual strategies for staying positive: 'It's lovely at night, so cool'; 'Hark at me running through the desert, I am a goddess'; 'My legs hurt but at least they are still attached to my hips'; 'Maybe that wet stuff in my socks is not blood but water dropped into them from when I tried to make my liquid cereal'; 'Mint tea at the end'; 'I am going to torture my friends with unending when-I-ran-the-MdS anecdotes when I finish'.

My mantras were beginning to lose their power when salvation arrived in the form of John Colquhoun, running in a camouflage kilt and the proud possessor of a very strong head torch. I asked him if he would mind sharing his light and going on together and he said he would like the company. Hours passed discussing the upcoming Scottish independence referendum, socialism, and the state of British politics. We got each other through that night, a comradeship forged in mutual suffering. If one of us felt tired, the other one made encouraging noises. John's stories were a distraction from the pain and the feeling that this stage was never ever going to end, that I was going to be walking across this rocky plateau in the dark forever. A couple of years later, I was talking to a Sahrawi, a native of the Sahara, and he told me that Moroccans are friendly but the Sahrawis are brothers, joined together by their struggles in the desert. After that night, I understood something of what he meant.

Then, the palest of dawns broke and the sun rose, swapping places with the moon. What an experience to walk and run through a day, through sunset, an entire night and into the dawn. Despite the exhaustion, I could still feel the wonder of what we were doing and that strong connection to Mother Earth. Only a couple of kilometres to go and we were starting to feel really perky thanks to the finish line being in sight and the thought of that mint tea, plus knowing that we would have completed the long stage and run/walked further than we ever had before. Then we glanced behind us and saw a black dot moving fast towards us. John and I looked at each other in horror. 'What the @£%?. No @£$%^& is going to overtake us at this stage,' was our mutual, outraged reaction. 'I bet he's French,' said John, as he gathered up his kilt and we started to run.

We ran and ran and ran, occasionally panting out a 'Come on, come on, he's gaining.' Every time I looked back he was getting closer. We were entirely fuelled by race fever – that feeling of absolute determination that Mr X is not going to pass you, even if you die in the attempt to fight him off. I reckon it is one of our primordial human emotions. The finish line grew closer, the footsteps behind grew closer, we speeded up. Then, HA!, it was done. We had got there first and beaten him. Forget the 79 kilometres that had gone before, it was those last 2.5 kilometres that mattered. John and I were ecstatic and triumphant. We hugged and raised a cheer for Scotland. Twenty-one hours and twenty-six minutes after I had started, I was done. Definitely done.

Coming back to the tent, I found the boys all lying out in a row snoring or moaning lightly. I was feeling elated to have finished and at the prospect of a whole day and night of rest ahead of me. Then I took my shoes and socks off. Armageddon. What had happened down there? Had someone stolen my feet and replaced them with monster paws? Instead of being a nice rosy colour, they were ridged in thick white skin, punctuated by deep, bloody or pus-filled holes at the heels. Every toe was blistered. Some of the blisters looked pretty innocent, just fluid-filled sacs, others had the red and yellow of blood and pus. Then the pain hit me like a train. Now I had stopped, every single piece of me hurt, throbbed or ached, or maybe all three. I lay there with my legs in the air, groaning inwardly and feeling very sorry for myself. How was I going to do a marathon tomorrow? I could barely bear to stand up.

There was a treat in store, though. We were to get a can of Coke along with our water rations. Oh joy, oh bliss, oh can of happiness. The camp that day was like something from *The Walking Dead*. People would shuffle past, zombie-like, on their painful feet, supporting themselves on their walking poles. I limped to Doc Trotters and got bandaged up. 'Will my feet make it?' I asked the doc. 'Yes, of course,' she said. 'You'll be fine. Look how tight I have made the bandages around your toes.'

That rest day taught me another thing about life in the desert. Time is very elastic. I did nothing all day except for rest, feed myself and get my feet seen to, and yet the day in camp flew past. I didn't have a book to read or signal on my phone or any outside distraction but I was perfectly happy, in fact euphoric, to just be at rest. I didn't even think about anything; my mind was a blank. All my energy was being taken up by my body, working away behind the scenes, rebuilding everything I had destroyed on that long day.

Waking up on the last race day, the marathon stage, was good. I had rested, my legs were relaxed, I only had two helpings of porridge left to eat, life was sweet. Then I stood up and the sky darkened. My feet were sore, really sore, not just as sore as they had been for the rest of the race, but white-hot needles being stuck into your toenails, sand being ground into open wounds, bursting pus bubbles with every step, swollen, tender, don't touch me and definitely don't stand on me sore.

I hobbled to the start line, putting my full weight on my

running poles. 'I know I am going to do it,' I said to Charlie, 'but I don't know how I am going to cope with the pain over the next few hours. I don't know how that is going to work.' And I really didn't. My feet were screaming at me to get off them and I was about to pound them across 26 miles. I was going to have to drown out those screams somehow. Charlie was reassuring and practical: 'How many painkillers have you got?'

Me: 'Ten. Ibuprofen, paracetamol, co-codamol.'
Charlie: 'Take six now and then take the rest through the race as you need them.'

Don't try this at home, but it was excellent advice, and I swilled them down. I basically started the day high on pain relief.

Three, two, one and we were off. I set out at a run and, to my amazement, after the first horror I didn't feel too bad. Painkillers work. My feet weren't as sore as when I was walking. I dared myself to actually feel good. My shoes were a mid-strike shoe, which means that they want you to hit the ground in the middle of your foot, and this helped me because this was the place where I had no blisters. When you walk, you hit heel first and this was where I had the most blisters (a little clue there into how much walking I had done over the six days), so running felt much better than walking. I was going to be fine.

I ran across the plain. I ran across the dunes. I ran across the dried river bed and through a little oasis. I ran more than I had run on any other stage. I overtook people. I popped some more painkillers. I actually felt the much talked-of and, to me until that point, entirely mythical, runner's 'flow' when everything was in tune and running was easy. The miles passed quickly and I saw my foot doctor at one of the checkpoints. I ran up to her and kissed her, 'Look, look. I'm doing it. I'm doing it.' 'Bravo, bravo, *courage*,' she replied.

I was crossing a flattish area with scrub and soft sand when I heard a shout and looked up. There, on top of a small hill, was the black outline of a runner against the sun. He was jumping up and down and waving his sticks. It could only mean one thing, he had seen the finish line. I speeded up and took the hill by storm. All I could think to myself was, 'I have almost done it. I am going to finish the Marathon Des Sables. I'm going to do it. I can't believe it. I'm so rubbish at running but I am going to have done it, run the toughest footrace on earth.'

I crested the hill and there, a few kilometres away, was the white arch. I could hear a few traces of the music at the line drifting back on the wind. THE FINISH LINE. All the hairs on my arms stood up, and my whole body was flooded with the most intense happiness I have ever experienced. My heart felt like it was going to explode with the sheer power of it. I roared my victory, shrieking into the air. The months of effort, the self-doubt, the pain all disappeared. I was left only, and purely, with sheer joy. Tears streaming down my face, I ran down the hill to cross the line. I had done it. I had run the Marathon des Sables. In my own small way, I had taken on the desert and survived.

The final day was just a short 10-mile walk to where the buses would pick us up and a chance to walk with Charlie and my other tent mates and new friends and reflect on what we had learnt from the experience and our time in the desert. One thing we were unanimous about was that we felt some-how cleansed and spiritually invigorated. Our bodies were tired but a week in the sand had recharged us fundamentally. We wanted cold drinks and hot showers and to reconnect with loved ones, but we all wanted to hold on to that feeling of renewal that the sands and sun had brought us.

Modern life is busy and crowded and full of variety, all of which is great but it is also exhausting. The majority of people live in an urban environment where their access to nature is limited.

The desert is the exact opposite of that. You can't do anything very fast because the environment just won't let you. There is nothing crowded or distracting about endless seas of sand. There is nothing ahead of you or behind you or around you except sand. There are no nuances in temperature, it is baking hot as soon as the sun is up and that intensity lasts till it goes down. Your sense of companionship is heightened by the feeling of being very small humans in a large world. And perhaps that is the real secret to the abiding allure of the desert: you feel life, you feel the universe. It is there. You are a part of it, but a tiny part, and you understand that long after you are gone, the wind will keep blowing the sand across the dunes.

That feeling of being spiritually connected to our planet is a precious one and the other place that I have felt close to it is in the wilds of the Atlas Mountains, a very different kind of wilderness.

3

THE ATLAS MOUNTAINS

Rachid and I were trudging along an unpaved road following a valley up to the next village through the jagged peaks
of the Atlas Mountains. It was hot and dusty, and we were
tired, fed up and parched. A high stone wall next to the road
guarded a terraced orchard dug out of the steep mountainside.
Overhanging it was a huge fig tree, with the purple-black
ripe fruit dangling temptation right in front of us. My mouth
started watering and, in that moment, I knew just how Eve
felt when confronted with the apple in the Garden of Eden.
Time to scrump, and Rachid got to work with his walking
poles. The first fig exploded in my mouth and the juice ran
down my chin. I was so lost in pleasure that I didn't immediately notice the immaculately dressed Hajj in a white robe
and skull cap who had rounded the corner on his donkey.
Caught! Rachid and I exchanged guilty glances, and he
scrambled down to explain.

'Honoured sir, we are so sorry, excuse us,' he said. 'We have eaten some of your figs. We were hungry and thirsty and they looked so good. Please, forgive us.'

'My son,' replied the Hajj, 'why do you think I planted the fig tree there, next to the road? It was so that travellers like you could enjoy its fruit.'

The Sahara desert may have brought me to Morocco, but the Atlas Mountains are the reason I stayed. A German friend of mine, Dennis Kiphardt, was walking with me one day and summed it up: 'Alice, it is not the beauty of the mountains – you have that everywhere. I live in the Swiss Alps; those are really beautiful. It is the completely different culture that you find here.' He was right. The mountains are an hour's drive from the airport, which means they are 4.5 hours from the UK, but actually they are hundreds of years away. The way of life you find here goes on as it has for centuries, and the people are the most hospitable you will ever meet.

The Atlas mountain range stretches across Morocco, Algeria and Tunisia covering 2,500 kilometres (1,550 miles) and the highest peak is Mount Toubkal in Morocco with an elevation of 4,167 metres (13,671 feet). In Morocco, the mountains form a natural barrier between the desert and the Atlantic and Mediterranean seas. In the Amazigh (Berber) languages the word for mountains is *adrar/adras*' which is thought to derive from Atlas. Atlas is also the root of the word Atlantic.

When you are walking through these mountains, it is easy to believe in the Greek myth of the fallen hero, Atlas. According to mythology, Atlas was a Titan who tried to rebel against the gods by leading his people in battle against them, hoping to win control of the heavens. As any of us who have tried have found, fighting the gods is a mug's game, and the Titans inevitably lost. Zeus, the head of the gods, condemned many of the Titans to a deep dungeon in the abyss called Tartarus, but he devised something extra special for Atlas and gave him the job of holding up the heavens for all eternity. Look up to the summit of Mount Toubkal towering above you at dawn or dusk, and you will catch a glimpse of the giant Atlas, frozen in stone, carrying out his grim and endless duty.

In Morocco, the mountains are divided into three sections; the High Atlas, the Middle Atlas and the Anti-Atlas. The High Atlas rises in the west at the Atlantic coast and stretches in an eastern direction to the Moroccan–Algerian border. At the Atlantic and to the south-west, the range drops abruptly and makes an impressive transition to the coast and the Anti-Atlas range. The High Atlas is the closest range to Marrakech, with hiking expeditions centred around the small but bustling town of Imlil and other centres for shorter trips such as Setti Fatma and Ouirgane.

One place I have to mention is Ait Bougmez, which is like the Garden of Eden and well worth the extra hours it takes to travel there. The Anti-Atlas also extends from the Atlantic Ocean – but further south. It then ranges 500 kilometres (310 miles) to the north-east to Ouarzazate and further east to the city of Tafilalt. In the south, the range borders the Sahara, and the easternmost point of the Anti-Atlas is the Jbel Saghro range. The Middle Atlas range doesn't cross any borders and stays firmly in Morocco. Its 350 kilometres stretches along the length of the north-east. It is known for its biodiversity and also for its animals. It is home to the Barbary ape and the macaque monkey, as well as the wild boar and the pole cat.

My experience of the Atlas has been shaped by two men:

Noureddine Bachar (Nouri) and Rachid Ait Elmahjoub. They have guided me for many hours through the peaks, sharing their knowledge of the landscape, its plants, insects and birds, and, most importantly, explaining the Amazigh way of life and introducing me to the people of the mountains.

Nouri is tall and skinny. Later he was often to complain of this to me in a way that was very galling to someone who finds it easy to gain weight: 'Alice, look at me. I am a skinny goat. I cannot get fat.' He has one eye that roves a little and wears thick glasses. He has a handsome, strong nose and high cheekbones inherited from his mixed Amazigh/Arab ancestry. His legs are very long and my nickname for him in Tashlaheet, the Amazigh language of the High Atlas, is '*Boyou Ghourash*', 'Daddy Long Legs'. His nickname for me is '*Tamkhilawt*', 'Mad Woman'. Noureddine means 'light of religion' in Arabic and Nouri is a shining light. He brings happiness and laughter with him and is irresistible to children.

Rachid is very easy to describe. He is the spitting image of a young Tom Cruise and has the charm to go with the Hollywood looks. He is pure Amazigh and very proud of his heritage, and lives in a village a few kilometres from Imlil.

I met Nouri on a holiday with some British and Irish friends, Karina, Cian and Jo. We wanted to do two days' hiking and two days' mountain biking in the mountains, so Epic Morocco organised it and sent us Nouri as our guide. My first impression was of a whirl of arms and legs and energy as we set off at a run across the mountains and valleys in the spring sunshine. Nouri likes to test his clients' abilities, so the first day is always fast. Panting away at the back, we started talking about music.

Nouri: 'Alice, do you like Michael Klaxon?'

Alice: 'Michael Klaxon?'

Nouri: 'Yes, you know, Michael Klaxon, the American singer.' (At this point, he burst into a rendition of 'Thriller' and started moonwalking. The penny dropped.)

Alice: 'Ahh, you mean Michael JACKSON.'

Nouri: 'No, Michael KLAXON, you know, with the Klaxon Five. Blame it on the boogie.' (By this stage we are all giggling helplessly, and still racing along breathlessly, and my sides were starting to hurt. Cian, Karina and Jo all backed me up.)

Us: 'No, no, no. Nouri, it's the *Jackson* Five, not the Klaxon Five.'

Nouri [with a face as innocent as an angel]: 'Alice, it *is* the Klaxon Five. I have seen them in Rabat.'

When I went back to the UK, I got him a T-shirt with the 'Klaxon Five' printed on it and he was to wear it for my first ascent of Mount Toubkal. Mount Toubkal is the highest point in north Africa and always has some snow on it – even in the height of summer you will find some small patches – and is a two-day climb from Imlil.

To start with you have to get to the base of the mountain. You stock up on any provisions you might need in Imlil. Typically for a walk I would buy freshly baked bread, sardines in tomato sauce, Laughing Cow cheese (it always tickles me that in Tashlaheet it is called Tamoogayt ('cow') HA HA!), a couple of apples and some nuts and figs or raisins, as well as plenty of water.

Imlil is similar to any other high mountain hiking centre you have ever been to. It lies at 1,740 metres above sea level so you will feel slightly breathless as soon as you start walking up the hill. It is a small place centred along one main road that drives through and up over the next pass. The road is always badly pot-holed from the snow and ice in the winter. There are a collection of kit shops selling second-hand equipment gifted to guides by grateful tourists, which are worth a look as you can get some great brands at very good prices. This is also where you hire your crampons and ice axe for Toubkal in the winter. There are lots of tea and tagine places, a couple of souvenir shops, two mountain bike hire shops and a great butcher's. The sheep and goat meat from the mountains is highly prized because the animals feed on the alpine plants and herbs, like wild thyme, which grow in the passes. The animals are very lean and the meat is not only delicious, it is also healthier and believed to be especially good for diabetics.

From Imlil, you walk through the abundant apple, cherry, peach, plum and walnut orchards – come in April for the blossom – across a wide, stony river bed overlooked by the typical Berber village of Armed perched on a hillside, the skyline pierced by the mosque, and over to the base of the Toubkal national park. It is 14 kilometres to the refuges at the base of Toubkal where you will spend the night at 3,207 metres (105 feet). That first day is misleading because it feels relatively easy, but you in fact ascend 1,467 metres (4,812 feet), which is higher than Ben Nevis. The first section winds up through a river valley. On each side are the high, pointed, brown, barren mountains against the bright sky. They are dotted with juniper trees, gnarled and dark green like trees from a scary fairy tale. These are protected by law in Morocco and grow to venerable ages. The oldest juniper tree in the USA is believed to be 3,000 years old. I disagree with my friend Dennis, because I find the mountains very beautiful.

They are not lush or covered in green pastures like the Alps, but they have a naked grandeur. You can see the bones of them reaching into the sky and feel how old the earth is.

Lunch on day one is at the shrine of Sidi Chamharouch, a place of pilgrimage. You will almost certainly have been passed on the route by a pilgrim sitting on a mule, sometimes wearing all-white. Non-Muslims are not allowed into the little white domed building that straddles the river, but you can go as far as the bridge. Pilgrims come to be healed and it is thought to be particularly good for those suffering from mental illnesses.

After the shrine and lunch the path immediately becomes steeper and the real work of the day begins. It is not like climbing a mountain, but it is a good pull up and over the boulders and becomes increasingly narrow as you approach the refuges. They can never come quite soon enough for me. You turn a final corner in the path and there are the two of them, cosying into the base of the sheer mountain face. There is quite a lot of water at this point, so you approach over grass, the green coming as a bit of a shock after a day of browns, greys and blacks. There are always mules grazing there. They've been used to transport baggage, food, gas, water and tired hikers. The refuges are well-equipped and serve hot, filling suppers, but they are always freezing, even in the height of summer.

That first time with Nouri, we spent the evening playing cards with a group of guides, and then got to bed early because the next day was going to be a big one. Thankfully, as I wiggled into my sleeping bag and piled on an extra three blankets, I had no idea how big.

It all started out so well. Nouri and I had got up just after 3 a.m. and were breakfasted and out on Mount Toubkal by 4.30 a.m. It was a beautiful night with the stars shining brightly and the Milky Way unfurling above us.

Crampons and an ice axe were absolute necessities and the beginning of the climb from the refuge was fiercely steep and really challenging. My legs felt like little stumps as I bashed my crampons in at every step to get purchase. An hour into the climb, I was starting to feel more confident and thought I had pretty well sorted my crampon gait, but not according to Nouri – 'Legs wider, legs wider'. He was obviously imagining the dreaded trouser catch and subsequent tumble down several hundred metres.

He's a merciful man, though, and I was allowed a sit-down on a big rock and to eat a Bounty halfway up to the first pass. Dawn was breaking with fingers of pink reaching out from behind the clouds through the peaks. The sun took another hour to come out and hit us just as we were about to reach the pass. From there, it was crampons off as we got to the scree. The gradient had loosened off a bit and the climb was lighter. There was just one really nasty section, which was a traverse from right to left across snow and boulders with a vertiginous drop to the side. 'I don't like this, Nouri, I don't like this.' Until then, we had been the only folk on the mountain, but at that point two young Moroccan men cheerfully passed us. I was jealous of their confidence and ease on the slope but trudged doggedly on.

In the final metres of the walk to the top, I felt great. I'd done it and had no altitude sickness at all. Here I was on the highest point in north Africa, with Nouri singing 'Billie Jean' in his Michael Klaxon and the Klaxon Five T-shirt. The sun was shining on the snow and it was time for a breakfast of Laughing Cow and bread on our own private picnic ledge, with a heart-stopping 360° view of the High Atlas.

But all good picnics come to an end and soon we started back down the scree. Within half an hour, the two lads we had met on the way up bounded past us. Nouri called out to follow the paths and watch their legs, but they were on a high and weren't listening. Disaster struck 150 metres later. One of them tripped over his crampons on the scree and flipped right over, landing on his back. I watched it happen in slow motion and felt sick with fear for him. He was about 300 metres away from us down one of the most treacherous slopes of the descent, which was covered in a mixture of loose scree and black ice. The boy was lying like a rag doll on the slope – unconscious, sprawled and bleeding – and his friend was distraught. All joviality disappeared and Nouri sprang into action. He ran down the slope with total control, showing his years of experience. He covered the distance in less than a minute. To put that into context, it took me nearly twenty to get down to him because of the difficulty of the terrain.

Nouri saved that boy. He got him into the recovery position, bandaged up his head and got a foil blanket and then my down jacket on him. By the time I got there, the boy, Ibrahim, was barely conscious but thrashing around. Nouri and I tried to support his head and stop him bashing himself. Nouri got some water and sugar into him but he vomited it straight up (an ignoble part of me felt momentarily sad for my down jacket). The gods were watching over that boy – by sheer good luck he didn't appear to have any fractures, just a very nasty bump on his head. When I saw him fall I thought he'd broken his neck.

At last, a second mountain guide appeared on the horizon and ran down when he saw what had happened. So there we were on the mountain with a barely conscious boy, who was alternately throwing himself around and lying limp, with no phone reception, air ambulance, or any way off except on foot. There was only one option, so Nouri and his fellow guide got Ibrahim on his feet between them and started carrying him down.

It was amazing to watch. They were so quick and sure-footed even when they were sinking thigh deep in the snow, which had now softened under the strength of the sun. They were quickly way ahead of me as I made my tentative way down. I am not that confident in the snow, and seeing such a horrible fall did nothing for my courage. Two-and-a-half hours later, I saw the refuge and Nouri walking back up to me – the man is a machine.

When I got to the refuge, Ibrahim was lying down, looking much, much better and waiting for a mule to take him down to Imlil where an ambulance was waiting to drive him to the hospital in Marrakech. Lucky boy that Nouri was so close to him when he fell, and a reminder that mountains have to be treated with respect and caution.

For me, there was still a long way to go, as we were going on to Imlil that day. The full walk is 38 kilometres, and by the end of it my legs were screaming. We were late due to all the drama but set off in good spirits and the walk down distracted me as the sun bounced off the valleys and gorges and deepened into dusk. Too many hours later, we finally arrived at the guest house, Douar Samra, one of my favourite places in all of Morocco. Nirvana. Fluffy blankets, a fire in my bedroom, a hot-water bottle in my bed and big fat cushions for my achy legs. Mohammed and Rashida, the waiter and chef, had saved me supper and even brought it to my room because I was too knackered to tackle the steps back up to the dining room. I'd seen the best and the worst of the mountains that day.

Until I came to live in Morocco, I had not appreciated the extent of the Amazigh/Berber nation. I had, ignorantly, lumped Morocco in with the 'Arab' countries and made my assumptions based on that. In fact, Morocco was an Amazigh country and was invaded by the Arabs at the time of the great Arab conquests in the eighth century. Many Berbers in Morocco do not like being called Berber and, understandably, want to be called by their name in their own language, Amazigh (singular) or Imazighen (plural). The word means 'free man' and the symbol of the Amazigh is a man standing with his arms upstretched to the sun. The word 'Berber' traces back to Ancient Egyptian and means 'outlander'. It then filtered into Ancient Greek where it means 'a person from the outside who speaks a language we don't understand' (blah blah blah). The pejorative 'barbarian' comes later.

At its height, the Amazigh nation stretched from Morocco across Algeria, Tunisia and Libya and through to the Siwa Oasis in Egypt. From north to south, it went down through Mauritania and Mali, stopping at the natural barrier of the Niger River. In modern Morocco it is estimated that around 40 per cent of the population is Amazigh, although intermarriage is so common that most people have Amazigh connections in their families. There are three main Amazigh languages: Tashlaheet, Tamazight and Tarifit. Tashlaheet is the most widely spoken, and is used by about 20 per cent of the population, with 13 per cent and 10 per cent respectively for the other two. All three are different but are mutually understandable to some extent. Although there are around 12 million people who speak the Amazigh languages in Morocco, they were only recognised as official languages in 2011, after the Arab Spring.

I like languages, so with every trip to the mountains, I

learn a few more words of Tashlaheet. I have an obscure but fine collection:

ifsi nizri – white wormwood
inghayi fed – I'm thirsty
tashwit – You are beautiful
tagint mzyayn? – Did you sleep well?
hashagh – I am on form
aswoo – stork
yaazadari wdrar – I love the mountains

One of the fantastic things for me about living in Morocco is that because I speak Arabic I immediately get a high approval rating and people are nice to me, which I like. When I speak Tashlaheet, that approval rating goes off the scale and I attain goddess-like status, which I really like.

The experiences I have been privileged to have, and the people I have met in the Atlas Mountains, are among the dearest to me. Nouri was instrumental in this. With his silly, jokey, extrovert personality, each walk I have done with him has been fun, no matter how much I have suffered, and he immediately brings people out of their shell so that even the shyest mountain child will be chatting away by the end of the night. If you are with him you become part of that and are soon treated as part of the family. At the beginning of my forays into the mountains I was reluctant to stay at people's houses, and felt that very British feeling of, 'Oh no, I couldn't possibly. I don't want to intrude. I need my own space. This is going to be awful. Where will I go to the loo?' Nouri smashed that barrier early on, simply by ignoring it, and plunging me into the heart of various unsuspecting Amazigh families.

One particular trek, we were going far into the hills and heading for the Yaghur plateau. The plateau is fertile ground and has been settled for tens of thousands of years, as evidenced by the prehistoric rock carvings that are littered across it. Now it houses a couple of hamlets and, in the summer, is home to the nomadic herders who bring their flocks up to feast on the rich grass.

Our first encounter that day was at lunch time. We were halfway up a steep slope when we came to a flattish point which was perfect for a break. We took off our packs and started rummaging around for food. Nouri got his blue tin teapot out, gathered some twigs and started a fire to get the water boiling. He had collected some wild mint on the way for the tea. The slope opposite was dark with dots of goats grazing on the scrub and as we sat there the shepherd boy who was herding them spotted us and ran down the mountainside to meet us and eat with us. In the loneliness of the mountains, any company is good company, and we quickly made a jovial threesome.

Hassan was a gawky fourteen-year-old with a long oval face and a wide smile. He had left school because his family needed him to work. His family didn't own the goats, but he was overseeing the herd of around 300 for a rich man in the village. He told us about his brothers and sisters, helped Nouri to blow on the fire to make it burn brighter and scraped away a load of stones and sticks so I could sit down comfortably.

I learnt two things from that lunch. The first was that there is no concept in Amazigh culture of a child, or anyone for that matter, not doing their share of the work. There is no nagging from parents to set the table, load the dishwasher, make a cup of tea. As soon as they can walk, the children are helping and working, and they want to be of use – they are proud to contribute to the family. All tasks are communal, and everyone takes their turn. The second thing I learned was that everything is shared. The concept of 'this is mine' is alien. We all got out our food and then we all ate it. No one had more or less than the other. We actually had a feast: the obligatory bread and sardines with Laughing Cow cheese and a couple of tomatoes, hot tea with lots of sugar and fresh mint from the mountain and then two flourishes. Hassan produced three rosy apples from his bag, and I came out with my bar of Kendal Mint Cake. Dessert of champions. I loved the apples, enjoying their crisp tartness, and Hassan thought he'd died and gone to heaven when he bit into Kendal Mint Cake: sugar and mint in a concentrated lump, a Moroccan dream.

As the night drew in, we reached the hamlet we had been aiming for. About half a kilometre from it a group of kids came running out to see who we were. Nouri told them and said he was heading for Hussein and Rqyya's house. The advance guard ran excitedly back to tell them we were coming. Nouri had not seen Hussein and Rqyya for seven years, but he had brought printed photos that he had taken last time he was there to give to them. He was greeted like a long-lost brother and I could hear the metaphorical fatted calf accepting his fate in the yard.

The house was typical: large to accommodate an extended family, built of red compacted mud with very small windows clad in iron grills. It was square with a central courtyard which had a byre for the family cow and a few sheep and lots of chickens. Three generations lived there, including two brothers and their wives and children, and we were immediately ushered into the main guest salon. This was a long rectangular room with hard banquettes on each side with cushions for your back. We took our boots off, sat down, and the tea was brought in on small wooden tables. I drank it, grateful for something hot and sweet to give me back some energy. The grandfather came in and we all got up and kissed his hand respectfully. He fixed me with a gimlet eye. 'I'm 103, you know,' he said. This was my first encounter with a mountain phenomenon. Whenever you meet an elderly person, they are always proudly declared as over 100 years old. Admittedly the mountain air is very pure, so who knows, perhaps my slight scepticism at the sheer volume of centenarians in the Atlas is misplaced.

Rqyya went off to cook a celebratory tagine and Nouri and I went too, to see what was going on and chat. Where Nouri goes the children go, so soon there were thirteen of us ranging from three to fifty gathered in the kitchen. It was a basic room with a clay floor, a cylinder-gas-fired two-ring stove and a clay bread oven with a chimney built into one wall. There were no windows, but since there was also no actual door on the doorway, that didn't matter. There were a couple of handy shelves and essential supplies arranged around the walls: oil, sugar, flour. Because everyone eats communally from one big plate or tagine using bread as the spoon and you also share the water glass, you don't need as much crockery or kitchen equipment in Morocco.

Rqyya busied herself with the tagine and Nouri set to entertaining the children with his amazing disappearing coin trick. It was a scene from Rembrandt as the light from the gas illuminated the rosy faces of the children, sitting in a ring with their eyes glued to the sorcerer.

When the tagine was ready, we decamped to the TV salon and sat on another set of banquettes round a low table. There were six of us. The TV was blaring out an Amazigh channel that no one was watching. One of the elder boys brought around water so we could all wash our hands. This water contraption is like a large kettle on top of a bowl. You hold your hands under the kettle and wash them as the water is poured over them and drains into the bowl. You are then given a little towel to dry them on.

Everyone was very pleased when I said I didn't want to eat with a spoon and a plate 'Christian style', but with my hands like everyone else. For just this occasion I had asked Nouri to explain to me previously how to eat a tagine politely. Rqyya had made a goat tagine with carrots, turnips, potatoes, courgettes and a chilli on top. It was arranged, as always, in a kind of volcano shape with the vegetables propped up artistically on the outside, the meat inside and the chilli on the top. This is what Nouri had told me in my tagine-eating lesson:

So, Alice, before you eat, say, '*Bismillah*' (in the name of God). The host will break the bread and give it to you. If you take a piece of bread you must eat it to the end. It is a sin to leave bread. Tear off a small piece and then, with your right hand, dip it into the juice at the bottom of the tagine. You must only eat from the section of the tagine in front of you. This is your portion, don't stray into someone else's part. You pinch the bread between your thumb and your first two fingers, and then you can use it to take pieces of vegetables. Small pieces at a time. When you come to the meat in the middle, leave it! Don't just eat it. You have to wait for the father or the mother. They will divide it for everyone, so that everyone gets a fair share, and then you can eat it. There is only a little meat and everyone needs to eat it.

Knowing what to do meant I could relax and enjoy the meal, which was delicious. A full day's hiking at high altitude is the right way to work up an appetite. My '*imim*'s ('delicious') were heartfelt. Nothing tastes as good as a hot tagine made from meat and vegetables fresh from the farm with a family of open-hearted, generous people.

After dinner and tea there was no lounging around; it was straight to bed. In our culture we have central heating to keep us warm, comfy sofas to sink into, TVs and the internet to entertain us and we live much more automated lives so we have time for leisure. In mountain culture, every resource is gathered or created and is sparse: there is no heating in the houses – there is no fuel for it; instead of sofas there are hard banquettes which double as beds; and you are going to be up at first light to start feeding the animals and working, so there isn't much time or comfort for watching TV.

Nouri and I were to sleep in the salon. Large, heavy acrylic blankets were produced and I searched out my toothbrush. There are so many beautiful things about Moroccan culture, but teeth are not one of them. I assume it is because of the high proportion of sugar in the diet and because they don't brush their teeth, but it is the norm here for people to open their mouths and show big gaps where teeth have come out, or, even worse, blackened stumps. In this house, there was no running water or bathroom and we were in the centre of the village.

'Nouri, where do I go to the loo and brush my teeth?' I asked.

'With the animals, Alice.'

I wasn't 100 per cent sure if he was joking or not.

'Are you telling me the truth? What do you mean?'

'Of course. With the animals, outside, downstairs in the courtyard.'

The alleyways of the Marrakech medina.

A tiled water fountain. These are traditionally gifted by rich people so that everyone has access to drinking water.

The water sellers dispense water from a goatskin bag and ring their little brass cups together like castanets to advertise their presence.

Majorelle blue from Yves Saint
Laurent's famous Majorelle
gardens.

Wading into pigeon shit with my friends in Marrakech's
tanneries.

Jemaa El Fna square: Marrakech's centre and a vibrant welcome to life in Africa.

Climbing the dunes during the Marathon des Sables.

Experiencing the Sahara desert.

Crossing the desert the traditional way. White camels can smell out water.

The rich colours of the Atlas Mountains.

Stopping for a tagine on the way up to Morocco's
ski resort – Oukaimeden.

In summer, you can
escape the heat by
eating with your feet
in the water at Setti
Fatma in the Atlas
Mountains.

Shepherd kids watch, fascinated, as Rachid prepares dinner during the Atlas to Atlantic trek.

Amazing hospitality. Eating *tannourt* bread with our host, the father of Fatima. We had met him as we walked into Ouizamarn and he had offered us a bed for the night.

Rachid and I wade straight into the sea at Agadir, filthy but happy to have completed our world first Atlas to Atlantic Trek.

Summiting Toubkal, North Africa's highest mountain at 4,167 metres.

The back streets of Fez.

Green tiling on one of Fez's many mosques.

The Merenid tombs at first light as I run up with Serena.

Another comfort zone exited, I was going to have to go and take a wee with the cows in the middle of the courtyard.

'Nouri, you have to come with me and stand guard.'

'Why?'

'In case anyone comes. I can't go for a wee if anyone comes. I will die of embarrassment.'

Poor Nouri, he has had to listen to me ablute far more than any person should have to, but I was not risking the 103-year-old grandfather coming across my mooning white bottom in the middle of his courtyard.

I had been in Morocco for about eighteen months when I decided that it was time for a bigger adventure. As always, I sought the advice of Charlie. We were sitting having our weekly lunch at the café near his office in Gueliz: tripe and beans. I was just having the beans because I am not a fan of tripe, but Charlie was tucking in appreciatively to the frilly, coral-shaped offal on the top of his plate. We had thrown around lots of ideas when Charlie had his brainwave.

'I've got it. A world first. You should walk from the top of Toubkal, the highest point in north Africa, straight across the Atlas to the low point, the Atlantic ocean at Agadir. Atlas to Atlantic. You'll need to carry all your own stuff and you need to make it hard, so an average of 30 kilometres a day. Epic Morocco will sponsor it.' I was in! A great idea and a sponsor rolled into one. Charlie rose even higher in my estimation.

Timing was always going to be a problem as we were already in May and Ramadan was coming in July, when it would be impossible to find a guide. Ramadan lasts for a month, and during that time all Muslims fast from sunrise to sunset. This means not only not eating, but not drinking anything at all, so, obviously, it would be far too much of a physical strain to ask someone to walk 30 kilometres per day in the heat and over the high mountains. Moreover, Ramadan is a big family celebration and breaking the fast every day is an occasion with special food. No one would want to miss that. We settled on a start a week or so after the feast that celebrates the end of the holy month, which took us into mid-August. It was going to be hot.

I also needed a guide and Charlie could not spare Nouri. Also, Nouri's wife had just had a baby girl and he didn't want to be away from home that long. We decided on Rachid. I had already spent a couple of days with him going up Toubkal with a friend and had liked him a lot. That initial liking was to be transformed into a lifelong friendship over the course of the expedition.

An expedition is different from a hiking trip or holiday. It's tougher, but it isn't just that: it is the fact that you have a goal to achieve and a purpose. That is very positive and moti-vating. On the other hand, you have the pressure of having to make sure that you succeed and that you do your best for your sponsor, too. There is also an expectation on you from the community. When Rachid told the other guides what we were doing, the response went something like, 'Nah, you'll never make it. She'll give up.'

The distance in total was around 350 kilometres, and we were aiming to do it in twelve to thirteen days. The only big barrier we faced was the high peaks of the Atlas, which we were proposing to go up and over as we headed west in a more-or-less straight line. There were lots of them. I had a tent, stove and sleeping bag in my pack and we had enough food for a couple of days, but we were aiming to stay in people's houses in the remote villages on the way and eat with them – of course for a payment – and we could restock water from the rivers.

Before we even started on our actual expedition, we had to scale Mount Toubkal. The mind is a strange thing. Usually, if I go up Toubkal, it is an adventure and a treat, but in this case it was actually a pain because I kept thinking, *This doesn't even count towards the journey.*

Within two days of leaving Mount Toubkal and walking through the mountains, we had entered a different world. The scenery was similar to that around Toubkal, but there were no tourists or mountain guides in their Berghaus and North Face jackets. The only people we met were local villagers and herdsmen. The scatterings of villages became more and more sparse.

On the third day, our up and over took us down to join a river and we walked along it for most of the day. In the morning, it was a large, silted course with the brown water of the river in the centre. There were little rock pools and sand pools at the edge and legions of fat, green toads, belching and burping at the sun. We saw two turtles, their little heads just poking up above the water and lots of tiny fish feeding at the water's edge on the abundant insects. The air was alive with the buzz of creatures going about their daily business without human interference.

As the river narrowed, it became fiercer and the silt gave way to rocks and big boulders. On either side were thick groves of oleander covered in pink blossom. We had to hack and push through them and clamber over and under the boulders using our hands and feet. The sun was still hot even though it was around 5 p.m. when we heard excited squeals and splashes up ahead. Around the next bend was a natural pool, filled with young boys jumping in from the rocks above and being carried down by the current. Rachid and I were hot and tired. There was only one thing to do. He stripped down to his pants, and I just took my shoes off and went in fully clothed.

The boys were ecstatic; a weird foreign woman swimming with them. This was a story to tell the family. They dived and plunged and somersaulted and showed off with all their might. 'Auntie, look at me! Look at me!' Rachid and I revelled in the cool Atlas water after the hot hours of walking. Happy times for sore muscles and a joyful end to the day.

Wherever there is water in the Atlas and some soil, there will be a village, a hamlet or just a family living off the land. The houses are long, low and built from compacted clay. They are often built with one wall backing onto the rock of the mountain to give them a strong foundation. The windows are small so that the sun is minimised in the summer and the cold is minimised in the winter, and are often unglazed. A thick square of white is painted round them as the bright white gets very hot in the sun and stops the ants from crossing into the houses, and they are covered by hand-crafted, ornate iron grills, decorated with spirals symbolising eternity in the Amazigh culture. They are usually two to three storeys high. The ground floor is for the animals and the upper floors for humans. The roofs are flat and used as an extra place to sleep when it is hot, somewhere to put the washing out, or just somewhere to watch the world go by from. Because the houses harmonise so well with the mountain, you can often be quite close to a village before you spot it.

The cultivated areas are heavily terraced up and down the sides of the mountains. The terraces are sustained by hand-built stone walls using the stones cleared from the little fields to leave the earth for the crops. The farmers then plant irises along the edges of the terraces which bloom their violent purple all through spring and summer. Iris roots are very tenacious and they help keep the walls and the terraces intact. A nice corollary is that they are also quite profitable and are exported to Germany to be used in stomach medicines.

Courgettes, onions, carrots, tomatoes, potatoes, alfalfa for the cows, barley and some wheat are the main crops. In the right conditions there are various fruit, almond and walnut trees. I have often passed a young man on the mountain carrying a big gallon tub of water, walking up to water two or three saplings he has planted. Once they are established their roots can reach down to the water deeper in the ground, but at the beginning they need to be carefully tended. The earth is rich and the sun is strong so the yield is good. Water is the key, and is jealously hoarded.

When you look closely at the terraces, you will see an arterial network of irrigation channels bringing in lifeblood. There are little gates at various points along the system which are opened and closed at set times so that each plot gets its share of water. Everything in the mountains is shared. The irrigation network is communal, built and maintained by the men of the village. When it needs to be cleaned they will be brought together by the village leader and organised into a work party with refreshments prepared by the women. If someone can't make it for some reason, they might donate a little money or some extra food.

One morning, we set off from where we had been staying at the entrance of the Agandis valley and headed towards Ijoukak. This area is highly cultivated with many orchards, almost like Ait Bougmez but not as extensive. Walking through the shade of the fruit trees in the summer and seeing all the perfect little squares of vegetables is a real pleasure and Rachid and I were doing just that close to the village of Alla when we heard a shrill, 'Help, help!' coming from about 100 metres away.

We ran through the trees and found a little old lady on her back, turtle-like, unable to get up. She had an enormous load of alfalfa strapped to her with ropes, which she had obviously just cut, and she didn't have enough strength to right herself. It's the women's job to look after the family cow and you often see them bent double under the weight of a load of alfalfa. They bind it into a block and then sling it over their shoulder with a rope that has a hand loop in it, or tie it onto their backs. I have tried to carry some of the loads and found them extremely heavy and unwieldy. Our turtle-lady looked at least eighty, and we scurried to give her a hand. We pulled her up and settled the load more comfortably on her back. Rachid offered to carry it for her, but she refused and after a lot of hand-, shoulder- and cheek-kissing and many blessings we went on our way. '*Do'a,*' said Rachid, which means extra credit in paradise.

Summer is when the cactus fruit aknaray comes into season and along our route they were everywhere. The plants grow in big clumps, often two to three metres tall and five metres long, with the green, fleshy, thorny leaves topped by the red or orange fruit. Men go out and pick them and then sell them for a couple of dirhams, and Rachid was an addict. He could spot aknaray from fifty paces and would always make a beeline for them. We would buy a few and the seller would carefully peel back the outer coat for us. It looks quite innocent but is covered with tiny prickles which leap onto you if you touch it and get into your skin and clothes and under your nails and are incredibly difficult to get rid of. It is not the bigger thorns that get you; it's the little prickles. A mantra for life, really. The flesh ranges from white to orange to red but most are a peachy orange and the taste is a gentle sweetness.

The other plant that was ubiquitous was the aloe. The bushy plant with fleshy leaves at the bottom is the base for a tall stalk reaching five or six metres into the sky, topped by a red or yellow poker-shaped flower at the top. You can break the leaves open to get out the sap, which soothes sunburn and skin irritations. I liked them for their architectural qualities and the way they soared into the sky. When I looked back at my photos after the trip, I had hundreds with aloes acting as a frame for the mountains or as punctuation for the valleys.

Deep in the mountains most villages don't have shops, so we had to make sure that when we reached somewhere slightly bigger we stocked up on sardines and Laughing Cow cheese. However, we could always buy bread as the women make it at home for their families. Water was the thing we had to be vigilant about. We would fill our bottles and CamelBak from clean points in streams, far from any humans or animals. Rachid was very particular as he didn't want either of us to get sick. On one very hot, dusty, sticky, sweaty afternoon, we walked into a cluster of houses that were rather cut off as a landslide had taken away the road some months earlier. Immediately, a couple of smiling villagers came out to meet us and we exchanged greetings and news. The invitations to drink tea came thick and fast, but we still had a very long way to go that day so we refused but asked if we could have some water. A man rushed off up the hill and came bounding back down with a huge grin on his face, carrying two plastic bottles filled to the brim with ice. The circle of people looked at us expectantly, and they were not disappointed; we were delighted.

'Wow! Ice! How did you get this? This is fantastic. Thank you so much!' we exclaimed, as we took off the lids and sipped at the newly melted water on top. It was so good.

Nothing tastes that good. They explained that they had one solar panel and that they powered the village fridge with it. 'May God be praised,' we chorused. 'It's a wonder!' There was enthusiastic agreement all round. We swapped out our empty bottles and went on our way. For the rest of the afternoon we had icy cold water to drink under the hot sun, and the memory of kindness.

By now, I had no shyness about staying in people's houses overnight. The Amazigh code is one of hospitality and all we had to do was show up in a village at dusk to be bombarded with invitations. People would bring out their best for us, prepare our tea and dinner, boil up water so we could have a wash and do everything within their power to make us comfortable. We would always leave some money as resources are tight and we didn't want to abuse people's hospitality, but sometimes it was a real struggle to get them to accept it.

Host: 'No, no, no. For shame. You are our guests, it is our pleasure to have you. You are welcome here any time. You must come again. No. We do not want payment.'

Rachid: 'My uncle, this is not payment. You have given the gift of hospitality and we have become friends, but we live far away and maybe you won't visit us, although you will always be welcome in my home in Asni or Alice's home in Marrakech. Because we are travelling far we do not have any gifts to give you. The only poor gift we have is this money. Please accept it. Please use it for the children, maybe they need something for school.'

The tea and the food were always very welcome, but it was the conversations that I came to appreciate the most during these stays. Each home was, of course, different. In some the men and women would eat and socialise together, and in others they would be separate. Sometimes I was with Rachid and he could translate for me, and sometimes I was on my own and had to get by with my very basic Tashlaheet and lots of sign language and goodwill, or Arabic if the people were slightly more educated. I would learn something new every time about this culture that was so far from my own and yet so warm and welcoming. In one house in Ouizamarn, Rachid had gone out to make an appearance at a wedding up the road – August is wedding season in the mountains – and I was alone with the daughter of the house, who was around thirty.

She spoke Arabic so we could communicate easily, and she told me her story. Her father was from this village in the mountains, but her mother was actually from the desert plains outside Agadir, which is where she lived for most of the year with her other, married sisters. Fatima was the one delegated to look after her father when he was in the village, and then they would go down to the plains to all be together at some parts of the year.

Me: 'Where do you like it better, the plains or the village?'
Fatima: 'I like the plains much better. I don't like it here.'
Me: 'Why not?'
Fatima: 'I have no one here. My mother and sisters are all away. I have no one.'
Me: 'Don't you have any friends in the village? Young girls your age to talk to and to be with?'
Fatima: 'No. They are all married and they have children so they don't want to know me because I am not.'
Me: 'But you have plenty of time. You are young and beautiful and I am sure you will get married soon and have lots of children.'

She turned and looked me full in the face and asked me if I really thought she was beautiful. She told me that she thought she was too old and no one would want her now, and then she asked me if I would like to see her hair. She took off her headscarf and shook out a cloud of dark hair around her face, and I realised that in her life in the village this young woman had no one to share this hidden beauty of hers with, that no one but me would give her the pleasure of telling her she was lovely.

Although we tried to go from village to village, with our up and over route we sometimes had to camp. Camping in the Atlas is a great option. Of course, you need to make sure you are near a source of good water and that you have somewhere flat enough to camp, but those two things aside you can camp wherever you want and enjoy extra hours under the sky. On this particular section we were going from Ouizamarn to Khmis Nait Zmlal and there was no village where we could stay over, so we were aiming for the Tichka plateau to camp on for the middle night. Every step of this day stays in my memory.

We set off in the early light from Ouizamarn along well-walked paths in the valley, crossing the river. We passed lots of small villages clinging to the hillside, almost invisible sometimes except for the jutting spire of the minaret from their mosque. The aloes poked into the sky and the aknaray plants were laden or bare, depending on whether they had been harvested or not. We encountered a few people on the way: women leading their one cow out to the pasture or carrying bags of laundry to the best spot for washing on the river; men on donkeys or mules heading for the bigger towns; children walking towards the fields to help out their parents but having a lot of fun on the way. The predominant colour was brown from the exposed earth on the mountainside and the clay of the village houses. The green of the small cultivated patches stood out vividly, pointing us to the water.

By midday, we had turned into the forests of the mountain and our world became greener. There was a lot of climbing on this day and we were in an area that was completely uninhabited. We entered an enormous basin surrounded by high peaks. I wished my cousin Charlie, a geologist, was there to explain the science of it, but even to my uneducated eye it was clear that great ructions in the earth had pushed up the mountains and hollowed out the valley. The area was large, several kilometres across, up and down – kilometres that feel even longer when you are on your own two feet. For lunch we stopped on a ledge of grass which had two handy boulders for our backs and a stream down below where we could refill our water. We'd been going up steadily for a couple of hours and the small patch of flat was a relief. I watched two white butterflies dance in front of me, listened to the buzz of the insects, and enjoyed the warmth of sun on my face, the taste of sardines on bread and the feeling of not moving.

We kept going, and the hours and kilometres passed. We had not seen anyone since early morning, not even a goat. This was the first time here for Rachid too and he was under pressure. He was navigating from some kind of inner compass and descriptions of the area from locals and other guides. There are no real maps and no reception for Google Earth when you are this remote. Our problem was that if we went up the wrong peak, it would add many, many kilometres to our journey, as we would then have to detour back to Khmis Nait Zmlal. Adding distance was not a great option when we were already on a heavy schedule of more than 30 kilometres a day.

The shadows were lengthening and we were back out in the deserted open plain, looking round at the encircling high peaks, trying to work out which one would lead us to Tichka. We decided that the only thing to do was to climb to the highest point and look out from there to see if we could see the plateau. Ahead of us were sheer scree slopes but that was the only option, so with legs that were protesting quite loudly that they had had enough, I followed Rachid up. About three-quarters of the way up I had a mini-revolt and demanded that we stop long enough for me to brew up some rooibos tea with lots of sugar on my mini stove.

Rachid: 'Alice, it is getting dark. We don't have much light left.'
Me: 'I have to have a break, Rachid. I will be quick but I need to stop.'

Girded, we carried on into the dusk. It is not a great feeling to be lost in the middle of the mountains, constantly climbing when you are exhausted and not knowing where the end is, and both of us were quiet. Then, suddenly, I smelt shampoo. Shampoo? I couldn't work out what was happening. At that moment, a head poked up over the top of the ridge about 50 metres ahead, followed by the body of an immaculately groomed young man. I actually pinched myself as Rachid bounded up to him.

It transpired that he was on his way to visit his family in the next valley. He was wearing an ironed shirt, spotless jeans, his hair was freshly washed, his feet were clad in loafers without a speck of dust on them and he was carrying a box of pastries tied with a ribbon. We, on the other hand, were filthy and sweaty. He told us that all Rachid's instincts were right and that if we carried on over the top of this ridge, we would reach the plateau. 'You know, Alice, he was sent by God, don't you?' said Rachid. I couldn't argue.

We climbed out onto the plateau with the last light and suddenly we were in Switzerland. Lush pastureland with a stream trickling down the middle being grazed by a whole herd of cows wearing bells. I had never seen a herd of cows in Morocco before. The sense of unreality continued.

This area is famous for its grass in the summer and nomads come to live here for a few months to fatten up their cows, goats and sheep. At the bottom of the slope was a set of *azeeb* – stone-built shepherds' huts. These *azeeb* are found all over the mountains. They are built to provide temporary accommodation for up to several months for shepherds, nomads and their families. They are built by a family or clan but often used by many different people. Below us, we could see smoke rising from the cooking fires and hear the sheepdogs barking. We set up camp under the interested eyes of a group of about seven children aged between five and twelve, who had spotted us as they were gathering wood and come over to say hello. They put down their bundles, which were bigger than they were, and settled down for the show.

Rachid has three predominant qualities which I had come to discover during our days together. He is a proud Amazigh and taught me new words of Tashlaheet and new things about his culture every day. If I ever slipped up and said 'Berber', I would be fixed with a gimlet eye until I corrected myself. He is deeply respectful and has impeccable manners. This is a wonderful quality as it makes life better all round if you treat your fellow humans, the animals who serve you and the environment we live in well. I watched him and tried to learn. One illustration of this only dawned on me halfway through our expedition. Whenever we stayed at someone's house he would go up to sleep on the roof. I thought it was because it was hot, but in fact he was, very delicately, preserving my reputation, and his, in the eyes of the villagers we stayed with. I'm old enough to be his mother, but for some of them it would be strange and shameful if we shared a room. The last quality is generosity. When we stocked up on food we would always get little sweets and chocolates to give to children we passed on the way.

They came in handy now. The kids came up and we doled out some sweets and everyone was happy. '*Merci bien, Madame. Comment vous appellez vous? Vous êtes d'ou?*' I couldn't believe it. The eldest girl was speaking to me in excellent French. When I investigated, they all chimed in and said they had a French teacher at school and their father, who had just joined us, said that he was a really good one. The children took every chance to talk to me and show off their prowess, and also practice because they said they didn't get much chance to meet foreigners. This I could believe as we were a full day's walk from the nearest habitation and I was pretty sure that almost no foreigners had ever got that far. Yet, here they were eager to learn and sucking up the experience like little sponges.

I had brought a couple of rations of dried food for overnight stays and we cooked one up on the stove, watched in fascination by the group. They weren't impressed when they tasted it, however, and scampered down the hill to their own dinners. We were invited to come and have breakfast the next day. It may have been the middle of the summer in Morocco, but the altitude makes for very cold nights and Rachid and I were both glad when dawn broke and we cleared up and set off for our tea. There is a sad end to this story, though, as the sheepdogs would not let us close enough to the *azeeb* to get our tea. Teeth bared, they chased us off down the mountain with our metaphorical tails between our legs.

The last part of our expedition took us through the foothills of the Atlas and out to the plains towards the sea. Soon, we were walking on the sandy, rocky flat with camels munching on the acacia trees and feeling the full force of the August sun. This is where I learned that buttermilk (*liban*) is the best drink you can have in the heat. It actually reduces your core body temperature and the effect lasts a lot longer than my old favourite, Coke.

We had three days of this before we reached our destination, the ocean, and the huge euphoria of successfully completing our mission. Running into the sea in our filthy clothes and boots under the eyes of astonished holiday makers was made even more wonderful by the fact that we did it together and no one had done that route before. But as this chapter is about the Atlas and its people, the last story belongs to Hassan.

It was the very end of the mountains close to Argana and we were suffering from the sharp increase in temperature and the sandy trails underfoot. We'd also run out of water, so when we came to a small hamlet we stopped in the shade of one of the houses and Rachid knocked on the door. It was opened a crack and we were handed some water but not invited in. Then, as we sat slumped against the wall, gulping it down, a man came running down the hill.

He had a lovely, friendly face, a neat beard and was medium height and slim, aged in his mid-thirties to early forties. His name was Hassan. His face shone with open-heartedness and intelligence.

Hassan: 'Greetings. How are you? You must come to my house and drink some tea.'

Rachid: 'And greetings to you. Thank you so much, but we just need a little water and a small rest, and then we are going to carry on. We still have a long way to go.'

Hassan: 'No, no, you MUST come. My mother-in-law phoned me. This is her house and she is so sorry but as she is alone she could not open the door to a strange man. But she told me to come down and get you. My wife is preparing everything for you. You must come. You have to come. Otherwise it is a shame on me.'

Of course, we went. When we got inside we took off our shoes and when Hassan saw my feet, which were swollen and blistered and bleeding and generally in quite a bad state, he immediately ushered me to the toilet and brought me a bucket of hot water to wash them in. I heard him saying to Rachid, 'My brother, what have you done to her? This is terrible. You must not walk any further. She is a woman, she cannot support this. No, you must stay here and let her feet heal. Stay with us as long as you like.'

His salon was a simple rectangle with thick patterned rugs on the floor and big cushions around the walls to prop your back on. His wife and daughters came in to say hello and bring trays of food. The very best of everything was brought out for us. The kindness of it and the respite after the heat and the hardships of the past days made me want to weep.

First of all, we had fresh, cold buttermilk with couscous, which immediately cooled us down. Then, a small table was placed in front of us laden with every kind of goodie: walnuts; dates; almonds; *bldi* butter (a preserved butter used in the mountains); honey from local hives; *amlou* (a paste made from almonds); argan oil and honey; and, of course, freshly-baked *tannourt*. *Tannourt* is the bread of the Atlas Mountains and is a bit like a thick naan. It is cooked in a wood-fired clay oven, shaped like a dome. You slap the dough onto the walls of the oven, and it cooks from the wood in the middle, so it always has a slight taste of ash and crispy bits.

'Eat, eat, drink, drink,' Hassan urged us every time we showed signs of flagging. Finally, we really couldn't eat any more. The tea was brought and we settled in for a chat.

Hassan told us that I was the first foreigner ever to visit his village and wanted to know all the details of our expedition. He was highly educated and spoke both French and, much more unusually, English, fluently. He was obviously delighted to have company and a chance to talk about life outside the village. I asked him why he was living in the village when he had his baccalaureate and such good language skills, which meant he had the chance of a well-paying job in the city. He said that he had had to choose: a wife and family life in his village or a career, and he had chosen the family. He told us, wistfully, that it was a hard choice and that he missed intellectual stimulus, but that he was content with the life and family that he had built. We talked about the world, politics, the differences between family in Europe and Morocco, religion, everything in fact, and the hours sped by.

We had to go, though; we had our goal to reach. Hassan pressed us to stay, and we were sorely tempted. Both Rachid and I put our boots on with a heavy heart, picked up our rucksacks and said our farewells. Hassan walked with us to the end of the village. We had only known each other for a few hours but, somehow, inexplicably, in spite of all our differences, the three of us had forged a friendship. We all got emotional as we said goodbye and Rachid and I walked on, looking behind us to wave until finally Hassan, and the extraordinary hospitality of the Atlas Mountains, was behind us.

A world away in terms of culture and history and a few hundred miles to the north-east lies Fez, once the most important centre of Islam in north Africa and a place rich in architecture, learning and food.

4

FEZ

Some places make an indelible impression on you, and Fez was one of those places for me. Fez is situated inland in the north of Morocco and is a crossroads for the major cities of Casablanca, Tangier, Rabat and Marrakech. When I was nineteen, I came to Morocco for the first time with my boy-friend Tim, a student budget and a Fodor's guide, which was hopelessly out of date but a tatty hardback, so had the whiff of romance about it so necessary to student travel. We came overland from the UK, travelling by endless train through Spain in a carriage full of Moroccans. This was when I got my first inkling that studying Arabic was going to be a very good thing. The miles and the hours passed and we all got cosy in our carriage. Food was produced and shared and, as the crumbs settled, we asked each other where we were going and what we were doing. We were speaking in French, but then I told them I studied Arabic and the fun started.

Family: '*Vous parlez Arabe? Non, c'est pas possible!* OK, count to ten.'

Me: 'One.'

Family: 'God is Great!'

Me: 'Two.'

Family: 'God is the Ruler of the Two Worlds!'

Me: 'Three.'

Family: 'Yeeeeessssssss!'

Me: 'Four.'

Family: 'Oh, Peace!'

Me: 'Five.'

Family: 'May God be Praised!'

Me: 'Six.'

Family: 'Go on, go on.'

Me: 'Seven.' (The applause starts.)

'Eight.' (The applause builds.)

'Nine.' (The applause is now ecstatic. The Rolling Stones at Wembley can't compete. Can she do it? Will she win the gold? Is the Oscar hers? Will she take the penalty to win the World Cup for Scotland?)

'Ten.' (The carriage erupts. Everyone cheers, jumps up and down and hugs each other. The grandmother starts ululating. Two of the sisters are in tears. Tim is slapped on the back and kissed enthusiastically (and to his surprise as it is the 1980s) by the men. I am congratulated, offered tangerines and made to take photographs with each of the family members on my little non-digital camera. It was a great start to the trip.)

We travelled to Fez by bus and my first impression of it was of a city lounging over its hills in the hazy, lazy light of late afternoon. It looked untouched and somehow secret, with green conifers and slim minarets standing tall. Thirty-five years on, of course it has changed, but it still has that mystical quality.

Fez is the eat, shop, pray destination of Morocco. Charlie always says that 'Fez is for connoisseurs', and he is right. It offers something more nuanced and refined than the brash delights of Marrakech or the malls of Casablanca. Perhaps this is because of its status as one of the great centres of Islamic learning and the home of the world's oldest university, Al Kairouan.

You enter the old walled city through Bou Jouloud, also known as the blue gate at the top of the hill. The whole of Fez is built on a hill, so my tactic is to start my tour at the top and walk down. The gate is decorated with blue tiles, hence its secondary name of the blue gate, and its arches frame the minaret of a mosque at the entrance. It gives on to a large street with cafés on either side, but don't be tempted to stop – there is a must-eat coming. As you go down you come to a split in the road. At that junction is the stand that sells boiled sheep's heads. The stall has two huge pots boiling away and being stirred demonically by the genial chef. The pots stand about two feet high and steam billows from the top. When you open the lid of the one on the left you are confronted with a dozen heads bobbing in the stock. If for some inexplicable reason you don't fancy a boiled sheep's head with popped-out eyeballs, then the other pot is full of whole boiled chickens which are also delicious. You can sit at the café next door, and they will add chips and salad to make a meal.

The road is now divided into Talaa Kabir and Talaa Saghir – big Talaa and little Talaa. *Talaa* means 'to rise' in Arabic and these two long streets take you from the top of the town all the way down till you start to smell the tanneries and come out to the river. Go down one and up the other and every step feels like it takes you further back in time. The streets and alleys are so narrow that at busy times of the day you have to queue to get up and down some of them even though it is pedestrian and donkey access only. They are lined with small shops and stalls with wooden shutters and doors, stuffed with everyday goods and treasure for tourists. Near the end of Talaa Kabir on the right is a haberdashery stall which is crammed with every colour, shape and size of tassel. Because most djellaba hoods are decorated with a tassel, they are in high demand. Much thought goes into whether you want the same colour or a contrasting one, a knotted tassel or a smooth one, a big showy number or a discreet silky style.

Even narrower alleys lead off the main street to left and right. Fassians (people from Fez) are proud of them and I was excitedly taken one day to what is proclaimed to be the 'narrowest alleyway in Fez'. It was so narrow that I regretted that extra 'moment on the lips, lifetime on the hips' chocolate bar and wondered if I would get stuck. As I was considering this, I got to the end of the alleyway. It was a dead end at someone's front door and just as I arrived, the door was opened by a scholarly-looking man who peered at me in surprise. I was embarrassed to be caught snooping on his doorstep and apologised for disturbing him, explaining I had been told that this was the narrowest alleyway in the city, at which he broke into a glowing smile and invited me in. I was too flustered to say yes and then had to do a complicated three-point turn and walk the walk of shame back out under his benign gaze.

Fas (Fez) in Arabic means a pickaxe and the story goes that

Fez got its name when the great-great-great grandson of the Prophet Mohammed, Idris I, founded the city by drawing out its lines with a golden axe in 789. He built it on the east bank of the River Fes and twenty years later his son founded another city on the west bank of the river. In time-honoured tradition, the two cities hated each other and spent the next 200 years fighting. They were united in the eleventh century by the Almoravids, the Berber dynasty who ruled Morocco until 1147 and founded Marrakech, and Fez began its rise to become one of the most important cities in the Islamic world, reaching its peak from 1269 under the Merenids, another Berber dynasty who held power from the thirteenth to the fifteenth centuries. It is one of the four Imperial Cities in Morocco, along with Meknes, Marrakech and Rabat, so-called because they have all been the capital of Morocco at some point. Rabat holds the title at the moment, but Fez has worn the crown at six different points during the centuries. Still, many of the leading families of Morocco hail from Fez and Fassians dominate the political, financial and cultural elite of the country.

Under the Merenids, the city flourished. It was a crucial depot for the trans-Saharan trade that linked the riches of West Africa's gold mines and slave markets with the salt and trading goods of Morocco and on into Europe from the north. It was also a centre for craftsmanship, becoming known for the finest leather and the most delicate ceramics. The Merenids spent part of the riches accrued from this trade to expand and consolidate their Islamic power base through an extensive programme of building and public works. Two buildings tell the history of Islamic Fez: the Kairouan University and the Bou Inania Islamic School.

Many universities vie for the title of 'world's oldest', so it's important to get these words right. It is 'the oldest existing, continually operating and the first degree-awarding educational institution in the world,' according to UNESCO and Guinness World Records. It is an extraordinary place and it began in an extraordinary fashion, because it was founded by a woman. Fatima Al Fihri was the daughter of a wealthy merchant who had educated both her and her sister, Miriam, to a high level.

The family had migrated from the town of Kairouan in Tunisia in the early ninth century. When they got to Fez they moved to an area that already had a large community from Kairouan and settled there. At that time there were lots of refugees coming into Fez from Andalusia and from Tunisia. When her father, husband and brother died in quick succession, Fatima and her sister were left heartbroken but very rich. Fatima started building the mosque and the adjoining madrassa or medersa (Islamic school), which was to become the university, in 859. The story is that construction started during Ramadan and she vowed to observe Ramadan until the mosque was finished. It took two years, at the end of which she was able to pray and give thanks in the mosque that she had built. The mosque, which can accommodate 22,000 people, still dictates the times for prayer and for the beginning and breaking of the Ramadan fast every day for the whole of Morocco. It has a special room called the House of Timings.

Today, the university still holds classes as it would have done hundreds of years ago. Students sit in a semi-circle around a sheikh who discusses texts or points of law and grammar with them. The age range is from thirteen to thirty and you can study towards a high-school diploma or a university degree. To be a student you have to be a Muslim, have memorized the Quran in full and be able to understand and use classical Arabic to a high level, although you can come and sit in on classes if you are a Muslim and have a reasonably high standard of religious knowledge.

The university concentrates on the Islamic religious and legal sciences, classical Arabic and Maliki jurisprudence. There are also classes in French and English. Students come from far and wide to study in Al Kaiouran, especially from the Muslim areas of west Africa. There are also lots of Spanish converts, who want to bask in the heritage of Muslim Al Andalus. Both women and men are admitted, as you would expect with a founding mother. Sit and drink a coffee near the university and you will see groups of earnest young men and women huddled in animated discussion, or hurrying past with piles of books. The dress code is a bit different from a university in the West, though, with the West Africans clad in brilliant white robes and skull caps and the Moroccans in traditional djellabas.

Fatima Al Fihri would appear to have been acting from the purest of motives and to have been a model of piety. If only the same could be said of the other major contributor to the Islamic infrastructure in the city, the Merenids, but for them religious fervour was balanced with political expediency. When the Merenids conquered Fez and established 'new' Fez in 1276, they had reputational issues. They were a Berber dynasty and were seen by the upper-crust Fassians as a bunch of wild barbarians come to destroy their cultured haven. The Merenids embarked on a hearts and minds campaign and set in place an enormous programme of public works: new mosques and madrassas, private residences and communal buildings. The programme wasn't just about creating new spaces, though – it was about building a new class loyal to the dynasty. To this end, they provided students of the madrassas with free bed and board, and even small payments to attend, and encouraged the rural poor to take advantage of them. New madrassas meant new teachers; new public buildings meant a new bureaucracy. In this way, they were able to secure a base of civil servants and pupils who were beholden to the state.

Sultan Abu Inan was fairly typical as a Merenid sultan. He was known for his vigour and action on all fronts. He came to power by deposing his own father and ousting his nephew from Fez. He then marched off to war and managed to take much of the north of what is now Algeria and Tunisia, although he was later to lose it again. His rule was marked by war and then plague with the arrival of the Black Death, but he had a very productive ten years when, legend has it, he managed to father 325 sons. He also did two great things which would surely guarantee him some leniency before his Maker: he built the biggest madrassa in Fez, the Bou Inania; and he commissioned his secretary to sit down with one of the greatest, if not *the* greatest, travellers of all time, Ibn Battuta, and write down his adventures in a book called *Al Rihla* (The Journey).

The Bou Inania is the biggest of Fez's madrassas (or medersas). Non-Muslims cannot enter a mosque but you are free to enter the madrassas and see for yourself the exquisite stucco work, lavish onyx and marble, and intricately carved Quranic inscriptions that cover the walls. You can also see the dormitories where the boys lived and imagine them sitting grouped around a teacher under one of the archways learning the Quran by heart. When Abu Inan was planning the madrassa, the religious leaders advised him to build it on the city's rubbish dump on the basis that good works can cure anything. Money was no object and he spent so much on it that when he got the accounts he threw them into the river saying, 'A thing of beauty is beyond reckoning.' His good works could not save him from a violent fate, however, and he was murdered by his own first minister, who had him strangled.

Between the madrassas and the university, with its growing library, Fez grew in importance as an Islamic centre for the whole region and beyond, a kind of Oxford or Harvard for Muslims. Understanding this is the key to unlocking the city. When you walk down the streets, you will see a tiled, arched water fountain on every corner. These have been donated by pious Muslims to provide clean water for drinking and also for washing before prayers. Look up and you will see the distinctive rectangular minarets of Morocco. Trying to find out how many mosques there are in the Fez medina is like searching for Nirvana – elusive. Between 100 and 300 is the best estimate. Peek through the door of a mosque or a shrine and you will get a glimpse of worshippers going in to pray or just to sit in the shade and think.

This intellectual capital did not only benefit the Muslims of north and west Africa; it brought light to Europe when we were languishing in the Dark Ages. While my ancestors were scraping a living from the cold and unforgiving frozen fields of Scotland, scholars in Fez were making breakthroughs in medicine, navigation and mathematics. Manuscripts from Ancient Greece and Rome were saved and brought to life again through their Arabic translations and then exported back into Europe through the link with Spain, Al Andalus.

A good example of this cross-fertilisation of ideas through Fez is the story of Rabbi Moses ben Maimon, known as Maimonides, a famous Jewish philosopher and medical pioneer. He fled his native Cordoba for Fez and spent two years there, studying at Al Kairouan from 1166 to 1168, during which time he wrote one of the seminal works of Hebrew theology, a commentary on the oral form of the Torah. It is thought he may have made a fake conversion to Islam to enable him to do this. He also produced a piece in Judeo-Arabic, aptly called 'Guide for the Perplexed', which brought together Aristotle and biblical faith that was to have far-reaching effects. This was, of course, written from his religious viewpoint as a Jew, but it went on to influence one of Christianity's great thinkers, St Thomas of Aquinas. Greek philosophy, Islam, Judaism and Christianity all interlinked through the thought capital of the age, Fez. He also worked on subjects that were far from these giddy heights of faith and intellectualism, which may not have enriched the cultural life of humanity but certainly helped make us all more comfortable. I refer, of course, to his 'Treatise on Haemorrhoids'.

Knowing about and looking at the monuments to faith is one thing; feeling that faith is another. In search of that, Serena, my Marrakchi flatmate, and I got up before dawn on a chilly January morning in Fez and headed up towards the Merenid tombs which stand on a hill overlooking the city. We were in training for the Marrakech half marathon at the end of that month, so were doing this at a run. Incongruously clad in our Lycra, we set off from our riad, Dar Roumana, which is a work of art in itself, in the centre of the old town, and launched ourselves up Talaa Kabira. Going down Talaa Kabira is all very well; going up it at a run is a whole different experience, more wobbly and with less breath. As we broke out of the city walls, there was a sliver of pre-dawn light, enough to illuminate the large hill in front of us which led up to the tombs. Serena is a woman of few words and I am a panter, so we maintained an agonised silence and pounded on up. Then the muezzins began their pre-dawn prayer – Al

Fajr – and the sound bounced and echoed from a hundred minarets across the city and up to the hills.

Allahu Akbar (God is Great)
[said four times]
Ashhadu an la ilaha illa Allah (I bear witness that there is no
    god except the One God)
[said two times]
Ashadu anna Muhammadan Rasool Allah (I bear witness that
    Muhammad is the messenger of God)
[said two times]
Hayya 'ala-s-Salah (Hurry to the prayer (rise up for prayer))
[said two times]
Hayya 'ala-l-Falah (Hurry to success (rise up for salvation))
[said two times]
Allahu Akbar (God is Great)
[said two times]
La ilaha illa Allah (There is no god except the One God)
For the pre-dawn (fajr) prayer, the following phrase is
    inserted after the fifth part above, towards the end:
As-salatu Khayrun Minan-nawm (Prayer is better than sleep)
[said two times]

We reached the top and the large golden arched gate that marks the tombs just as the sun rose up, a red disc through the clouds, glancing off the minarets and silhouetting the flocks of birds wheeling around them. Our goosebumps were only partially from the cold.

Our run was to go from the sublime to the ridiculous. We sat and admired the view of the city spread out below us and watched a convoy of donkeys coming up to take the animal hides that were drying on the hill behind down to the tanneries. Then it was time to head back down to Dar Roumana and some fluffy scrambled eggs in the ornately tiled and stuccoed courtyard. Back down the hill, through the gate and onto Talaa Kabira. I was thinking how much more I enjoyed trotting down it than puffing up it when I heard, 'Nice ass! Look at that backside. Wow.' This comment was clearly not directed at me – I have many attributes but would struggle to place my bottom among them – but at my young and beautiful co-runner, Serena. I looked at her and her face was a picture of annoyance and resentment. This hassle happens to her every time she steps out of the door. Moroccan men claim they are just being appreciative, but it is very, very wearing for young women here to be constantly targeted with sexual comments. My protective instincts rose to the fore and I turned back. Serena did a double take.

The perpetrator was a skinny, almost spotty youth standing next to a group of older male shopkeepers who were opening up their businesses. His eyes widened in alarm, or expectation, as I strode back up the hill. I hope it was alarm, as that would have prepared him for what was to come. Under the interested eyes of the shopkeepers, I began my one-to-one reformation of young Moroccan men who accost women on the street.

Me: 'My brother, why did you say that?'
Perpetrator [with goggling eyes]: 'Uh ...'
Me: 'Do you kiss your mother with that mouth?' (This is an excellent phrase that can be whipped out on many occasions.)
Perpetrator: 'Uh, uh.'
Me: 'Do you think that is a nice thing to say to this beautiful young woman who has come to visit your city?'

(By now the shopkeepers have formed an appreciative circle and are weighing in with a few choice comments of their own.)

Shopkeepers: 'Shame on you. Why did you say that to this guest in our city? Apologise!'

Perpetrator (crestfallen, shrivelled and beaten): 'Madame, I am so sorry. I didn't mean it.'

Me: 'You don't need to apologise to me, you need to apologise to the young lady.' (I am severe and yet gracious in victory. Serena, who is a gentle soul, is cringing quietly beside me, not having asked for this intervention.)

Perpetrator: 'Miss, I am so, so sorry, please forgive me.'

Serena: 'I forgive you, may God guide your steps.'

Shopkeepers: 'God be praised. You are welcome in Fez. Blessings of God be upon you. And if you would like to buy a carpet, we are here.'

Serena had by now recovered from her embarrassment and I was basking in victory, so we giggled our way back to our scrambled eggs and we actually did go back and buy a couple of carpets.

We also stocked up on the pottery that Fez is famous for. There is a whole group of pottery shops clustered round a courtyard which has an ancient tree in the middle. The tree has been appropriated as a kind of display cabinet and draped in every shape and size of bowl, vase and plate and also outstretched female hands that you can attach to a wall. We were both tempted by these but then decided there was something a bit creepy about them – they look too much like severed human hands.

There are two strands to the pottery produced in Morocco: the masculine, which uses geometric or symmetrical designs and calligraphy; and the feminine, which uses designs from nature and arabesques. In Islam, depiction of the human form or face is actually forbidden, so calligraphy and plant, flower or natural forms have become highly developed and stylised. The Islamic influence prevails in every piece, whether it be in symbolic geometric designs or actual words from the Quran. Fassian pottery is distinguished for its use of cobalt oxide that creates every shade of blue. What I like about the pottery of Fez is that it is so fine. It is like bone china, rather than the more solid, rustic pottery of Safi that dominates the shops in Marrakech. My preference is definitely for the more feminine designs from nature in greens and reds and blues, but I have got a couple of older Fassian bowls decorated in blue calligraphy.

Praying and shopping completed, eating is my other Fassian preoccupation. Moroccan food is based on excellent ingredients and is good and hearty and perfect after a hard day in the mountains. However, and I hope I am not going to be shot for this, I find it a bit restricted, certainly if you want to eat out. I can't help looking longingly to the East and the superb cuisine of Lebanon or Turkey – and don't even start me on the world-famous almond and honeyed pastries of Damascus. In Turkey, there is a kebab called Imam Bayildi. Apparently, at its creation it was sampled by a revered imam from Istanbul, who was so overcome with ecstasy at its deliciousness that he lapsed into oblivion and collapsed on the ground in a dead faint, whereupon it was named 'The Imam Fainted' (Imam Bayildi) in commemoration

In Morocco, you basically have a few set staples. Tagines in all shapes and flavours; some are sweet with dates or prunes and some are tangy with preserved lemon and olives.

Couscous is the special dish and it too comes with different meats and sauces. Then there is *bastilla*, which is a layered mille-feuille pastry stuffed with meat, seafood or vegetables and almonds or walnuts and dusted with icing sugar on top for the sweet twist. There are also skewers, meat grills, aubergine and tomato (*zaaluk*) and, of course, *harira* soup. *Harira* soup is always drunk during Ramadan. It is also great during the winter as it really warms you and is full of lentils, beans and vermicelli. Moroccan salads come in a wide variety and are often served in little dishes as a varied appetizer: grated raw carrot with lemon juice; pepper, onion and tomato; beans with tomato sauce and lots more.

On my visit to Fez with Serena, we had feasted on Mediterranean treats at Dar Roumana, chunky burgers and a trendy vibe in Café Clock and Thai green curry in Maison Moi Annan, whose owner is also a fashion designer so you can eat and then buy a frock (maybe buy a frock first). This had set Fez firmly in my mind as a culinary destination, much more so than Marrakech. This first impression was cemented when I got the opportunity to spend a day food shopping and sampling with the incomparable Najat Kaanache, chef and owner, with her partner Charles, of El Nur.

Najat is a tornado of colour, big hair and energy. She is always dressed in an array of layered dresses, shawls, wraps, artificial flowers, tassels and spangly things, all in vibrant pinks and blues, stripes and patterns. Her dress sense reflects her personality, which is full of life and vigour, embracing everything new and radiating vitality. When you are in Najat's presence, there's always the sense that something is going to happen.

I first met her when we were fellow speakers at TedX Marrakech. She talked about food and I talked about adventures, and each of us had a love for the other's subject. Najat is a Berber from the mountains, but her father wanted a better life for his children and to educate his daughters, so he took the family and migrated to Spain in 1975. There they started again with nothing. I was really struck by what she said there about the experience of growing up poor as a stranger in a foreign country.

We lived in a very, very, very poor house, it had no roof. I know people don't want to say this. People think, 'Oh you grew up in Europe, everything is marvellous.' You come back to Morocco and you bring your Mercedes. You know that is the big old story among a lot of families but that is not the whole story. That is not the truth in many cases and was not the truth in mine. We don't have a roof and I am sleeping in a little bed, with Mama coming every two hours to see if I was frozen purple or blue or if the bed was wet, but I had something very magical – I could see the moon. It was like a connection with this light which transformed us every night. One morning, this woman shows up under my mother's window yelling, 'Oh, Fatima!' with a tray with aluminium foil. I look out of the window – what's that? That's food. Oh no! That's too embarrassing, that's not happening. But yes, this woman has walked all the way from the village and came with a tray and a huge chicken, a huge chicken for us. It was her way of accepting us, a way of being kind. I was so upset for the next week, I was so embarrassed.

Her father always called his daughters 'champions' and told them they could do anything they wanted. He pushed them, making them study and work hard. That focus clearly stuck as she is now a top international chef who has worked at the best restaurants in the world, including El Bulli, and has her own cooking show. She brought her modern, international take on Moroccan cooking back home and opened a restaurant in the medina called El Nur.

When we were looking for someone to illustrate what kind of food the trans-Saharan traders might have eaten five centuries ago for the BBC Two programme, getting her involved seemed like an ideal opportunity to plug into all her energy and knowledge, so the team and I went up to film her in her stomping ground in the medina.

We started off our day together in the neighbourhood bakery. A bakery in Morocco is rather different from Greggs because not only can you buy bread and biscuits there, it is also where you go to get your own bread baked. Since not all homes have an oven or a cooker, it used to be the norm, and is still common, for housewives to bring their dough to the communal bread oven at the bakery.

The clay oven is big – about two metres squared – and fired by wood. The baker stands at the entrance with his long bread shovel and slips in the individual sets of dough, batches of biscuits and all sorts of other good things. As you can imagine, the smell is divine, and that day it was chilly outside so sitting in a warm bakery being given things to taste was about as good as it gets. The baker chatted away to us about how he knows all the different doughs from his ladies by the little marks they leave on the surface, or from the basket they bring it in, or the cloth they cover it with. All the time, he was keeping one eye on the red-hot furnace and expertly flipping over the loaves, which are round and flat.

As well as the sheer functionality and eco-friendliness of a communal oven, what I really like about the idea is that the bakery also functions as an information centre. The baker knows everything that is going on in the community. He is a repository of secrets, some whispered to him and others overheard, as the women chat and he flips his loaves. The bakeries sell their own goods, so next time you are passing one, fish out one dirham (8p) and invest in a hot, fresh loaf.

Our next stop on the culinary tour was the market to buy the ingredients for lunch. Food shopping in Morocco is never quick and it is always fun. The quality of produce is usually high because everything is produced locally and ripened in the sun. The Moroccans have also mastered the art of the glossy vegetable pyramid and every stall gleams with red peppers, shiny aubergines, purple onions and orange carrots.

We weren't there to shop for veg, though; our mission was to get some camel meat. The meat stalls are all together in a row, just on the left as you enter the food market. They are spotlessly clean and surprisingly fly-less, and I wonder if it is because it's quite cold. It is easy to spot who is selling camel meat as there is a severed camel's head hung proudly above the stall. I eat meat, but I am a full-on hypocrite when it comes to admitting it comes from real animals that have to lose their lives so I can enjoy mine, so I suffer pangs of guilt looking at the glazed eyes with the long eyelashes suspended just above my head.

I had done my research before I came out, though, and had discovered that camel meat is very healthy: 98 calories per 100 grams as compared to 150 calories for 100 grams of beef, very rich in potassium, and only 1 gram of fat as opposed to 5 grams in beef. One per cent of fat is nothing, and the reason is that all the camel's fat is stored in its hump, and there, lying on the table, was a skinned camel hump, basically a big pyramid of pure fat.

Najat told me that we were going to buy both the meat, which did look beautiful and lean, and the fat, because the fat would add the flavour. The butcher shaved off slivers of the fat and wrapped it in paper. Before we left, there was a little treat in store for me: a glass of cold camel's milk. I had never tried it before so I was a little bit apprehensive but took a tentative sip. Fortune really does favour the bold; it was delicious. I like milk anyway, and this was a cleaner, richer version of cow's milk. It is expensive and so reserved for special occasions – like the camel meat. In Morocco, camel meat is eaten at feasts and celebrations like weddings, and now most camels in the country are actually sold for their meat rather than for transport.

Najat and I headed back to El Nur so that she could cook up a storm with our purchases. On the menu were camel meatballs. There were around ten of us in the end that sat down in the light-filled covered courtyard as dish after delicious dish was wheeled out of the kitchen. Charles and Najat had made sure that all of us were invited, including Mohammed, who had been pushing around the camera equipment for us in his cart, which is the way all heavy things are transported in the medina. This is the true spirit of hospitality in Morocco. Each mouthful of each dish was an experience: the camel meatballs literally melted on my tongue, and who would ever dream up a beetroot and blanched radish salad with grapefruit? Najat and Charles flitted in and out of the kitchen with juices and desserts and would only sit with us at the very end. I can truthfully say it is the best meal I have ever eaten in Morocco. Fez: a place to eat, shop and pray.

Of course, it is impossible to leave the city without finding out a little bit about its most iconic product: that little red felt hat with a black tassel, beloved of Tommy Cooper. The fez came to be called the fez, a bit like the vacuum cleaner became known as the hoover, through market dominance. For a long period the city became the principal manufacturing base for this hat that has been worn all over the world and been, at various times, a symbol of modernism and a symbol of tradition; a symbol both of freedom and of oppression.

A historical battle rages as to where the hat first emerged from, with Greece and the Balkans as the combatants. Whichever it is, it first came to universal prominence in 1826 when Sultan Mahmud II started reforming the Ottoman army. He replaced turbans with fezzes and decreed that they could be worn by civilians too. It became the ultimate symbol of modernity and fez production in the city boomed – the Ottoman Empire was enormous. So much so that a large group of Fassians emigrated to Constantinople and set up shop there, where they plied a lucrative trade until modern trade imperatives took over.

They got priced out of the market by the factories of Strakonice in the Czech Republic, which was then part of the Austrian Empire. The innovative Czechs had invented cheap, synthetic dyes to take the place of the expensive scarlet produced by the Cornelian cherry, used by the Fassians. In 1908, disaster struck the Czechs when the Ottomans boycotted all Austrian Empire goods after the Austrians annexed Bosnia Herzegovina. The boycott was called the Fez Boycott because it was one of the main things affected, and the supply of new fezzes dried up overnight. Ah, how the old Fassian manufacturers must have rubbed their hands in schadenfreudic glee. But the hat's time of being a symbol of modernity had passed, and when Kemal Atatürk started on his massive reforms of Turkey in the twenties, he banned it.

In Morocco, it is still worn on ceremonial occasions and also by different military units around the world as part of their ceremonial dress, including the Senegalese and the Italians and, as you would expect, is widely available for sale on the streets of the city that gave it its name. It was the final item on my Fez shopping list, although, in fairness, a pirate's hat would be more suitable for my journey further up north to Tangier, or perhaps a soft fedora. Either would do to get me in the mood for this city of pirates, spies and drug-, sex- and booze-fuelled literati.

5

TANGIER AND THE PIRATE COAST

Major Heinrich Strasser: 'What is your nationality?'
Rick Blaine: 'I'm a drunkard.'
Captain Louis Renault: 'That makes Rick a citizen of the world.'

It would also almost certainly have made Rick ('Of all the gin joints in all the towns in all the world, she walks into mine'), the anti-hero of the film *Casablanca*, a citizen of Tangier. It is Tangier, not the bustling, modern metropolis of Casablanca, which evokes the romance of the film so strongly, and at the cost of rewriting cinematic history, I can't help but wish all those great lines came from *Tangier*. Tangier has at various times in its history been designated a neutral international zone by the great powers; become a haven for spies and espionage; a magnet for the louche writers of the beat generation;

a stepping-off point for the Arab conquest of Spain; and a bolthole for pirates.

The city is just eight miles from Europe and on a clear day you can see Spain across the water. It is one of the most fought-over cities in the world. Its strategic importance, perched as it is within spitting distance of Europe and offering a gateway into Africa, is incalculable. If you hold Tangier and Gibraltar you control access to the Mediterranean, and everyone has had a stab at conquering it: from the Romans and Phoenicians to the Portuguese, Spanish, French and British.

The British involvement first started in 1661. Charles II had been given Tangier as a wedding present by the Portuguese, which certainly beats a canteen of cutlery, and he sent over Lord Sandwich to take control of it from the Portuguese fleet. The British government then spent a fortune fortifying it but, like so many wedding presents, it languished unused. This entry is in the diary of the greatest of all diarists, Samuel Pepys:

This place so often mentioned, was first given up to the English fleet under Lord Sandwich, by the Portuguese, January 30th, 1662; and Lord Peterborough left governor, with a garrison. The greatest pains were afterwards taken to preserve the fortress, and a fine breakwater was constructed at a vast expense, to improve the harbour. At length, after immense sums of money had been wasted there, the House of Commons expressed a dislike to the management of the garrison, which they suspected to be a nursery for a popish army, and seemed disinclined to maintain it any longer. The king consequently, in 1683, sent Lord Dartmouth to bring home the troops, and destroy the works; which he performed so effectually, that it would puzzle all our

127

engineers to restore the harbour. It were idle to speculate on the benefits which might have accrued to England, by its preservation and retention; Tangier fell into the hands of the Moors, its importance having ceased, with the demolition of the mole.

The suspicion that Tangier was a hotbed of Catholic plotting was a result of the garrison there having a very large number of Irish Catholics in it, who at the time were disallowed from serving in the army in Ireland. Ex-soldiers from Tangier were called – no surprises – Tangerines, and a group did go on to plot to depose James II. They were also known as innovators as they brought back experience of active service and used it in the formation of Britain's first standing army, which took place over the next few decades. Life for the soldiers stationed in Tangier was never dull as there was plenty of fighting to be done with local tribes, Ottoman troops and the ferocious Barbary pirates.

Tangier was also where the great Arab conquest of Spain started, although the initial invading force was made up primarily of Berbers. In 711 the great general Tariq Ibn Ziyad left Tangier, crossed the straits and landed at Gibraltar, which took his name – Jebel means hill in Arabic so Tariq's Hill, Jebel Tariq, morphed into Gibraltar. From there, he swept across Spain and laid the foundations of the Cordoba Caliphate. The story is that when he was crossing the straits, the Spanish didn't take much notice as they thought the ships were just traders, and thus were caught unawares.

Today, the small city is a pleasant place to spend time wandering through the old markets or enjoying a tea in the main square. Cruise ships and daily ferries from Europe ensure that there is always a steady influx of foreigners coming through the busy port. Its history is clear from the enormous iron cannons that stand on the ramparts, now used very peacefully as a background for endless tourist selfies.

In the central fruit and vegetable market you will see women who have come in from the countryside with their produce, dressed in the traditional clothes for this region. They wear a distinctive red and white striped shawl wrapped round their waists like an apron and big wide-brimmed conical hats decorated with lots of coloured threads and sometimes with added pompoms. They sell all sorts, but my favourite thing to buy is the fresh goat's cheese, which is in a big round wheel, wrapped in dark green leaves. It's got a tangy, salty taste and is good with freshly baked bread and chilli olives.

This tranquil idyll, though, is far removed from the north African coast, which was once the domain of the notorious Barbary pirates. Their story is a fascinating one. They ruled the seas for hundreds of years, causing havoc along the coastlines of Spain and Italy and grabbing any unwary ships. They were hunting for rich cargoes but also for slaves. It is estimated that 1.25 million European Christian slaves were captured by Barbary pirates between the beginning of the sixteenth and the middle of the eighteenth centuries. In our culture, 'pirates' conjure up Johnny Depp and fancy-dress costumes, but these pirates were not the jolly villains that we see on the screen. They were professional and rapacious hunters. Slavery was big business. In the mid-sixteenth century, under the Ottomans, it became even better organised. Slavery was legal in the Ottoman Empire and a vital part of the economy. The pirate ships were fitted out and owned by investors. The captains carried out the raids and then the money was divided according to the deal in place for that ship, with 10 per cent of the value of the booty paid to the local ruler, the Pasha, as a tax.

The main centre of the Barbary pirates in Morocco was Salé to the south of Tangier, but the rocky coves, with their natural lagoons and the mountains behind for shelter, made the entire northern coastline right across Morocco, Tunisia and Algiers ideal for the trade.

It wasn't just about taking ships and stealing everything aboard them; the pirates would raid whole villages, taking slaves and then killing the rest of the inhabitants. It was so bad that large parts of the Spanish and Italian coast became deserted as the villagers moved inland for safety.

Salé's golden era was in the seventeenth century, under the command of its first president and grand admiral Jan Janszoon van Haarlem, a Dutch convert known by his Muslim name of Murat Reis the Younger. *Reis* means 'head of, chief, or president' in Arabic and was the name given to the pirate commanders. Janszoon began his career legitimately from his native port of Haarlem. He was hired by the Dutch state to harass Spanish shipping as part of their war effort against Spain in the Eighty Years' War. The spoils of war tasted very sweet and he soon found that Spanish shipping wasn't enough and went freelance. He sailed to the rich waters off north Africa and started attacking everything that sailed. If it was a Spanish ship, he would fly the Dutch flag; if it was from any other nation, he would fly the flag of the Ottoman Empire.

One day his luck ran out and he was captured by Barbary pirates and taken to their stronghold in Algiers. There he converted to Islam. If you converted you escaped slavery and a life on the galleys, but history tells us he actually became a fervent

Muslim missionary and thereafter tried to convert all those he captured. He started sailing for the corsairs with another converted Dutch captain and they grew in power within the Ottoman state. The Salé Rovers were a group of pirates who wanted their own capital, so they formed the independent republic of Salé and elected their best pirate, Janszoon, as president and admiral of their eighteen-ship-strong fleet. The Moroccan sultan took umbrage and besieged the city, but he had no chance against the privateers and plumped for a dip- lomatic solution by recognising Janszoon as governor. It was during his time as governor that the histories of Morocco and Ireland met in a story that sounds made up, but isn't.

In 1631, the fleet set sail from Salé to Ireland under the command of Janszoon. The Irish authorities apparently knew that an attack was imminent but did not know where it was to take place, so had no real way to guard against it. The unlucky place was Baltimore in West Cork.

It must have been as shocking as if aliens landed in Trafalgar Square on Boxing Day. The villagers would have been going about their daily business. The men would have been fish- ing, mending nets or cutting peat. Presumably the women would be cooking and cleaning and yelling at their children, or maybe tending a small plot of land. Then, suddenly, out of nowhere, a fleet of savage north African pirates appeared in the harbour and launched themselves into the village, screaming in a language that was completely unintelligible to the petrified villagers, cutting down those that stood in their way, burning and sacking the small cottages, and rounding up the fit men, women and children to take on board.

Treachery had led them into the village. The pirates had captured a fishing boat and the captain, a man called Hackett, was promised his freedom if he would lead them into the harbour. He did so, betraying his friends and neighbours, but death was waiting for him that day: when his act was discovered, the remaining villagers took him and hanged him on a clifftop. Those who survived the attack moved to Skibbereen, and Baltimore was left deserted.

One hundred and seven villagers were put in chains and led off to slavery. They were a mixture of English settlers and local Irish people. The pirates had a number of ways to make money from the people they captured. The first thing they did was ransom them, and three of those captured at Baltimore were ransomed and saved and made it back home. If no one came up with the money then there was a life of hard labour on the land, or as a galley slave, for the men; and a life in the harem, or as a domestic worker, for the women. If you were a man, you had better pray to be working on land. The life of a galley slave was heinous. You were chained to your oars and some never set foot on land again. That seat became your life. It was where you worked, ate, slept and even defecated. There was no escape and the only movement was to work the oars.

Janszoon went on to become a very rich man and something of a diplomat himself, helping to negotiate a peace treaty between the French and the Moroccans. Eventually, he retired and died in domestic tranquillity at a ripe old age.

The stories of the Barbary pirates still catch at the imagination. The Darkness wrote a song in 2015 about the raid on Baltimore called 'Roaring Waters'. One of Lord Byron's most famous poems was 'The Corsair', and Miguel de Cervantes wrote the 'Captive's Tale' in *Don Quixote* based on his own experience of being captured and held for five years until a ransom was finally paid. In fact, there were so many tales written by ex-slaves and captives that it became a separate literary genre. One part of the history attracted a much more titillating kind of author, however, and the theme of white women being sold into harems to endure a life of exotic sexual practices at the hands of a ruthless owner became the central theme of a slew of pornographic novels such as *The Lustful Turk*, published in 1828.

Three pirate facts for the pub quiz:

- The obligatory pirate eyepatch is modelled after a pirate called Rahmah ibn Jabir al-Jalahimah, who lost his eye in battle.
- Moroccan pirates captured and held the island of Lundy in the Bristol Channel for five years.
- One of the most famous corsairs was a woman called Sayyida al-Hurra. Her name means the 'Free Woman', and through her privateering she became rich and well-known enough to catch the eye of the sultan of Morocco, who pursued and, finally, married her. Free to the end, she would only marry him if the ceremony was in her own town of Tétouan – a massive break with royal protocol, which demanded that the sultan marry in the capital. He was a keen suitor, though, and capitulated.

Walking through modern Tangier is a cosmopolitan experience. Formed due to its geographical and strategic position, all the faces of the world are in this small city. It really is unlike anywhere else in the country and its social structure feels looser and more liberal. Tangier is a pretty tolerant place, and that is what made it so attractive for the young, rich and wild of Europe and America. When homosexuality was still illegal in those places, gay men would come to Morocco, where attitudes were much more relaxed – as long as you behaved discreetly.

Homosexuality is a complicated subject in Morocco, where what is said is often very different to what is practised. It is illegal and, except in the biggest cities and among the most modern families, is not even discussed openly, but at the same time there is an active gay sex tourist trade and a gay expat community. When I try to talk about homosexuality with my straight male Moroccan friends, they just won't engage. 'It's wrong', 'It's unnatural', 'It's forbidden' ends the discussion promptly and there is no room for my interjected, 'But why do you feel like that?'

The reality, though, is nuanced. In this society, traditionally men and women have socialised separately, being brought together mainly in a family context. This is changing with mixed schools and universities, but it still holds true. Men and women aren't really friends outside of marriage in the way that is normal in the West, certainly not after marriage. Behaviour that would be marked down as 'gay' in Western culture is not in Morocco. Men will walk down the street holding hands or with an arm over their friend's shoulder, and will kiss on the cheeks when greeting their friends. Instead of a night out at the pub, the boys will go to the steam bath together for a scrub, and I have spent many an evening listening to female friends moan (with reason!) that their boyfriend is out again with his mates smoking shisha till three in the morning, while they are sitting at home with his mother watching Turkish soap operas dubbed into Arabic.

The bookshop La Librairie des Colonnes, on the boulevard Pasteur, is owned by the former boyfriend of Yves Saint Laurent, and there you will find shelves of books by the many famous gay and bisexual authors who spent time in the city: Tennessee Williams, Truman Capote, Gore Vidal, Jean Genet, André Gide, Joe Orton and Paul Bowles.

Although the hotel El Muniria on Rue Magellan doesn't do very well on TripAdvisor: 'Noisy club next door', 'My son found a bedbug crawling across the sheets', 'The area is run down', if you go and stay you will be steeping yourself in the beat generation. I don't think the décor has changed significantly since the fifties. At one stage, William S. Burroughs, the author of *The Naked Lunch* – the clue is in the title; it became the last book (without pictures) in the USA to become the subject of an obscenity lawsuit – was in room nine typing up his manuscript. Allen Ginsberg and Jack Kerouac had rented rooms four and five on the floor above, and sometimes Paul Bowles, the author of *The Sheltering Sky*, would use number seven on the top floor. I bet there must have been some serious partying going on up on the roof terrace.

If you want to soak up a bit of that decadent beat sensibility but don't fancy the bedbugs, then a good alternative is to head down to the Petit Socco in the medina. It means 'the little square' and it is, in fact, a little open square in a network of narrow streets. There are three or four cafés positioned round it and my favourite is the one at the top end, looking down onto the square and adjoining streets. This is where the literati used to take their in-between-drug-and-absinthe-binge coffees and is a good place to soak up some history and some sun. A small cup of thick black espresso and a quick perusal of the Moroccan newspaper *Al Sabah* of a morning will set you up for the day. You can have a chat with your neighbour about what's in the paper. Mention football, government corruption or terrible bus crashes and you are onto a winner – they feature every day. Or, of course, you could whip out your copy of *The Sheltering Sky* by Paul Bowles and join him on his magical mystery tour of Morocco. It perfectly captures the fly-blown desperation of the small desert towns and the strange languor that overtakes you there.

Tangier's secret gem is the Art Deco cinema on the main square before you enter the medina. The square is large and open with a small garden in the middle leading to the mosque. Opposite the cinema are a row of imposing French-style colonial buildings which have been transformed into cafés and restaurants. The cinema itself is in a classic Art Deco building, painted mainly white, with one multicoloured section, with the name 'Cinema Rif' picked out in red. You can sit at the café outside for your pre- or post-film juice and snack. Inside, there is a splendid gold-speckled mirror on your right-hand side and an equally large light fitting made of big frosted-glass globes. The whole place is an antique dream and worth visiting just for a look.

Even better, though, it is the independent cinema set up by an association to promote Moroccan and international independent and arthouse film. Its programme is always joy-ously eclectic: January 2018 was showing the thriller *Cairo Confidential*, 'Thirty million residents are waiting . . . waiting for something to happen'; *Hayat*, 'A road trip from Tangier to Agadir'; and *Headbang Lullaby*, 'An exploration of political and social conflicts through a surrealist and psychedelic fresco'. Best to check what languages the films are in and what lan-guages the subtitles are in to avoid disappointment when you arrive, ready to practise your French, only to find the film is in Serbo-Croat with Russian subtitles. I speak from bitter personal experience.

Tangier was where I landed in Morocco the very first time I came to the country. Our train dropped us off at the ferry in Spain, and Tim and I crossed by sea. Even though just eight miles separate Africa and Europe, they are two continents, and the minute you step onto Tangerine soil it is somehow very different. There is the scent of spice in the air and waving palm trees vying with minarets in height.

Of course, when we arrived as fresh-faced students from the chilly winds of an Edinburgh summer, one of the first things we did was head to the beach, which was to be the scene of a great triumph for me and a story that gets retold every time our group of old friends meets. The beach is a long, pristine curve of golden sand, with the blue wavelets of the Mediterranean lapping onto the shore. Tim and I plunged in and splashed around. Later we decided that we wanted to have a proper swim and we headed for a wooden raft anchored about a kilometre offshore.

The water was clear, the sun was warm and all was right with the world. We pulled ourselves up onto the raft when we got there and basked in the sun like walruses. I think I may even have made some snorting noises of satisfaction. Eventually, though, it was time to head back and we slipped into the water again. I was forging my way towards the shore when I heard a polite, 'Alice?' from Tim. I half turned around to see what was happening and Tim said, 'Alice, I think I might need a hand.' I am a very bad girlfriend, because my immediate thought was not, 'Oh no, you poor thing.' It was, 'Hooray! I am going to get to life save. This is fantastic!'

My mind flashed back to my lifeguard's badge from school. When I got this badge it involved a very strange procedure that, to this day, I have not understood. We were lined up on the edge of the swimming pool in our pyjamas, with our drowning victim halfway down the length of it. When our swimming instructor blew the whistle we had to jump into the pool, take off our pyjama bottoms and knot the legs at the feet, then try and scoop air into them like a balloon and knot them at the waist. Now I come to think of it, highly reminiscent of trying to capture air in the goat skin in the Marrakech tanneries. This could then, allegedly, be used as a buoyancy aid with which to rescue our victim. Obviously, the amount of time it took trying to get air into knotted pyjama bottoms would have caused any actual person in distress to drown, however that is a detail. Then, you would swim to the victim, go behind them and cup their head under their chin and swim backstroke back to the side, with them holding onto the air-filled pyjamas.

Now, my conundrum with Tim was that I didn't have any pyjamas. It has since struck me that it is highly unlikely that you would ever be wearing pyjamas when called upon to life save, but I improvised and just went for the supporting of the head and backstroke swimming. All went smoothly and we were soon on dry land, where Tim with admirable generosity of spirit thanked me for saving him, and I, not in the slightest bit gracious in victory, whooped and crowed and generally lorded it for the rest of the holiday. This was over twenty-five years ago but the memory is still sweet.

In spite of all its rich history, and my own personal story of heroism, Tangier is probably still best known for the humble tangerine. These are in season in December through to January and when I was a kid we always used to get one in the toe of our Christmas stocking as an extra treat. Of course, they taste even better in their homeland. In winter, juice carts pop up all over the city, piled high with the juicy orange globes, where they will press you a fresh glass for around £1.20. In fact, they most probably originated in south Asia and were brought to Tangier via the trade routes from the Orient. The soil and climate conditions were perfect for them so they flourished and became synonymous with the city. In this city that gave them their name they are served everywhere as a dessert, lightly dusted in cinnamon. A fitting end to a meal and to tales of Tangier.

6

CHEFCHAOUEN AND THE RIF

My first experience of Chefchaouen could not have begun under more inauspicious circumstances. Owen Prowel (one 'l') and I had met while we were both working on a journalism training programme for the BBC. It covered seventeen countries across eastern Europe, the Middle East and north Africa, and while I was focusing on training mentors in countries as diverse as Moldova and Egypt, Owen was doing the admin involved in getting 1,200 journalists through the process – a master of organisation. We used to spend quite a lot of time silent-screaming in the office together. Fortunately, he has a well-developed sense of humour and is also very dapper, with hair gelled just so, and excellent efforts made in the gym. After one course in Jordan had ended, Owen and I had taken a couple of days' leave to go on a road trip together to visit Wadi Rum and the fabulous ruins of Petra. We hired a car, switched on our Google Maps and set off.

First, we made a stop at the Dead Sea. Owen had kept up the grooming and had shaved that morning. This is a big mistake when you are about to go into a sea so salty that you are more buoyant than a helium balloon at a kids' party. I had maintained no personal grooming so looked on with some amusement as he ouched his way through the experience. Of course, we had to cover ourselves in the black mud, dredged up and put in basins for the purpose, and take photographs that I hope will never come to light.

Emboldened by the pain, Owen decided he was going to take over the driving. He hadn't driven for several years because he lived in London (in fact I have a nasty feeling this may have been only the third time he had got behind the wheel since his test). Five hours later, in the pitch black, he was manfully revving the car through sand drifts covering the one-track, sandy and deserted hilly road in the middle of nowhere that we had managed to get ourselves on to. I was navigating. I am very bad at navigating. If the car had stopped or swerved off the road, we would have been truly stuck – kudos to Owen.

Obviously we learnt nothing from our experience and decided we wanted more of this type of adventure, so Owen came over to Marrakech and we planned to road-trip it to the north, up to the town of Chefchaouen. The morning after he flew in we set off from my flat to the car hire place, which was about a five-minute walk. Passport – check, driving licence – check, £500 in cash for car – check, iPhone – check.

The sun was shining through the purple bougainvillea, the birds were singing their spring song and we were catching up on a couple of years of news. I was in one of those happy, oblivious moments of life when suddenly a moto passed me, and as it did, the guy on the back reached out and snatched my bag from my hand. We both yelled and ran after them, but we had absolutely no chance. They sped on to the end of the lane, turned into the main road and were gone. I swear the one on the back turned around and laughed at me. Unfortunately, moto crime is a real problem in Marrakech. The modus operandi is to approach a person from behind, cut the strap on their bag, grab it and then ride off before they realise what has happened; or to do what they did with me, which was to approach from the opposite direction, snatch and then speed on. A strong bag with thick straps that can't be slashed easily, as well as keeping vigilant, really is necessary in the city.

This was a total disaster. I had lost everything important, including a shedload of money and an uninsured iPhone, as travel insurance doesn't cover you when you live in a place. Inside I was distraught. Being an Adventurer is a great job, but I can exclusively reveal that it is not hugely well paid, and this was a really big deal for me. However, Owen had flown all the way over and we were booked and ready to go, and I didn't want the moto thieves to ruin that for both of us too.

The upshot of this was that Owen had to drive as I had lost my licence, and there are lots of police stops where they demand to see your licence and fine you if you don't have it. So, we were late in starting after the drama and, to top it off, I had planned the route and was navigating. I am wildly optimistic about driving times and distances and, as discussed, very bad at navigating. It was to be a baptism of fire for Owen. In most respects, Moroccans are absolutely delightful people. They are kind, generous, funny and welcoming. However, put them behind the wheel of a car and, to a (wo)man, they transform into demons from the deepest, darkest pits of hell. I am prone to a bit of road rage myself, but nothing compared to the sweetest of Moroccan grandmothers when she takes possession of the keys. With this in mind, I gave Owen my top-ten tips before we set off:

1. Get horny (tee hee). Your horn is of much more use to you than your brakes, rear-view mirror or accelerator. Use it long and hard and often.
2. Ignore indicators. Drivers in Morocco use their indicators a lot. There they are blinking away merrily and arbitrarily. Putting on your left-hand indicator does not mean you are turning left, no, it does not. What it might mean is that you are pulling into the kerb on the right. Or, that you just forgot to switch it off. Who knows?
3. Don't ignore someone coming in the opposite direction flashing their lights at you. This means there is a police checkpoint ahead. There are police radar points everywhere. On the motorway they hide in bushes in the central reservation or behind artful clumps of palm trees, ready to leap out and fine you.
4. Don't presume you have right of way on roundabouts. You do and you don't. Where there are traffic lights on the feeder road, the incomers have precedence. Why oh why? If you are in Essaouira, it gets even more complicated with the small roundabouts on the so-called 'autoroute' – actually just a road with two lanes – giving precedence to vehicles on the main road, but the big roundabouts reverting to normal practice.
5. Tailgate. You have to really. I like doing this to big 4×4 BMWs in my Toyota Yaris. Bumper up with your lights on full beam to someone who is slowing down for a red light and then toot impatiently.

6. Give some money to the beggars who are lined up at the traffic lights or buy a box of tissues. Well, would you like that job?

7. If you are out in the country and someone needs a lift, give it to them. They can't afford a car and you are in one – simple.

8. Don't mess with a moto. They are tools of the devil, driven by Satan's helpers. They will dart up your inside when you are trying to turn, push your wing mirror in so that they can get past you in a queue, and veer into your path with no warning whatsoever. But they are carrying live and breakable human beings . . .

9. Do make sure you have lots of good-luck charms, verses from the Quran, hands of Fatima and other symbols to protect you from bad luck, the evil eye and accidents, hanging from your rear-view mirror. Much more effective than driving sanely.

10. Don't do it. Take a cab, a bus, a train, or even a horse and carriage . . .

Our aim had been to drive straight through from Marrakech to Chefchaouen that day, which is doable if you know where you are going and start at a reasonable time and use the motorways as much as possible. But our late start and my navigation, which took us on the scenic mountain route, was a combination ripe for disaster. One thing to say about this drive, though, is that the scenery is worth the time. It was March and the trees had their early spring foliage on, when everything is fresh and green and newly made. You pass through wide, flat plains, grazed by fat cows and wind up on escarpments through the pine forests. Everything feels satisfyingly lush and well-fed. There are no skinny goats feasting on scrubby thyme clinging to a rocky mountain here. The miles spooled past and I basked in the green. Owen, meanwhile, was white-knuckled as he took on the hairpin bends and the speeding container trucks, who had absolutely taken my advice and used tip number one at all times: horn over brakes.

The sun set, and we were still just south of Meknes, a long way from our goal. With the prospect of narrow mountain roads and suicidal truck drivers ahead, we decided to cut our losses and stay in Meknes – one of Morocco's imperial cities. Meknes was the brainchild of Sultan Moulay Ismail, who built it in the seventeenth century. As a northern Moroccan city, it reflects a lot of Spanish influences. Like all Moroccan cities on the tourist trail, Meknes has its fair share of gorgeously renovated riads secreted in the medina.

A night there, even though unscheduled, would surely be an ideal opportunity to stay in one of them and soak up the imperial vibe? Absolutely! But when you are knackered and stressed from driving, the last thing you want to do is find your way round an ancient walled city. Owen and I stopped by the side of the road to consult TripAdvisor. 'Hooray, an Ibis on the outskirts, with parking.' This was genuine joy that could not be dimmed even by the hideous flaccid pizza we ate in the fast-food outlet next door. I am as much of a hotel snob as the next person, but living in Morocco has given me a deep appreciation of the Ibis: comfortable beds, WiFi that works, power outlets that work and plenty of them, a guaranteed hot shower with good water flow, easy access and egress ... What's not to like? As a bonus, the police station was just a five-minute walk away. Because I didn't have my passport and I hadn't registered it as stolen in Marrakech, I had to report it in Meknes and was given a letter and a number that I could use at all the other places we stayed in on that trip.

One unexpected positive of our unscheduled stay in Meknes was that we hit Volubilis, Morocco's biggest Roman ruins just to the north of the city, as it opened and before the tourist rush. I am a bit of a history nerd and aside from the history of the Arab and Islamic world have two particular interests. The first is the Georgian period in Britain and the Napoleonic Wars, which I attribute to an early love of Georgette Heyer thanks to my mum and a later love of Sean Bean in *Sharpe*. The second is the Roman Empire, which is down to a big kids' book on Ancient Rome, thanks again to my mum, which led to a constant passion for novels, histories, films and plays about this long period of history. A favourite moment in film is the scene of Marlon Brando as Mark Antony in *Julius Caesar* on the steps of the forum decrying, 'For Brutus is an honourable man.' My favourite novels on Rome are the series by Colleen McCullough, which I have read many times and which never pale.

Volubilis was actually the capital of Mauritania, which became a client state of the Romans after Carthage fell in 146 BC. Over 100 years later, in 25 BC, Juba II of Numidia was put on the throne by the government of Rome. His blood may have been Berber, but he was more Roman than the Romans, having been educated there. He married Cleopatra Selene II, the daughter of the ill-fated but oh-so-romanticised union of Mark Antony and Cleopatra, and it was he and his son Ptolemy who built Volubilis into a proper Roman capital for the region. It stayed that way for 250 years, and at its height probably had around 20,000 occupants and covered about 42 hectares (100 acres), with the town surrounded by 2.5 kilometres of walls. It was conquered by local tribes in the 280s, by which time the Romans had rather lost interest in Mauritania and didn't go to the trouble of retaking it.

Paintings and sketches throughout the centuries showed that it stayed more or less intact until it was hit by a big earthquake in the eighteenth century and devastated. The rulers and businessmen of nearby Meknes then came and scavenged it for their buildings in the city.

My mind was full of heroic figures from the history of Rome as we approached. I was about to walk in a place where Cleopatra and Mark Antony's daughter had walked, to physically be in the place that she had been. Volubilis lies in a slight dip below the mountain of Zerhoun, on a ridge overlooking the rich plains of Khoumane. It's slightly hidden, and you walk down and then up to get to it. When you are at its highest point you can look back to the mountain and then across the fertile fields of the valley and imagine the legions marching, or a messenger galloping his horse towards the city.

We were almost the first to arrive, and, having decided we didn't want a guide, we walked up to see what we could find. It was a perfect March day, with warm sun and blue skies, and the site was absolutely quiet except for the sound of the wind ruffling the trees and the birds singing. Twenty thousand people used to live there, and yet now it was silent. You can still see the outline of the streets, the temple and some mosaic floors. An impressive triumphal arch guards the city at the end of a colonnade of pillars. It is the atmosphere that is most captivating, though, and the feeling of being connected to people through millennia. When the Romans were here there were lions hunting in the mountains. They've gone now, but the fields are still being tilled and the olive trees, known for their produce even then, are being harvested, over 2,000 years on.

We finally reached Chefchaouen, Morocco's prettiest city and the jewel in the crown of the Rif mountains, 173 kilometres later. It is surrounded by hills and lies terraced up one of them, a big splash of vivid blue and white against the green of the trees and the red of the earth. In Chefchaouen the houses in the old town are typically painted bright blue – a shade somewhere between cobalt and turquoise. It is this blue that is the trademark of the city and one of the reasons it is so pretty. It also gives the place its name, the Blue Pearl. There are lots of theories as to why the blue paint started being used. Some say the blue keeps mosquitos away; another theory is that the blue is a metaphor for the sky and heaven, and so reminds the citizens to lead a spiritual life; some residents say it is to represent the sea or the importance of the Ras El Maa waterfall which provides the city with its water, while others claim that it helps to keep the houses cool in summer.

The most convincing theory is that the colour was originally brought over in the 1500s, when Chefchaouen received an influx of Jews escaping the Spanish inquisition. There is a Jewish religious tradition of weaving prayer shawls with tekhelel (an ancient natural blue dye) to remind people of the presence of God, which formed the basis of painting houses blue for the same reason. In 1492, Ferdinand and Isabella of Spain issued the Edict of Expulsion, which ordered all practising Jews to be expelled from Castile and Aragon. Isabella had come under the influence of a new and fanatical confessor and had been led to believe that Jews were trying to convert Catholics. The edict stipulated that the Jews were trying 'to subvert their holy Catholic faith and trying to draw faithful Christians away from their beliefs'.

Many Jews converted to Christianity to avoid persecution

during this turbulent time, but many others refused and were forced out of the country. It was not until 1968 that the edict was formally withdrawn. Morocco, with its close geographical proximity and existing Jewish community, was a natural haven for those fleeing, and Chefchaouen became a large refugee camp. The Chaouens still repaint the houses blue every year, and when you are walking round the old town you are sometimes in a cocoon of blue light.

Chefchaouen's proximity to Spain has shaped its more modern history too. In 1920, Spain seized the town and, although most of the rest of the country was under French control, Spain held it and the rest of Spanish Morocco until independence. There are still two Spanish enclaves on Moroccan soil: Ceuta and Melilla.

Spanish is still the first foreign language spoken in Chefchaouen, above French, so you have to readjust your ear from a '*Bonjour*' to an '*Hola*'. We had chosen to stay at Casa Perleta, which is a traditional Andalusian house in the old town, owned by a Spanish couple, of great charm – both the house and the owners. They recommended we walk to the intriguingly named Spanish Mosque for some good views. The mosque was, in fact, a gift from Spain to the city and sits on the hill opposite. You leave the old town through Bab al Ansar, the eastern gate, and cross over the Ras El Maa river where women still do their washing. Then the trail goes uphill, not too steep, on a little path spiked with cactus fruit plants and agave. Within ten minutes you are in the countryside and we passed farmers with their donkeys and a herd of sheep going up to pasture. The mosque itself is nothing special, but the views over Chefchaouen are, especially if you time it to catch the light hitting the blue houses of the city on the hill opposite at midday.

There are some nice things to buy in Chefchaouen that you don't find anywhere else in the country, particularly the striped blankets that the women wear as aprons. Traditionally, they are red and white, but they also come in pinks and blues and make really nice throws. The old town is small but takes ages to explore as you stop every other step to take a picture. Geraniums placed against a blue wall, or arranged in pots up a blue staircase; corners of blue and turquoise, accentuated by ornate black cast-iron window grills; a boy playing with a red football in a luminous blue square – Chefchaouen is somewhere where you get greedy for photographs.

The main square has several restaurants for locals and tourists. The nights were still cold so we wanted to eat inside and headed upstairs in the busiest one. I knew it wasn't going to be the best meal of my life because I was trying out a vegan diet for a diet-comparison article I was doing for a health magazine. It was three diets in three months: Paleo in January, calorie-counting in February and vegan in March. Paleo, according to Serena and Olivia, my Marrakchi flatmates, had turned me into a 'hangry' nightmare. It does make you really hungry, even though you can eat as much meat and as many vegetables as you like, and if I wasn't around food at 5.30 p.m. my temper went into the red zone. Serena actually did it with me for two weeks and got so hungry one day that she ate two cooked chickens, bought off the spit, at one sitting. Calorie-counting was by far the most sensible one and had the extra bonus of really improving my mental arithmetic, although I did get slightly anal about weighing courgettes.

Vegan was the one I had been looking forward to the most, as cooking vegan at home is not a problem in Morocco, where the fruit, vegetables, nuts and grains are local and plentiful. Eating vegan on a road trip, I was to find, is not so good, as the choice in restaurants and cafés gets very limited once you eliminate not only meat but eggs and cheese. In places like Chefchaouen, there are no specialist restaurants or health-food shops where you can buy a variety of delicious alternatives as there are in the UK and the USA (not all of Europe though; trying to order a meal for a vegan friend in Paris remains a painful memory of abject failure). It was going to be bread and jam for breakfast and vegetable tagine or couscous for lunch and dinner for me, with not even a little crème caramel to alleviate the tedium. I watched glumly as Owen gnawed his way through hunks of beef sweetened with prunes, or lemon chicken contrasted with sharp green olives. On the upside, I was able to look at every goat or sheep we passed with a clear conscience.

Although a wonderful place to visit, Chefchaouen does not rely on its tourist trade for income. Kif – also known as hash-ish, marijuana, dope, grass – is the cash crop for this region. Morocco has the doubtful honour of being the world's larg-est producer of cannabis, according to the United Nations Office on Drugs and Crime's annual 'World Drug Report 2017'. The report estimated that 38,000 tonnes of the drug is produced in the country annually, most of which is exported to Europe and other north African states. As in many other countries, in Morocco the whole subject of drugs and the law is a confusing one. It is illegal to use hashish in Morocco. It is also illegal to grow it. However, it is very obviously being grown widely in the Rif mountains where the poor, rocky soil means that many other crops fail and local farmers rely on it for income. Eighty thousand people in the Rif live off the crop, but it is not a safe living, as although the fields are left intact, the farmers are often imprisoned for growing it. Unsurprisingly, it is the buyers and smugglers who make the cash, not the farmers who grow it. They earn around £6 per kilogram.

There is debate within the Moroccan parliament about legalisation of some part of the crop for medical sale and use, but there is also opposition to this from the more conservative elements.

While we were planning the BBC Two documentary *Morocco to Timbuktu*, Charlie and I had suggested to the producers that we should include the dope fields in the film, to show a new form of trade in the country and to provide a contrast to the trading goods of old. When it came time to do the reconnaissance trip in September with Alicia, the director, and Laura, the assistant producer, Chefchaouen and its fields of green were high on the list. Charlie and I, Alicia and Laura piled into the car with our driver, Mohammed, to find them and see whether we could get a story.

It did not prove difficult to find them. About three-quarters of an hour from the city, we turned onto an unpaved road and got out of the car. We were surrounded for as far as we could see by lush cannabis plants growing at least eight feet tall. We all dashed in to take silly selfies in the middle of them. The air was thick with the smell and it may have been purely psychological, but I felt quite high just standing there. A couple of women walked past with big bundles on their backs, dressed in the local red-striped apron and big straw hat. The fields were neatly tilled and clearly well cared for. It could have been a series of turnip fields. After we had taken lots of photos of ourselves, we continued further up into the hills, passing hectare after hectare of the plants and planning how we could use them in the story. At the top of one of the hills, we came across a group of workers, and so we stopped and I went over to chat to them and ask them what was going on.

I was in a bit of a social conundrum. How should I go about this? Was there some kind of special approach to narcotics growers? Would they talk to me? Or would they chase me off, maybe even threaten me? My experience of drugs is very limited, and I had never been in contact with people in the 'trade' before. The preconceptions I have are from American TV shows about evil but glamorous gangsters or twisted chemistry teachers. These well-tended fields and normal-looking farmers did not fit these tropes at all. However, we were thinking about using the story and I needed more information, so I strode over and decided to approach the whole things as if I actually were in a turnip field.

Me: 'Peace be upon you.'
Farmers: 'Upon you be peace.'
Me: 'How are you? How is the crop?'
Farmers: 'Thanks be to God. We are fine. Are you fine? The crop is not very good this year.'
Me: 'But the plants look so tall and healthy.'
Farmers: 'Ah yes, but there are not as many. There has not been enough rain. You should have been here two years ago. Then, it was a good crop.'

And there it is. Whether you are running a carpet shop in Marrakech or growing cannabis plants in the Rif, life was always better a couple of years ago. It is a universal law. By now the farmers and I were on excellent terms and, naturally, I got invited to share a pot of tea. This, I thought, is not what I expected. This, I thought, is nothing like *The Sopranos*. Sadly, there was no time for tea, but I did manage to find out that the harvest was going to be in about a month and would take a couple of weeks. They would be working in this area, camped out at that time, if I wanted to come back and visit. I had told them we were making a TV programme about the trans-Saharan trade routes and that had not seemed to faze them, so I left it at that, said my goodbyes and mounted up with the team again.

The process for extracting the drug is that, when the plant has been harvested, the farmers take the dried bundles of leaves and put them on top of a fine wire mesh. They then beat them with sticks to extract a powder which is made into hash bricks for sale. If you come through in autumn, it sounds as if there is one massive drumming festival taking place.

The harvest time did not work very well with our filming schedule, so we worked on a plan to get Séamas McCracken, the director of photography, over just for a couple of days in advance to shoot this segment. We all loved the idea, but then, that evening over dinner, Charlie, the voice of reason, made a very salient point. The trade is completely illegal in Morocco and it would be highly unlikely that the Moroccan government would grant us a filming licence to cover the subject. Filming permits are very well administered, and you have to state what you are going to film and where. We were to find as we actually started later in the year that you could be in the remotest spot and, as if by magic, an official would pop up to ask for your permit. If we wanted to go ahead with filming, it would have to be clandestine. None of us wanted to go down that road. Our actual aim was to make a great documentary about the historic trade routes across this fantastic country and this didn't fit, so the idea hit the cutting room floor.

What intrigued me was the attitude to kif from an Islamic point of view. The plant had been grown in the north for centuries and was actually legal, by Royal Mandate, in several regions until 1974. There is no specific ban in the Quran against it as there is for alcohol (*khamr*), and I have certainly seen plenty of men enjoying a long-stemmed hash pipe of an evening in coffee shops in the mountains. However, it would seem to be disapproved of, not surprisingly, by most religious leaders. They argue that *khamr* actually means an intoxicant rather than just alcohol, and therefore kif comes under that heading. When I have asked Muslim friends, they say that marijuana is '*makrooh*', disapproved of, rather than '*haram*', which means unlawful or banned. I have also heard many people compare using dope to smoking cigarettes rather than to drinking alcohol.

On that same recce trip we were trying to find good routes through the Rif mountains that would reflect the trade routes to and from the coast. This meant another big day out in the hills for the team, joined by a local guide, Ismail, searching out hidden roads in the pine forests. No vegan diet this time meant I could feast at breakfast on the local goat's cheese that the Rif is famous for, accompanied by bitter black olives and homemade fig jam.

We were heading into the wilds, but our first stop was at a village called El Kalaa not far from Chefchaouen. It is a tiny place with a café, shop and the usual mosque at its centre. What distinguishes it is that this mosque leans totteringly to your left as you look at it from the main square. You can't resist bending your neck to the same angle to try to straighten it up in your brain. It is a simple brick building, whitewashed rather shabbily, with a large square courtyard to the back of it down the hill. The lean gives it charm, though. It seems that it is caused by natural movement in the mountain, which shifted after it built, shifting the minaret to the left along with it.

Rif means 'next to the sea', or 'the edge of the land' in Tamazight, the Amazigh (Berber) language, and this region is exactly that – a wide, mainly mountainous arc stretching inland from Morocco's northern coastline. This area gets the most rain in Morocco and used to be heavily forested. In the west and centre of the region are forests of Atlas cedar, cork oak and holm oak as well as the Moroccan fir, which is found only here. The eastern slopes of the mountains don't get as much rain and mainly pine trees grow there, including the Aleppo pine and the maritime pine, which has become a complete pest in South Africa, to where it was exported, colonising the countryside and pushing out native species.

While we were driving through the kif fields, we had seen for ourselves that acres of forest had been chopped down to make room for the growth of more plants. Overgrazing and forest fires have added to the problem and there has been deforestation on a large scale with its attendant problems of soil degradation and the loss of topsoil.

Our road took us up and soon we had come to the end of the tarmac and were on the piste. Quite often, it felt like we would slide out of the back of the car as Mohammed revved us up a vertical incline. Pine and conifer woods on a sunny day in good company, with a mission to discover hidden places, proved an excellent recipe for a great day out. We stopped at the edge of a gorge which slashed down into a valley to take a closer look at the dark red, deeply ridged bark of the pines and just to listen to the wind soughing through them. It's like the distant sound of the sea.

A few kilometres on we stopped again, not at the edge this time, but in the very heart of the forest. We all tumbled out into a womb of green. The shade of the trees completely blotted out the sun and the ground underfoot was soft with thick moss. The pines were impossibly tall and we had to crane our necks to see up to the top. I was busily snooping around the bottom of one looking at some interesting mushrooms when Alicia yelled, 'Look, look!' I jerked my head up and saw the top of the tree waving and jerking around. Monkeys! A little family of Barbary apes had come to see who had ventured into their forest. We stared up at them, fascinated, and they stared back down at us, equally fascinated.

The Barbary ape is a species of macaque specific to north Africa. Macaques are the biggest primate group in the world, aside from humans, and the only other primate living freely in Europe. They are actually monkeys rather than apes and are of medium size with yellowish-grey fur and pretty little faces. They live off plants and insects, and conifers are a major part of their diet. They eat every part of the tree including flowers, fruits, seeds, seedlings, leaves, buds, bark, gum, stems, roots, bulbs and corns.

They have a structured social order and group together in bands of ten to 100. We were looking at a small family. The society is matriarchal and nepotistic, with your importance on the ape scale being judged by your blood links to the lead female. Mating is a woman's game and when she is fertile the macaque mates with as many of the males as she can. Then, unusually, the males take an equal part in rearing the young, apparently to make sure that they are recognised as the fathers and to help with that proximity to the female leader. It is believed that females may prefer to mate with males that have shown themselves to be good fathers.

Sadly, the place that you are guaranteed to see macaques in Morocco is in Jemaa El Fna in Marrakech, dressed in a nappy and on a chain, ready to have their picture taken close up. Here in the forest, our pictures were happily guaranteed to be terrible, at best little blobs of greyish yellow against the green. More likely, just snaps of leaves which the monkeys had darted behind, laughing at our efforts to capture them on camera.

Dark was approaching but we were still in the middle of the forest. Ismail had developed a mantra: 'Just over that ridge we will be able to see the sea.' The hours passed, and when the ridge finally appeared and we saw the sea there was general rejoicing as we knew that now we were set for home.

We continued up and down and down and up and more hours passed. Car sickness spread round the interior and Laura curled up in a corner, no longer fascinated by the parade of conifers. I need regular feeding and our stash of very unhealthy snacks was finished and my stomach was rumbling. The mood in the car started to turn ugly. Ismail's mantra had altered slightly to: 'Just over that ridge we will see Chefchaouen.' This gave us no comfort given his track record.

My mantra is: 'When things get bad, rest assured that they will get worse.' At this stage, Charlie and Mohammed the driver were murmuring quietly to each other in Arabic, trying to be unobtrusive, which of course made me instantly suspicious. What were they hiding? What they were hiding was the fact that the petrol gauge was pointing at empty, as in 'you are on your last prayer' empty, and we were out in the middle of nowhere with Ismail and his 'over the next ridge' delusions. This was not an ideal scenario for any of us and I started to gear myself up mentally for a long, hungry walk in the dark. Every time Ismail said, 'Just over that ridge . . .' I could sense Charlie gritting his teeth and Mohammed grinding his. Then, as we were on the brink of being stranded and all of us were beginning to suffer a sense-of-humour failure, we summited a ridge and saw Chefchaouen in all its twinkling magic.

We coasted down the hill (Mohammed had taken to turning the engine off to conserve fuel) and then drove into the blue city triumphant, with the promise ahead of the two things that every traveller in Morocco needs: a hot tagine and a comfortable, warm bed.

7

CASABLANCA

It is tempting to get swept away by the romance of Morocco and its history. You often do feel as if you have stepped back 1,000 years when you walk through the streets of the old medina, or watch a man tilling his fields with a wooden plough drawn by donkeys. However, Morocco is a modern state, a country that is growing and thriving in the twenty-first century.

No place in Morocco epitomises this as much as Casablanca. Rabat is the official capital of the country and is where all the embassies are based, but Casablanca is Morocco's main city and the centre of the modern state.

Before I arrived in Morocco, my only contact with Casablanca had been with the film of the same name, so I was deeply disappointed when I got off the train there for the first time. I wanted wartime and romance and heartbreak. Instead, I got a city which, in many parts, could have been anywhere in the world. Skyscrapers and traffic jams were my first impression, not seedy men in fezzes, baddies in uniform and heroes in trench coats and trilbies.

Three-and-a-half million people live in Casablanca and it is distinguished by its port, one of the largest man-made harbours in the world and the base for the Moroccan navy. When it was first built by the native Amazigh, it was called Anfa, but when the Portuguese conquered it in the fifteenth century, they rebuilt it and called it Casa Branca, which means 'white house'. This got modified to Casablanca during a Spanish–Portuguese union. In Arabic it is Dar el Beida – a straight translation from the Spanish – but almost everyone just calls it Casa.

In part, Casa has Britain to thank for its early growth. In the nineteenth century it became a major supplier of wool from the surrounding region to the booming textile industry in the UK, especially to the north where the great mills were situated. While Britain imported wool, it exported tea to Morocco, grown in its colonies. I was told the story of how the Moroccans came to start drinking mint tea as I was sitting in a sidecar, being driven round Marrakech.

'Alice, what are you doing tomorrow? Are you free to test out a new Marrakech tour for us? It is round the city in a vintage sidecar,' said Charlie on the phone one morning as I was slaving away over a hot keyboard. Woo hoo! I was digging my Biggles goggles, jodhpurs and leather jacket out of the cupboard before he could finish his sentence.

At 9 a.m. the next day, Felix from Insiders Experience roared up to my front door on his motorbike with sidecar and raised my street cred to previously unattained heights. I donned my helmet and goggles, waved to my awestruck neighbours and clambered in. The bike and sidecar have a great backstory. The original version, the BMW R71, was designed by the Wehrmacht to transport them across the steppes for the invasion of Russia. When they discovered their existence, the Russians secretly bought five and took them through Sweden into the Soviet Union. There, they reverse-engineered them and started producing them themselves as the URAL M72. The one we were riding had evolved a bit, with concessions to better brakes, bearings and suspension, but, as Felix said, 'They kept the heart and look of the original machine and even though the rest of the world has moved on and forgotten about these machines, in Russia they are still going strong.'

Felix is a spinner of tales and regaled me with many as we sped round the city, not to mention some fantastic facts. 'Do you know that in the butchers' stalls in Morocco, the butchers hang the testicles above the meat to let you know it comes from a male animal?' he said. I did not and now cannot pass a butcher's without spotting lots of hanging testicles, so thank you, Felix. Then, there was his tale of how tea came to Morocco and the link with Casablanca, which, although elements of it may well be apocryphal, remains the story I tell to visiting friends as they sip their hot, sweet glass of the beverage.

The Crimean War was raging across the peninsula in the years between 1853 and 1856. All the Baltic ports were shut or severely curtailed for trade due to the fighting. The war itself was a disaster for British trade with Russia, as you don't normally want to trade with a nation that you are fighting. Florence Nightingale and the Charge of the Light Brigade both bore witness to the effects of the new, mechanised type of warfare that the Crimean conflict introduced. In terms of tea, the problem for Britain was that it had been carrying out a lucrative trade from China to Russia of the black, bitter gunpowder brew that was so suited to the Russian samovar and taste for sugar. Now, it was left with huge stocks of the stuff that it couldn't offload.

Meanwhile, across the water in Morocco, so Felix's story goes, the Sultan Abderrahman Ben Hicham was worried about his people's growing fondness for alcohol, which had been introduced by Westerners. Enterprising British merchants persuaded him that the very thing would be to introduce tea instead, so he bought a large consignment to come in through Casa. Moroccans made it their own by adding vast quantities of sugar and fresh mint. A national drink was born, the British trade problem was solved, and Casa thrived. Allegedly, the sultan then propagated its popularity by taking a deep gulp of the fragrant golden liquid and uttering the immortal words, 'Mmmmm, delicious Berber whisky,' in an effort to get his people off the hard stuff. It is still called Berber whisky to this day.

Today, Casa is Morocco's industrial and commercial hub. Agriculture, phosphate minerals and tourism are the mainstays of Morocco's economy, but there is also a substantial manufacturing base which includes garments and cars and is concentrated around Casa. All the newspapers, banks and major companies have their base in the city and it is the biggest employment centre in the country.

I came to Morocco to train for the Marathon des Sables but one of the things that attracted me to it as a place to live was that I could see that women were relatively free, which meant I would be able to do the things I like – such as cycling and running – without too many problems. Nowhere is this more apparent than in Casa. I had previously lived in Syria and Egypt and travelled widely in the Middle East and north Africa, but Morocco was the first place I had seen schoolgirls riding to class on their bikes, or young women dressed in office clothes dodging through the traffic on their motos.

The very first weekend I arrived, a running friend of Charlie's, MdS veteran Amine Kabbaj, invited me to run a half marathon with him and his friends as a practice. The half marathon was part of a charity drive by a young Moroccan runner, Ali, to run a half marathon in every province in the country to raise awareness and money for the disadvantaged. It was being organised by a woman from Casablanca, Zineb Bennouna, and she emailed me with maps and start times.

I decided that this would also be a good chance to practise running with a backpack, as I would have to for the race, so I turned up with 10 kilograms worth of couscous, lentils and dried white beans, all wrapped up in a sleeping bag, stuffed into my pack. It is quite intimidating turning up on your own, in a new city, when you are not a good runner and I wasn't feeling very confident, especially when I looked around me at the start line at a whole pack of lithe figures wearing the Casablanca running club kit.

Zineb was one of them. Tall, with shoulder-length brown hair, smooth olive skin and big brown eyes, she is a typically gorgeous Moroccan girl. Moroccan women are famous for their beauty, and rightly so. She works in sports PR, doing the publicity for events like the Casablanca marathon, and was helping to organise the race for Ali, who was a friend of hers. She was suffering from a slight injury and so was running more slowly than usual, which was fantastic for me as she ran a lot of the way beside me. My other companion was Yassine, who was about to start up a surf resort on the Atlantic coast and who gallantly stayed with me all the way.

I am not a fast runner anyway, but add on 10 kilograms in a backpack that was entirely unsuited to running – so I was glad I tried it out early – and I could have been overtaken by a tortoise. This was my introduction to modern young Moroccans – the Casa set.

Zineb and I became friends and I got to learn a little bit more about her. At that time, she was in her mid-thirties and living alone in a flat in Casablanca. She had been educated partially in France and spoke fluent French and English as well as Arabic. Her passion was running and she was a very active member of the Casa running club and went out with them before work three times a week. She also loved her job and clearly thrived on it. She could just as easily have been a Londoner or a Parisian as a Casablancite. She busted all my stereotypes about women in an Islamic country and is very much emblematic of the modern, middle-class Moroccan woman.

One of the main questions that I get about my life in Morocco is what it is like to live here as a woman. The hinterland to the question is the assumption that it is more difficult, because women are considered repressed in Islamic states. The answer is complicated but also very personal and is affected not only by gender but by age, personality type, money and language.

For me, personally, Morocco is by far the easiest north African/Arab country I have been in for a number of reasons. This is not only due to the openness of the country; it is also down to a number of other factors. Being a woman in your fifties in a north African/Arab country makes life a lot easier, as you don't have to deal with nearly as much sexual harassment. Now when someone calls me a gazelle, I take it as a compliment, whereas when I was in my twenties the attention was constant, and sometimes physical, and I found it mortifying.

Age also brings confidence, and people generally are less likely to try to take advantage of you, no matter whether you are male or female. Money is another factor. Having enough money to live in a decent area and take taxis if you are in a sticky situation makes things more comfortable. Being able to speak Arabic is, of course, a massive help. I can understand what is going on around me, so I don't have that nervousness about not being sure of what is being said or exactly what's happening. I can also talk to people on their terms and this makes the most enormous difference. All doors are opened and I get a 99.9 per cent approval rating. It is still relatively uncommon for Westerners to speak Arabic, so I usually get star treatment.

The final thing, before we actually get to the being female part, is personality type. I am by nature an extrovert (my description) or a massive show-off (my brother's description). I like meeting people and finding out about them and am generally friendly and curious (my description) or incredibly nosey (my friends' description). These traits are really useful when you are living in a foreign country and have to push yourself out of your comfort zone every day.

Now for the being female part. Of course, it is different living here as a woman than it would be as a man, but that is almost certainly true of every place in the world. On the surface level, I have modified some of my behaviours to fit in better. Dress is the obvious one. I don't wear vest tops or show a lot of cleavage and I don't wear shorts. The dress code here is more modest, but that also means I have access to different clothes. I wear a lot of djellabas, which I really like as they are so pretty and feminine, as well as practical in this climate.

When I open my wardrobe now, I have lots of clothes that are suitable for Morocco but horribly few that work in the UK. If I were to wear my Moroccan clothes in my village, Hayfield, in the Peak District, I think I might be marked down as at best an ageing hippy, at worst a raging eccentric.

On a deeper level, the things that have had most impact on my life are the lack of female friends who want to do the same things I do, and the lack of male friends full stop. Zineb and the Casablancites are a minority compared to the rest of the country, where most women over thirty are concerned with their children and their families and not available for hiking or running or taking off to the mountains for a couple of days. When it comes to male Moroccan friends, the problem exacerbates.

Typically, men and women here socialise separately and then come together for family occasions. It is not usual for men and women to be just friends after their school or university days. Again, the Casablancites are excluded from this description. They seem to mingle much more freely, as I could see from the running club, and there will be many other exceptions. Nevertheless, my experience has been that it is hard to make male friends because of the way that is viewed by society. Reputation is very important, and in this very social country your neighbours' eyes are always on you to an extent that is quite surprising. Michelle, a friend of mine who went on to marry her boyfriend, Faisal, told me of her experience. She had just arrived in the country and was trying to make contacts so was open to guys asking her to a local coffee shop she frequented called Mama Africa. She said yes to two different men to meet up casually and then was shocked when she found she was being talked about. It was all so innocent, but wasn't perceived as such.

There are also definite pluses to being a woman in Morocco. If you need help, it is given instantly and ungrudgingly. There is never a shortage of men to push the car when it doesn't start or to help lug kilos of cat litter up the three flights of stairs to my flat. In fact, I find being a woman at this age in Morocco really enjoyable. I get called 'Lalla', which is a term of respect for an older woman and means the equivalent of 'Aunty'. Once I had got over the horror of realising I was being put in the Aunty category, I came to really like it and to appreciate the goodwill and good manners behind it.

Morocco is changing, and the role of women in it is changing, but there is still a world of difference between the Casa set and the way Amazigh women live in the Atlas Mountains. This contradiction, or tension, has to be navigated and the best example for me of that delicate balance can be seen in regard to women's rights as enshrined in the Moroccan constitution. The 2011 constitution guarantees equal protection and enjoyment of its laws for both men and women. The country's progressive Family Law secured important rights for Moroccan women, including the right to self-guardianship, the right to divorce and the right to child custody. The legal marriage age was raised to eighteen years of age and women can now get married without needing approval from a male guardian. But, there are big gaps. For example, the ban on early and forced marriage can be over-turned by a judge, allowing it to go forward.

Polygamy is one of the tightrope issues that faces a Moroccan state determined to move forward but with Islam at its heart. Four wives are permitted in Islam, but many women in modern Morocco find the idea of their husband taking on more wives unacceptable. In 2004, Moroccan law makers came up with an interesting compromise. They put in place very strict financial qualifications that a prospective husband would need to meet before he could take on a second wife. In addition, the putative groom would have to get written permission from his current wife (or wives) to marry another woman. Breaking these rules can, and has, resulted in arrests and prosecutions.

Walking around the Casa mall, the second biggest in Africa, sitting on the coast, looking out onto the waves, it's hard to think of Morocco as anything other than a modern nation. This huge shopping mall has all the international brand names like Zara, Lee Cooper, H&M and so on. It may not be the thing that you want to visit when you are on holiday, but when you are living far from everything you are used to, the mall becomes a kind of haven. Back in the UK, I am a big supporter of the high street as opposed to the shopping mall. However, in Morocco, it is a real treat to have an occasional trip up to the mall in Casa. You don't have to expend any energy: there's no chatting; as all the prices are on the tags, there is no bargaining; there are no surprises, and everything is familiar.

For all its modern comforts and sense of twenty-first-century life, Casablanca will always be firmly rooted in my mind in the misty black and white of the classic film which took its name, and you really can't visit the city without going to have a drink, or preferably a meal as the food is excellent, at Rick's Café. Even though I still do think it would be better placed in Tangier.

Rick Blaine: 'Of all the gin joints in all the towns in all the world, she walks into mine.'
Ilsa: 'Play it, Sam. Play "As Time Goes By".'

Rick's Café reeks authenticity, from the charming tiled courtyard to the grand piano where Sam ran his hands across the keys to the discreet waiters in their red fezzes. If you've watched the film – and if you haven't, please do! – then you can almost hear the 'Marseillaise' being sung in brave defiance of the Nazi occupiers as you sit at your table waiting for your cocktail. The only catch is, the whole thing is a fake. The bar was built because of the film. It isn't real. Well, it is real, but you catch my drift.

It was actually developed by the enterprising Kathy Kriger, a former American diplomat to the Kingdom. It was transformed from a traditional Moroccan grand mansion with a central courtyard, built in 1930, to its current film-friendly state by fellow American Bill Willis. There are two entrances. The main one with its heavy wooden doors looks just like it did in the film and there is also a door out to the port and the Atlantic.

Inside, they faithfully recreated the set of the film, using the existing arches and balustrades and adding an intricate antique brass floor and table lamps with metal shades strung with beads, carved wooden screens, tables and chairs from Syria and fireplaces of carved marble. The piano is an authentic 1930s Pleyel. Everything is so exact and perfect that I defy you to go there and not toast with a 'Here's looking at you, kid.' It may be corny, but you do feel like Humphrey Bogart could walk in at any moment.

Casa may be the modern heart of Morocco and I find it fun to go there and enjoy the relatively Western delights of shopping and eating something that is not a tagine in the restaurants, but my heart really belongs to the wild places of the country. I would swap you five-star dining in Casablanca any time for a few days' hiking across the brutal, barren plains of the Jebel Saghro, which lies to the south and east.

8

JEBEL SAGHRO

It is about 550 kilometres (340 miles) from Casablanca to Jebel Saghro and about five centuries in time. Jebel Saghro is one of the most impressive places in Morocco because of its brutal landscapes, vast nothingness and unchanged nomadic way of life. It is a special place full stop, but I also want to tell the story of Zaid, a nomad from the Ait Atta tribe, and his family, who are the reason it is so special to me.

I had the chance to walk with this family during their annual migration from winter to summer pasture in 2014, with their flock of 210 goats, 7 mules, 10 camels, 3 donkeys, 2 dogs, 22 people, one sheep and one chicken. I then went back to spend time with them at the end of 2016. They epitomise all the beauty of a simple life, completely in tune with nature, and they live in the way their ancestors have for hundreds of years. It is something that is truly wonderful to experience, but that life is a really hard one and now they want to change.

They want to profit from progress, have their children educated and not spend every night in a freezing tent. When
they leave the Jebel Saghro a whole way of life will die, but
who could argue against a father wanting an easier future for
his children?

Jebel Saghro is not that easy a place to explore. It is not on
the beaten track, which of course makes it that much more
alluring. A good place to start is on the southern side in the
small town of N'kob, which is around a two-hour drive from
the desert launch pad of Ouarzazate. N'kob has some decent
guest houses, so you can spend the night there ahead of your
entrance into the wilderness.

Jebel Saghro means Mountain of Drought, and it is aptly
named as it sees only a tiny amount of rainfall each year – as
little as 100 mm on the plains and 300 mm on the highlands.
To contrast that with other highlands, the Highlands of
Scotland gets ten times that amount annually with 3,000 mm.
Jebel Saghro is a spur of the Anti-Atlas Mountains and,
although mountainous, is nothing like the High Atlas in
terms of summit heights. The highest peak, Amalou n'Man-
sour, is only 2,712 metres (8,897 feet), 1,455 metres (4,773 feet)
short of the mighty Toubkal.

The area is distinguished by its savage, prehistoric, visceral
wildness. When you are walking in the High Atlas there is
always a small village or minute farm carved out of the rock
wherever there is water. In the Jebel Saghro there is nothing.
Once you leave the few settlements on the fringes, you are
alone in nomad country.

The landscape itself is primeval. You can see where the
earth moved all those aeons ago and belched up fire and rock
from its innards. Flat plains are punctuated with monumen-
tal plugs of rock which must have been rocketed up with

immense force. There are the individual ones, nicknamed the Camel and the Elephant. Then, looming out at you from a distance, there are the outcrops that look like enormous cities of stone placed in the desert by aliens, housing giants and their families. There is a feeling of endless space, with views for miles and that sense of the smallness of human beings caught between the earth and the sky.

And yet, in this vastness, families of nomads still make their living from the land. Indomitable humans, not fighting the harshness of the landscape, but co-existing with it. Zaid Ait Atta and his family are one of the last few living that nomadic life.

Zaid is a small, wiry, weathered man in his forties. He has the body of an acrobat and the soul of an entertainer. Language, or lack of it, is only a minor barrier to communication and Zaid is the master of the joke. I met him when I went to walk with him and his family for a week as a writer and secondary (very secondary) guide/helper for Epic Morocco. Charlie had struck up a friendship with Zaid some years ago and had arranged to have the occasional small group join him and his family for part of the journey as they crossed the Jebel Saghro on their annual migration to better pastures. This was a unique experience, an opportunity to participate in something so far from the modern world. Nouri was the main guide and Omar was to be the cook for the guests. It was a top team.

Zaid comes from the Ait Atta tribe, who are a large tribal grouping covering the whole south-east of Morocco. Ait means 'family' in Tamazight, which is the Amazigh language spoken by this tribe, and Atta is the name of their common ancestor, Dadda Atta. He was a fertile chap and had forty sons, from whom it is thought all the Atta tribe descend.

The tribe is divided into five clans. Its heartland is the Jebel Saghro, but from the sixteenth century onwards it became increasingly territorially ambitious and conquered the area to the north and then southwards. The tribe's war raids became more and more daring and successful, and within 300 years it had established a presence as far as Taouat, which is now part of Algeria.

Morocco, or parts of it, has long been fought over by the great powers. Carthaginians, Phoenicians, Romans, then, in the 600s, the Arabs invaded. The Ottomans held it as part of their empire; the Spanish, Portuguese, French and British grabbed different bits throughout the centuries. In the early twentieth century, the French and Spanish agreed to carve up the country between them, with Britain agreeing to mainly stay out of it. In 1912, the Treaty of Fez formalised the arrangement and the French became the primary colonial power in the country, through force wherever they met resistance. Spain held on to pockets of territory, and in fact still do as there are two enclaves of Spanish territory in the north of the country. Tangier became an international zone in 1923. When the country came under its government, France set about building an infrastructure and exploiting its mineral and agricultural wealth. Immigration from France was encouraged and land was given to the colonialists to farm. It was to be forty-four years of conflict. French colonialist rule lasted until 1955 and French is still widely used in Morocco and is taught in schools. The French also left their bureaucracy, which is nothing if not thorough.

The Ait Atta, with their tight-knit clan structure and their centuries of fighting experience, resisted French colonisation bitterly, the last tribe to do so. They did not have the modern weapons of the French but they had the advantage of being on their own territory and the extra impetus of fighting for their homeland. The French had still not defeated them by the 1930s. In 1931, the French army finally managed to conquer the Middle Atlas, but around 1,500 Amazigh fighters, along with 6,000 civilians, had congregated in the Jebel Saghro area to carry on the resistance from this wild fortress. Europe was troubled and the French wanted to have their troops available rather than tied up in an endless conflict in a faraway colony. Also the French allies in Morocco, the Glaouis, were complaining about raids on their trading caravans by the Ait Atta, so a big push under generals Giraud and Catroux was ordered.

The French brought in tanks to push across the plains, but the fight in Jebel Saghro was led by the infamous Foreign Legion and nine companies of *goumiers*, as well as 7,000 other local fighters. A *goumier* was the name given to Moroccan nationals fighting on the side of the French. Despite being terribly outmanned, the Amazigh, under the leadership of Hasso ou Baslam, did not give up. They fought like wolves for two weeks and the French army suffered many casualties. In one *goum*, a unit of 200 auxiliaries, it was reported that six out of the seven French officers leading it were killed.

Then General Huré, who had taken over supreme command, ordered a blockade, and over the next three weeks the Jebel Saghro fighters were pounded from the skies in an intensive aerial bombardment. They could fight the tanks and the machine guns, but swords, homemade rifles and stallions are no match for airborne bombs, and the fighters' families were being slaughtered from the air, so they finally surrendered. The terms of peace were generous: there was a general amnesty and the tribesmen were allowed to keep their weapons. Also, no taxes were to be levied for one year. The French recognised Hasso ou Baslam's courage and leadership and made him a *caid* (governor). When Morocco gained its independence in 1956, he was one of the very few French-appointed *caids* that the new King of Morocco kept in power.

These men were Zaid's descendants, and that brave spirit felt really evident in the way he kept his family and his way of life alive in a landscape which, though beautiful, is ultimately very hostile.

Zaid and his family are semi-nomadic, which means that they settle for the winter months in Ighazoun and then set off in the summer to trek to their summer pastures near Ait Bougmez, where the grass is richer. They stay there all summer, feeding up the goats, and then walk back in September. That May I was going to walk with them for a week along the route, along with Nouri and Omar and our little bunch of Australian, American and British adventurers. The aim for all of us was to get a little taste of life as a nomad by actually living it.

DAY ONE: The first day was to be one of the longest of the whole trek as we had to walk to our rendezvous with Zaid and his family in their camp in the mountains. Until lunch we were walking along a dried river bed and then over gently rolling, stony hills. The gradient was relatively easy, but that belied the difficulty of the walk. It was rocky and uneven underfoot and the sun was beating down hard. The hills were bare of vegetation and forbidding in the heat haze. I felt for our poor guests who had arrived fresh-faced off the plane and found the transition to desert walking a shock.

On the way, we passed a group of men working to mend the pump to a groundwater well which sustained the families of the four houses built around it. Of course we had to go in for tea, and it was nice to lean against the cool clay of the brick walls and take in the sugar and mint. The father of the house brought his pride and joy out to show us – a beautifully engraved sword – and Nouri, ever the clown, proceeded to demonstrate his fighting moves. I told him about sword dancing in Scotland and immediately the sword was on the ground, crossed with a staff, and he was flinging like a Campbell, to the hilarity of the children who had come to stare at the strange foreigners. The last hour before our lunch break was especially tough as the sun was at its zenith and there was not a drop of shade. Cue mass relief when we came to the oasis where our picnic was laid out.

I had been bringing up the rear as helper, and when we stragglers finally got into camp, we found we had arrived to a mini drama. One of our guests had been horribly afflicted by the sun and the walking en route and had started hallucinating and feeling extremely ill. Of course, safety is the first concern, and so Nouri had shepherded her to the nearest rest spot and was staying with her until she could recover and travel back in a 4x4 to Marrakech. In truth, she had taken on too much by coming on the trek. I admired her for giving it a go, but it was just too ambitious. Hiking in desert areas has to be taken seriously, because even if the mileage and uphills look easy on paper, you have to factor in the heat and the harshness of the sun. It really makes a difference.

The oasis was typical of the area, where every small amount of water is fully exploited: date palms, fig and pomegranate trees, vegetables and barley were all planted out and providing enough food to support three or so families and some welcome shade for hot hikers. We all collapsed on the rugs that Omar had spread out for us and had great gulps of cool water, then tucked into the feast he had prepared.

Going forward, because Nouri was out of action, our muleteer became lead guide and I stayed in my backstop position. He went on ahead with the bulk of the group and I followed with the slower walkers. The next part of the hike was a steepish walk uphill to reach Zaid's winter dwelling, which was sheltered by the high rock faces on top of a small plateau. We were about 300 metres in when one of the ladies with me began to flag. The sun was still hot, and when we left the shade of the palms and started climbing, it hit her quite badly. I decided to head back to the shade where she could rest a bit and I could call in reinforcements. When the family in the oasis saw us coming back, they immediately rushed off to get a blanket for her to lie on and offered more tea. I called our muleteer and thanked my lucky stars that I had learnt the words for 'mule' ('*tasardount*') and 'I'm tired' ('*ormich*') and that they were similar enough in the two languages. After an hour or so he arrived with a mule. He'd got the other guests up far enough to be met by someone who could take them the rest of the way, divided up the luggage and freed up a mule to be our ambulance.

In all we had six mules with us to carry our food, gear and water for the week, but one of them doubled up as transport for when the going just got too tough. In Morocco, there is always a solution. Animals here are not really given names, but we decided to call our ambulance mule 'George' after George Clooney, as he was so handsome and shiny with just a hint of grey around the muzzle. Also, they both kind of worked in the medical profession.

The only disadvantage of the ambulance mule from my perspective, was that I had to try to keep up with him. His four long legs were definitely quicker than my two shorter ones, so the second half of my day was a panting trot up a perpendicular hill. I also felt I had to keep a brave face on as a semi-guide and expended quite a lot of energy mendaciously pretending to be totally fine.

I was very grateful when we crested the peak and saw Zaid's winter camp ahead of us. It was perched on a small, flat plateau surrounded by huge outcrops of black rock straight out of *Lord of the Rings* – volcanic plugs that had been smoothed and weathered into sheer faces. In the centre was the round stone-walled enclosure filled to jamming point with the flock of goats. There were three main tents pitched: the family's, the mess tent and, most crucial of all, the toilet tent complete with a beautiful white toilet seat and a view of the far valley. The guests were putting up their small sleeping tents wherever they could find a flattish, smoothish patch.

Zaid was waiting for us with a very warm welcome. We were immediately brought down to the family tent, and given the obligatory tea, made by Zaid's mother, Aisha, the spiritual leader of his little tribe and the boss in many ways. There were nine family members to meet: Zaid and Aisha, Zaid's wife, Izza, and half-sister, Fatimah, his three sons – Mohammed (fourteen), Maymoun (eight, and at school) and Hassan (three) – and his two daughters, Zahra (ten) and Aisha (one). Over the next few days we were to get to know, and fall a little bit in love with, all of them.

Family in Morocco is everything, particularly in the nomadic communities where they spend so much time solely in each other's company. They work, eat and sleep together, sharing everything from the communal food dish to the communal tent at night. Everyone does their share of the work. Even little Hassan would make himself useful in camp by collecting twigs for the fire or carrying things back and forth for his mother. The rules governing social interaction are absolute. Zaid was the king of his family, and Aisha was the queen mother. During the time we spent together I saw how much he deferred to her and asked her opinion. She was tiny and weathered but with a proud nose and jawline. Her movements in everything were quick and deft and when she held my hand, hers was hot and full of life. She laughed when she felt my cold fingers and rubbed them back into warmth. Aisha, Izza and Zahra were all dressed in a multitude of vibrantly coloured layers with plenty of spangle in them. They may have been tending goats and living out of a tent, but they still retained their femininity and a love for bright, pretty things.

As the dusk deepened, a caravan of camels driven by a tall blue-clad figure straight from a cinema screen came up over the ridge, ready to join us the next day. He was Mohammed El Kabir (Mohammed the Great) and was the camelteer and a relative of Zaid's. I could never work out if he was his cousin or his uncle (is it possible to be both?). Whichever, he was a very fine figure of a man, a picture-book hero. Zaid had to hire him and his camels for the annual migration as the family had all their gear to carry to set up camp for a few months when they arrived at their final destination, the grazing of Ait Bougmez. After tea we had a formal greeting ceremony, with Omar, who speaks both Tamazight and French, as our interpreter. The guests had all brought gifts for the family: thoughtful things including warm clothes, perfume for the women and a football and pump for the boys. Aisha oversaw the giving out and doled out a toy each to the children, then squirrelled the other things away for later, or perhaps to sell.

By this time it was dark and everyone was exhausted from the walk, and also the intensity of meeting each other, and it was time for dinner and for bed. I had imagined sleeping in the deep quiet under the majesty of the night sky, but the reality was rather different. The stars were indeed majestic, but quiet was there none: goats are noisy and so are shepherd dogs, especially when they spot rival shepherd dogs and get into a barking stand-off, and that barking stand-off is doubled through the amazing echoes of the rocks. But my mattress was comfy, my sleeping bag was warm and my legs were tired, so it wasn't long before I drifted off. I was sleeping in the mess tent with Omar, Nouri and the muleteers and can report a strange and interesting fact: Imazighen men don't snore or move in the night at all. Maybe it is because they are all so lean and fit, but I slept in that tent for a week and there was never even a rustle.

DAY TWO: We woke before dawn and Omar was up and getting the gas rings going for tea. Because we were with guests, we had brought our own food and cooking gear. We didn't want to impose on Zaid's scant resources, and it would have been hard for us to get accustomed immediately to a nomadic diet of bread, oil or butter, dates and some meat. It also meant we could share our food with the family, which they relished. Seeing it through their eyes, I realised how luxurious it is to have so much fresh fruit and veg and protein with every meal. It seemed almost sinful, but those feelings of guilt were quickly overcome by the delight of the family, and the fact that Omar is a very good cook and I was hungry with all the exercise.

We didn't eat breakfast with the family because they were busy working and had eaten long before us. Striking camp was like a military operation. The first thing to go was the herd of goats. Izza and Zahra opened the gate into the stone circular enclosure where they had spent the night and they leapt out. There are always some lead male goats and they went off after Izza first, followed by the rest. Zahra nipped in with the stragglers and soon they were moving en masse towards the hills. They would graze as they went, searching out the scrubby mountain plants that make their meat taste so good. The transport animals were gathered off to one side waiting to be loaded up. Zaid, Aisha and the boys took down the tent, packed it and the sleeping and cooking equipment up and loaded up the animals. The last thing to go on was the sole chicken, which was tied onto one of the camels.

It was crowded in the early morning light as we kicked off the first proper day of the migration. We set off in grand convoy, up to the first pass out of camp and down past the last road we would see for days. We were a motley bunch, from Mohammed El Kabir, resplendent in robes, turban and proper moustache, to us with our fleeces, hats and walking poles. Mohammed El Kabir was very taken with my solar phone recharger and wanted to swap it for his enormous dagger. After a spirited negotiation, he was even willing to throw in a donkey, but I wasn't sure my landlord in Marrakech would go for that.

Our route was undulating with some sharp rocky passes. Early on we passed one of the monolithic plugs of rock thrusting up out of the plain. Nouri had rejoined us, having seen our sick guest off to Marrakech safely, and made me walk around it till I could see why it was called 'The Camel'. The rhythm of the walk was completely new to me as I have never walked with a big convoy of animals before. We were slowing down and speeding up with them. Sometimes it was hard even to watch. One small donkey was very heavily laden. Twice she fell over a boulder as she was going uphill and had to be hauled up to standing again by Zaid and the muleteer.

Looking over the rooftops of Tangier.

A hillside view of Chefchaouen, the Blue Pearl.

The leaning mosque outside Chefchaouen in the Rif mountains.

Play it again, Alice. Playing the piano in Rick's Café in Casablanca.

Rooftop view over Casablanca.

Nouri looks out over the plains in Jebel Saghro.

Izza counts in the goats for the night in Jebel Saghro.

Zahra with her special charge, Shaun the Sheep.

Getting the fire ready to cook our goat in Jebel Saghro.

The fantastic rock formations of Jebel Saghro.

Essaouira beach.

The blue fishing boats in Essaouira port.

My hand hennaed during the big celebration, Eid Al Adha, by Hayat's daughter, Sara.

Looking across the sea wall of Essaouira.

The landscape around Guelmim in the south.

One of the granaries where the villagers used to safeguard their harvest from marauders.

Tighmert oasis –
a lush paradise.

A painted door in Tighmert.

A ksour – the fortified settlements where merchants could safely stop overnight.

I was fascinated by the camels, especially by their feet. They walk very elegantly and precisely and the soles of their feet puff up and down like little hovercrafts. No obstacle seemed to faze them, and whenever they caught up to us, they would just stop and wait till we had gone a little way ahead and then start again. It was intensely restful walking with them, hypnotic somehow.

We got to camp by lunchtime. The camp was on the migration path and had all the basics. It was in a slight dip between the hills and the ground was relatively flat. To the right was a stream which provided a trickle of water both for the animals and for us. In the centre was an enclosure for the goats and blackened spots where previous fires had been burnt. The first order of business was to repair the enclosure ready for the goats. Actually, the very first order of business was to build a tiny chicken coop and release the chicken from its perch on the camel so it could scratch around and enjoy a bit of freedom. The enclosure was made of big stones piled on top of each other. We all worked together to repair the parts of the animal enclosure that had tumbled down and make it high enough to discourage the goats from scrambling out. Zaid chucked up rocks with ease while the rest of us hauled and puffed.

Once that was done to his satisfaction, we turned to the tent. This was made of brown goat's hair from the flock, spun by Aisha. She showed us her spindle later that evening and was delighted to experiment with one that a guest had brought along from Australia to show her and leave with her. The tent was big enough to house the whole family and supported by a sturdy wooden pole in the centre. The side flaps were kept up but could be brought down for rain or at night when it got cold. It had guy ropes but was also sewn to the wooden frame with a needle as long as my finger using thick twine. Aisha laid out handmade rugs and some mattresses on the ground to lounge on.

Then, we were all despatched to gather wood and water. We spread out over the hillside picking up brush and any twigs we could find. There weren't any trees at this spot, just dried up shrubs and some wood from old bushes. I had made my scarf into a bag and was quite proud of the bundle I had gathered until I saw Aisha leaping over the ridge with a pile ten times as big strapped to her back. For water, the family carried plastic gallon containers and we walked up to the stream to the second little waterfall where there was no chance of contamination from the animals drinking below. Waterfall is a very grand word for what was a couple of rocks which kept the water moving and fresh.

With water, wood and shelter, it was time for tea, and the men soon had a small fire burning brightly and the kettle bubbling. No roaring fires here where wood is in such short supply, only enough for the necessities. That tea really tasted good and we all gathered together under the shelter of the tent to drink it and have a bit of down time.

In the late afternoon we walked up to a ridge and looked far down the cliff to a tiny farm carved out beside some water, which we could see supported one family. We waved and called down to the wife and her children tending the vegetable patch and our voices bounced back to us. At that spot Nouri appointed our tribal leader for the week. Paul, one of our guests, became the new Dadda Atta. Nouri wrapped his scarf around Paul's head and he was transformed. It is amazing how a well-wrapped turban can bestow authority. All week Nouri would ask Dadda Paul to rule on some decision we had to make, whether it be to have eggs for breakfast or to stop for a tea break. With his turban in place, Paul rose to the occasion.

We didn't see Zahra and Izza with the goats till much later, around six, as they had spent all day foraging, Izza walking with baby Aisha slung on her back. Their arrival was heralded by a cacophony of bleating. The goats poured up the hill and headed straight for the enclosure, scrambling and climbing over each other to get in. Any who went out of line were barked back in by the dogs or by a well-thrown stone. We all gathered round to see if our handiwork would hold and thankfully it did. By sundown, shortly after supper, we were all ready for bed.

That night it was cold and I drifted off easily. Then, in the middle of the night, I woke to feel a warm breath on my cheek. Half asleep, I turned round, vaguely wondering who this brave fellow moving in for a kiss was. Was it Mohammed El Kebir? I could certainly feel hair and he had a moustache, so part of me rather hoped it was – he did look like a matinee idol. It felt lovely, a little peck and nibble – nibble? I sat up with a yelp to find the little lone Shaun the Sheep looking at me earnestly. He had come into the tent to try to get warm and clearly thought I was his best bet. I'm not proud – Mohammed El Kebir, Shaun the Sheep, any port in a storm – so the rest of the night was spent nestled peacefully and cosily together.

DAY THREE: By now we were getting into the rhythm of it. Up early, a quick breakfast and then work together to pack up all our belongings. Once the animals were all loaded and secure, we would set off. The day's march wasn't long, between 15 and 20 kilometres, but we would usually also climb quite a bit, which always adds a bit of excitement to proceedings. Walking behind the camels, watching their hovercraft feet, was strangely hypnotising, and an hour could go by without me realising.

The landscape was filled with rocky inclines and declines, giving out to far-reaching views of the horizon. The vegetation was still sparse, scrubby wild thyme and low bushes with small dark green leaves that the goats hoovered up. Everything else was rock and compacted earth. The occasional juniper tree would jut up artistically, holding its gnarled hands up to the sky. The sensation was of time with no barriers or end points.

Maymoun and Hassan, Zaid's two youngest boys, had been appointed by Nouri as assistant guides, and I decided to lend Maymoun, the elder of the pair, my walking poles as a sign of authority. Oh, the delight. We had a serious ten minutes telescoping them to fit his height perfectly and checking that they were properly fixed. Off he ran to the head of the group, full of importance. Then something happened that illustrated for me the essence of the Amazigh ethos. The minute he got up to the top of our little caravan, he handed one of the poles over to his brother and explained to him how to use it. There is no pleasure without sharing. The two of them scampered off hollering and giggling and spearing every piece of goat poo they could find along the route – and there is a lot of goat poo along that route.

That afternoon after we had set up camp there was a violent rainstorm. We watched it approaching. Big, black clouds rolled in and smothered the blue of the sky. As it drew closer, the whole family sprang into action, covering the tent with a big sheet of plastic, doing the same to all the piles of provisions, bringing in anything that might get ruined by the rain and making sure the firewood had somewhere dry to sit.

There we were, our mixed crew of foreigners and Berbers huddled together with no languages in common but masses of goodwill. We did what all good people do when stuck in a rainstorm: we played games. Dadda Paul, of course, had first say, and he chose a version of Liar. Each of us had five pebbles and we had to secret some, all, or none of them in our hands, reach out our hands in front of us and then say how many we were holding. The person next to us would guess if we were telling the truth or not and if they got it right we were out; if they got it wrong, they were out. In the UK it is a drinking game; here we did it with just mint tea. Everyone loved it and the tent was rocking. It transpires that nomads are truly excellent liars.

Rain and water are the big preoccupations for Zaid and his family. There had been a drought in the region for the past three years and it had affected him badly. We could see the lack of water even in the little wells and springs that dotted the route. All were just puddles. This year he could not find enough grazing for the animals and told me he had spent over £900 on feed for the sheep in his flock, but he still lost thirty-five of them through starvation. Goats eat anything, but sheep are fussier. Shaun the Sheep was the lone survivor. Rain is an obsession for everyone in Morocco. People here, just like the British, talk about the weather, but in the opposite way. When it rains everyone is really cheerful and happy; it is our equivalent of a hot, sunny day in May. There is lots of 'Thanks be to God' and discussion about how long the rain will last. Even when it is pouring down and you are wet through, there is general celebration.

When it doesn't rain, it has a very serious effect on not only the people in the countryside, who are still, for the large part, subsistence farmers, but also on the Moroccan economy as a whole. Forty-one per cent of employment in Morocco is in agriculture. In terms of export, Morocco sends a lot of fruit and vegetables to Europe. Check your Tesco's tomatoes, strawberries and tangerines and chances are you'll find a Moroccan tag on there.

Rain is such a preoccupation that when it doesn't come the state intervenes. Fast-forward a couple of years to November 2017. There had been almost no rain all through the autumn, leading the World Bank to downgrade Morocco's GDP forecast for the first quarter of 2018 as the prognosis for the following year's harvest was dire. The king issued a proclamation for state prayers to be held for rain and the whole country joined together.

Alyson, a forester living in the countryside outside Essaouira, told me what used to happen in Morocco when the king called for prayers for rain. When they got the proclamation, the men of the village would gather.

In the olden days, there was a ritual designed to bring rain by asking together as a community. Muslims, Jews and Christians would first pray separately in the mosque, the temple and the church. But the important thing is that after the prayers they would walk together in a procession. They had to walk with their djellabas worn inside out and holding their *babouches* under their arms. It was believed that this walking together, wearing their clothes in this way, would bring the rain to Morocco. God would answer the prayers if everyone – Jewish, Christian and Muslim – walked together.

Whether you are a believer or not, something akin to a miracle happened after the national prayers in 2017. In January, not only did it rain, it snowed. It snowed in the Sahara for the first time in thirty years. There is always snow on the Atlas because of the high altitude, but snow in the desert is a once-in-a-lifetime event. The entire country went wild. I was woken up the morning of the first snowfall by my iPhone *ping ping pinging* with WhatsApp messages from friends down south sending me pictures of palm trees covered in snow and camels looking confused, up to their ankles in white stuff. The kids, naturally, got to it straightaway and lots of snow-men appeared. The only difference being that these ones were wearing turbans and headscarves. Most still had carrots for noses though. The whole mood of the country lifted as, in the truest sense, the people's prayers were answered.

THE PENULTIMATE DAY: Today we walked with Izza and Zahra and the goats rather than with the caravan. After breakfast, while the men were loading up the animals, we opened the rough gates to the enclosure and counted them out. There were the goats, of course, and the little sheep – my bedmate and Zahra's special charge. The dominant males in the group led the way directly up the hillside and the rest followed, spreading out to grab any vegetation they could find. Our aim on this day was different: it was not to get to the next camp, but to find enough food for the flock. That meant we weren't following any path but were scrambling up hill and down dale.

As we started up the hill, the air filled with scent as the goats trampled on the ubiquitous thyme shrubs. Izza led the way and Zahra was back stop, keeping an eye out for any stragglers and expertly throwing stones round the group to keep them together. She was also in charge of carrying the little sheep when he got tired and was in danger of being left behind by the fitter, fatter goats. Zahra was ten at the time.

She had been shy all week but, out in her element, she was smiling and laughing and even got brave enough to tease me by calling me Nouri's name for me, *'Tamkhilawt'* – 'the mad girl' in Tashlaheet.

An hour into the walk, she popped over the crest of a hill and came skipping back down. She reached into her pocket and brought out a beautiful white crystallised rock she had found on the trail as a present. She gave it to me with the biggest smile and my heart melted like a Thornton's chocolate in the microwave. Fortunately, I had on two little bracelets and had something to give back, so we could cement our new-found friendship. Top tip for walking in Morocco: have some little things with you to exchange as gifts.

Zahra was constantly vigilant. The goats spread out all over the mountain and were oblivious to everything but the shrubs underfoot. Our aim was to feed them, but at the same time we did have to reach our destination, so she was constantly urging them forward. With the caravan we would be in camp by lunchtime, whereas Izza and Zahra were always out until just before sunset, maximising grazing time and opportunity for the flock. I have no idea how she knew when a goat was missing, but she did and would rush off over a crest from time to time and come back with a couple of stragglers. The nomads use sheep dogs and Zaid's family had two with them. The dogs are treated well and fed well but there is no sentiment involved. We had a salutary illustration of this. Their bitch was pregnant and disappeared one night to give birth. In the morning, Izza went up the mountain to find her and came back leading her on a rope. The puppies were left, perhaps she killed them, as there was no need for them and not enough food. The bitch cried all day and for the first couple of hours kept pulling on the rope to go back but eventually settled down.

At lunch, we left Zahra and her mum and took a short-cut down to camp. Because it was our last full day with the family, we were having a feast with special dishes: bread baked in hot stones, couscous made by Fatima, Zaid's sister, and special kebabs made from offal.

The women bake fresh bread every day on a griddle on top of the fire, but this celebration bread was different and was made by one of the men, another Mohammed. To make the bread you need a bonfire, and our first job at camp was to go and get the kindling. Then, a fire was set under and over a pile of biggish, flattish stones. When these were really hot, the proven dough, which Mohammed had carried over in his satchel, was set on top of the flat stones and small pebbles were poured over the dough. Highly decorated leather satchels are traditionally carried by the Amazigh men to store food, knives, money and other personal goods in, a bit like a sporran in Scotland. When the dough was completely covered with pebbles, another fire was set on top of the pebbles, and the dough was left to cook for around forty minutes. When it came out, Mohammed dusted off any residual sand and twigs and brought it over to us. It was hot and fluffy and totally delicious, with a slightly smoky flavour.

In the meantime, Izza and Zahra had got back to camp, and it was time to choose a goat for our feast. Zaid and Mohammed picked a good-looking animal from the enclosure. They held it firmly and carried it out of sight of the camp up the hill to one of the small waterfalls in the river with a flat space beside it. The goat was bleating with the strangeness of it but didn't seem terrified. Away from the water, Mohammed held its head back and Zaid slit its throat. It immediately went silent and limp. Then, about three seconds later, it gave a mighty shudder and was dead. I don't see many dead things and the transition from life to death is somehow surprising. It is so absolute.

Then the men got to work on skinning and gutting. First of all, Zaid made an incision with his knife high up on the neck of the goat. Then he put his mouth to it and basically blew up the animal like a balloon. It filled with air and looked just like the fat animals on YouTube. This separates the skin from the meat and makes it easier to peel off. Zaid made the skinning look slick and effortless. Then, it was time for the gutting and butchering.

In Morocco, like in Scotland, offal is highly prized, and is the part of the animal that is eaten first at feasts and high days. Back at the tent, it was the men who were charged with preparing the celebratory kebabs. Izza and Aisha busied themselves with the couscous. The goat's heart, kidneys, lung, trachea and liver were chopped up into half-centimetre pieces and pushed onto metal skewers: heart, kidney, liver, lung, trachea . . . repeat. Zaid then moulded fat around them to make them tasty and help them cook. Separately, the intestines were squeezed out like tubes of toothpaste, ready for the fire. I was glad that the intestines were being cooked and kept for later. I have had goat's intestine soup once before and it had been a grim experience. It looked like dishwater with bits of spaghetti in it. When you took a spoonful, it tasted like dishwater and felt like chewing rubber tubing.

A small, very hot fire had been set and banked. Night had fallen, and the men squatted round the fire, with their faces flickering in and out of the light. Zahra brought over some small glasses of sweet tea and Zaid kept an eagle eye on the kebabs, turning them over regularly, chatting and laughing and speculating on how delicious they would be.

We all decamped to the centre of the tent and waited with varying degrees of anticipation. I like my offal and my tummy was rumbling, but some of the other guests didn't look as though they were looking forward to the kebabs much. The family, however, was virtually drooling. The children didn't take their eyes off their father, waiting for the treat. The kebabs arrived to acclaim, we all said, '*Bismillah*' ('in the name of God'), and silence reigned as we tucked in. The kebabs were delicious. The fat gave them a slightly sweet flavour and the liver, in particular, melted in the mouth. The trachea was a bit crunchy, which was challenging, but I just chewed it up quickly and swallowed it down. The kids wolfed down their first ones and went for second helpings. There were a few kebabs remaining after we had all eaten our fill so Aisha gathered them up and tucked them into the side of the central tent pole, where it joined the fabric, to keep them for later.

To the relief of some, it was time for couscous, and Izza proudly set a huge platter in front of us. Couscous in Morocco bears no resemblance to what you buy in the supermarket and whack in the microwave. It takes a long time to prepare and there is a definite competitiveness between women as to who makes a good one. You first prepare the onions, spices (salt, cumin, ginger, cinnamon) and the meat, frying them and then adding water and leaving them to steam. Later, you add the vegetables. This takes around an hour to an hour and a quarter. The couscous itself, the semolina, is first rubbed and mixed with oil. Then you cook it in a couscous steamer until the steam rises. It is taken off the heat and mixed again. This happens three times. The couscous is plated and the meat and vegetables arranged on top. Caramelised onions are the crown, and the whole thing is served with a clear gravy made from the stock.

Eating it is a messy business. With your right hand you make a ball of the semolina and add a bit of meat and vegetable to the middle – the semolina acts like a little spoon. Once you have got your little ball together, you flip it into your mouth. There are many dangers to avoid: the couscous is hot and burns your fingers; the ball can disintegrate humiliatingly just centimetres from your waiting mouth; and it can be hard to get any meat or vegetables into the little ball when you are starting out. Perseverance is the key.

We finished off our feast with the luxury of fresh watermelon. Then it was time for tea and tales. I wanted to find out from Zaid how the economics of his business worked and whether he could make enough money to keep his family. Yes, he had the animals and his tent and lived very simply, but I noticed he didn't eat meat regularly, it was for feast days, so what did he exist on and how did he afford it?

He told me that he had decided to build up his flock of goats after his sheep died. He has bucks and ewes so they breed naturally, a good goat can get £110 at market, a medium one makes around £65, and at Eid time, it can go up to £200. There are markets in the various towns they pass and he sells between three and five goats at a good one. The money is then used for essentials like flour, tea, sugar, vegetables and anything else his family needs. He also needs money to buy transport animals and sometimes hire them in. Then there are some school expenses for Maymoun, although he lodges with Zaid's brother when he goes to school. His flock is his entire capital and livelihood as he has no house, no car and no possessions that can't be carried on a donkey or camel.

This way of life has existed for centuries, and from my out-side perspective it seems very hard but also good. The family was healthy and happy and worked together in harmony in a beautiful environment. I asked what Zaid wanted for his children and he said, 'It is very hard to carry on as nomads. Electricity, television are coming and everything is changing. The government is building roads everywhere. I want my youngest children, Aisha and Hassan, to go to school. Maybe we will settle down with a small farm so they can do that. I have no choice. Change is here.'

The next day marked the end of our journey with Zaid and his family. They were carrying on to their summer pasture where they would spend the next few months, but we were heading back to the city. It was a sharp disconnect to get back into the cars and head to Marrakech, and in the months that followed, I often thought back to that experience in the wilderness.

That's why, when we were planning the TV programme and thinking how we could show something of life in the caravan and also describe the role of the Ait Atta, who were guides for the caravaneers during the time of the trade, Charlie and I contacted Zaid to film with him and the family for a couple of days.

Driving back into that wide open landscape with its explosive rocks, we were all full of anticipation. I had seen Zaid once in the intervening three years, when he was the muleteer on a hike I did up Mount M'goun in Ait Bougmez, and it had been a happy reunion, so I couldn't wait to see the family again. The crew were drinking in the scenery and we had a drone with us buzzing overhead like a swarm of bees to try to capture the sheer scope of it. The family were all gathered at the tent on a flat plain of sand, a colourful splash in the distance. There was a new addition, a baby, and the children were grown. Zahra had lost her girlishness and was now the double of her mother, Izza. Aisha looked exactly the same and her touch was as warm as ever.

For the next two days, we walked and lived together again. The scale and space and the rhythm were all as I remembered. The family worked as one and the goats ran and ate and bleated as before. There was, however, a clash of civilisations between the rigours of filming, when you have to stop and start and do things over, and Zaid's need to get to camp in time to set up and get his family and animals settled. It was a war of Titans, with victory fluctuating between both sides and me feeling a bit like a foot soldier caught in the middle.

When we had walked previously it was May and this time it was November. Living a modern life, the changing of the seasons is something to enjoy rather than fear, but in the Jebel Saghro the difference between May and November was enormous. At night, it was bitterly, bitterly cold. The minute the sun sank, the temperature plummeted. When we stopped to set up camp, the youngest children were cocooned in blankets and propped up by the bags to keep warm. The rest of us got to it, keeping warm by working.

At dinner, we huddled round the cooking fire, trying to steal a bit of its heat, and we were in bed as soon as we had eaten. I slept in the tent with the family and was glad of both the warmth and the company. The floor of the tent was covered in handmade carpets and we had mattresses underneath us and blankets and woven rag rugs on top. Once under you were immobilised by the weight, but grateful for the warmth.

The next morning, we were up with the dawn and soon drinking a hot tea. The experience of sleeping in the tent when it was so cold and that feeling of not warming up properly had given me a tiny bit of insight into the rigours of the family's life when winter was coming. Aisha was sick with a cold and Zaid was worried about her. The last time we had met, Zaid had said change was coming, and I wanted to know where the family was now. I sat down beside the head of the clan, Aisha, and we talked over a breakfast of bread with preserved butter and tea.

I asked Aisha what life was like for her, fully expecting her to say it was wonderful to live in this way. But she didn't. She told me that she was old now and this life in the mountains was too hard for her. She would prefer to stay down in a village. She said that everything was changing for them, and that it used to be better before. Then, there were more people living and herding in the mountains, more families, more goats. Now, the way of life was dying and it was getting harder.

It was difficult to hear that, sitting as I was by a glowing campfire under a newly minted dawn, surrounded by a family working in harmony, living a life that looked so good in so many ways from the outside. The reality, though, is that for all the wonderful things pertaining to this traditional way of life, it is really tough. The constant movement, the freezing cold, the never-ending work, the scarcity of food, and the huge contrast with the easier life of the towns and cities. It's even harder now with that easier life being brought into the camp every day through mobile phones and the internet.

For Zaid, the future is clear. 'I want something different for my children. I want them to be educated, to get better jobs – maybe even as a tourist driver. I want them to have an easier life, a good life.'

9

ESSAOUIRA

Essaouira, the windy city, an old walled citadel perched on the edge of the Atlantic, with waves crashing onto its outer battlements and endless stretches of white and golden beaches to the north and south, was to become my home for over a year. I moved here on a total whim. I had driven down one day in January to collect a cat carrier I had bought from an American lady called Freya. It's around three hours from Marrakech and it was a bright blue sunny day. I had given a lift to Olivia, a young Peace Corps worker who I had met through Project Soar, a girls' charity in Marrakech. We had passed the hours admiring the rolling scenery, desert in some parts giving out onto the mountains in the distance and cultivated green in others, punctuated by olive and argan oil trees. Trump had just been elected, so Olivia, a liberal young American, was in despair, and we indulged in three hours of righteous indignation at the state of the world.

After I dropped her off on the outskirts of town, I continued down to the corniche. The sun was bouncing diamond sparkles off the sea and the conifers that line the approach were swaying gently. The walls of the town rose white in the distance, guarded by tall palms. 'I'm going to move here,' sprang into my head out of nowhere. And so I did. As it happened, Freya was leaving her flat, and the day I visited it met the landlord and landlady, Abdullah and Hayat, and said I would take it when she left in two months' time.

A couple of weeks later, Freya very kindly invited me down to stay so that she could show me round and introduce me to people. After an evening of revelry which included fire eaters, magicians and chocolate fondant, I fell asleep the minute I got into bed, but was woken before dawn by the muezzin in my bedroom yelling the call to prayer into my startled ear. Of course he wasn't actually in my bedroom, but the flat is flanked by two mosques so he may as well have been, with a loudspeaker. Since I was awake, I decided to get up early and go for my run on the inviting beach.

Do you always forget something when you go on a trip? I do. Unfortunately, in this case, it was my running shoes. I don't know how I managed to remember a hydration pack and bottles but forget trainers. However, since it was sand, it didn't really matter, and Freya lent me her bathroom flip flops to get me out of the city.

Dawn was breaking in pink splendour as I left the old city through Sbaa Gate and headed for the deserted beach. I secreted Freya's flip flops behind the wall of a local café with a rock on top of them and set off on my gallop across the sands. Perhaps it would be more accurate to say my trot across the sands. What a glorious run. Clear sky and clean air. None of the craziness of Marrakech. No cars and no pollution and not even any people. It was heavenly.

But disaster awaited me on my return. No flip flops. The rock was cast aside, and the scene was empty. Grrrrr! How was I going to walk back into the city in bare feet? I could do it at a pinch, but didn't really want to risk a cut on an old bit of glass or tin. I nobbled one of the workmen who was digging up the pavement nearby.

'My brother, did you see anyone come by and take my flip flops? They were just there.'

'No, Lalla, where did you leave them?'

'Under this stone behind the wall. Someone must have taken them. *Hashooma*!' I said, brandishing the stone in the air. '*Hashooma*' is one of the most useful words in Darija and means 'shame' or 'oh no'. 'How am I going to walk back into the medina?'

'You know, Lalla, not everyone is good, may God forgive them. Next time you must leave them here with us. We will look after them for you.'

By this point a little crowd had gathered and we were all enjoying a mutual headshake and tut over how people had gone to pot and things weren't like they used to be in the good old days. Then my knight in a shabby, striped robe arrived, carrying a fishing rod and an old plastic bag. He reached into it and presented me with a pair of white, plastic sandals.

'For you,' he said, pressing them into my hands.

'But, my brother, I can't take these, I don't have any money to pay you.'

'Don't worry, my sister, it is not always about the money,' he replied, with the sweetest of smiles.

That sealed the deal, and I knew Essaouira was the place for me for the next stage of my adventure in Morocco.

Essaouira's history tells in microcosm the story of Morocco, with its waves of conquest and trade and its mix of peoples and languages. The area has been settled since prehistoric times, but first comes into historical record with the arrival of Hanno the Navigator, a Carthaginian, who established a trading post and whose travels were recorded in Greek. In Roman times, it became famous for supplying the Tyrian purple dye that was used to colour the robes of the highest men in Rome. The dye was made using mucus from the glands of seashells, which are commonly referred to as 'murex', and are found in abundance off the small islands opposite the city, which subsequently got given the name 'The Purple Islands'.

The city and area used to be called Mogador, possibly named after a saint who was active in the Middle Ages, Sidi Mogdoul, although an alternate explanation is that it comes from the Phoenician word '*migdol*' meaning 'a small fortress'. In the 1500s, the Portuguese arrived and built a fortress which became the base for the city. The next couple of hundred years were marked by everyone and his mother trying to conquer the city: the British, French, Dutch and Spanish all had a crack. Meanwhile, trade was flourishing and the port became known as a centre for the export of sugar and molasses. Later, it became the major valve in the Europe–Trans-Sahara trade and got nicknamed Port Timbuktu, as so much of the lucrative commerce between the two continents passed through it.

When Mohammed III came to power in the mid-1700s, he wanted to have a base at the closest possible point to

Marrakech, so Essaouira, which is in a straight line from the Rose City, was the obvious choice. Politics being what it is, he also had another aim, which was to teach Agadir, the main port to the south, a salient lesson for favouring one of his political rivals. He hired a French engineer, Théodore Cornul, to reimagine the city along modern lines (for the times) and for twelve years Théodore applied himself to the task, coming up with what we now call the old medina. The new town that emerged under his craftsmanship was first called Souira (the small fortress) but morphed into Es-Saouira (the beautifully designed).

Théodore didn't have the building of the city all to himself; others were brought in, including the rather romantic Ahmed El Inglizi (Ahmed the English), also called Ahmed El Alj (Ahmed the Renegade). He was a pirate from the infamous Salé Rovers gang and also an architect and engineer. English was one of those who left Christianity for Islam when captured and then went on to become a pirate, yes, but also a man of standing within Morocco. He built several fortifications in Rabat for the king and restored the Kasbah mosque there, before coming down to Essaouira where he built the harbour entrance.

As well as building Essaouira, Mohammed III also encouraged Moroccan Jews to settle in the city. He needed them to run the increasingly lucrative cross-Atlantic trade with Europe and the Jewish community grew. At its height, most estimates put the percentage of Jews at around 40 per cent of the entire population of Essaouira, and the Jewish quarter, or *mellah*, which abuts the sea wall behind Bab Doukkala, is extensive. In 2017, the census found that there were only three Jews remaining in the town, the rest having moved out of the country, mainly to Israel, in waves of emigration that began in 1948. The *mellah* is currently undergoing a big renovation programme, which is much-needed to repair the decay that comes quickly with the salt air.

My flat is in the medina, the part of the city designed and built by Théodore. The Essaouira medina is very different to Marrakech. It is very small and calm, and you don't risk death by moto every time you step out your door. Typically, the walls of the buildings are painted white with celestial blue window shutters and woodwork. My building is on three storeys. Hayat and Abdullah live on the first floor; Lavinia, an Australian artist and cat lover, lives on the second; and I am in a garret on the rooftop, which makes me feel like a real writer and is great for my two cats, who can roam free on the terrace and roof.

My flat is very Moroccan, with wooden ceilings, decorated cast-iron window grills and pretty tiling in the bathroom. The sitting room is long and narrow and I have divided it into three parts: the lounging area, where there are two day beds facing each other, covered in woven blue and yellow striped covers and stacked with blue tasselled cushions; the more formal reception area with two hand-carved wooden armchairs made by Abdullah, who is a carpenter, and a small table in front of the open fireplace, which is a total blessing in winter; and my work area in the middle, which is my desk and screen and growing piles of books and papers. I have lots of Moroccan pictures, carvings, rugs and old Arabic film posters to decorate and it feels like a nest. In the warm months I eat and relax out on the roof terrace, and even in the winter I manage to get breakfast out there most days, listening to the sea. I can also hear the sea from my bedroom, which is a great luxury.

Moving from Marrakech was a wrench, and one of those things you have to find out how to do in a country that is not your own. I would not have managed it without the help of Mustafa, the guardian at my Marrakech flat. A guardian is a factotum and Mustafa and I had become friends over my three years there, when he would arrive, toothless and beaming, to fix my lights, block up ratholes, transport and install a new fridge, or turn off the water and clean up after an epic flood when one of the taps exploded and came off in a startled visiting friend's hand. Mustafa is in his forties with two children and a wife who live in a village outside Marrakech, and who he visits once a week. He spends the nights in a little cabin on the street guarding the houses and when Alex moved into the flat he helped her clear it of cockroaches, paint it and make it habitable.

Once he had got over the horror of me leaving Marrakech, he took everything in hand. First we had to book a lorry to take my stuff. I was getting rid of as much as I could as I was moving to a furnished flat, but I still wanted to keep some things like my bed and my precious fridge that I had saved up for six months to buy. We toured the house saying 'leave' or 'take' and Mustafa decided we could make do with a medium-sized truck. Then he sourced cardboard boxes and arrived at regular intervals on his ancient bike piled high with boxes. Packing was a joint affair and I organised a clear-out house sale for everything I wasn't taking. Everything I didn't sell was divided between Naima, my cleaner, and Mustafa. Nothing is wasted in Morocco.

Abdullah had told me that the best time to arrive in Essaouira was around midnight, as all the shops and restaurants would be shut and we would be able to carry everything through the streets from the outer wall to my flat. You have to carry everything as you can't drive a car into the medina. The truck pulled up outside my door in Marrakech at six p.m. We loaded up, put the cats in last in their new cat box, and Brahim the driver, Mustafa and I piled into the front seat with a bag of crisps, sweeties and Cokes to sustain us.

It was a very jolly ride. I was squished in the middle and had to lift my leg up to let Brahim change gear, plus the truck swayed slightly alarmingly in the wind, but the mood was excellent. I had never really thought about what truck drivers talk about on long trips, but if I had, I would have guessed at normal stuff like football, the weather, etc. I also knew that Mustafa, and probably Brahim, had had almost no education, so I had built up a bit of a stereotype based on that. There is nothing more pleasurable than having your prejudices busted, and as we spent the entire journey talking about Amazigh nationalism, the stalemate in government following the recent elections and Morocco's growing role in Africa, mine were well and truly shattered.

We arrived at the city gate and Abdullah was there to greet us with a small battalion of *carossas*. A *carossa* is a hand-drawn cart and how you transport anything heavy around the medina. I always use one if I have done a supermarket run and have lots of bags, but in this case we had really big stuff like a fridge. It's Morocco. No problem. The fridge was tied on, the bed too, and everything else was piled up. I carried the cats. Three sets of narrow, uneven stairs faced us, but Abdullah had chosen only the fittest carters and they whipped up and down the stairs. Within an hour, we had everything installed. I paid a suitably hefty price for all the work we'd done and all parties retired amicably.

Mustafa stayed over so he could help me unpack and reassemble, and the next day we set to and got it all done. We drank tea together and reminisced and then the time came to say goodbye. This was the man who had looked after me with kindness and humour for three years and I didn't want to part with him. I told him how grateful I was for everything and as the final moment came, big tears rolled down his face. I felt truly bereft as his footsteps faded down the stairs.

However, it's Morocco, and you are not allowed to feel sad for long. My landlady, Hayat, soon arrived with more tea and homemade lemon cake, and a beautiful friendship was begun. Hayat is a year younger than me. She is medium height and weight with shortish brown hair, always concealed under a headscarf, intelligent brown eyes behind spectacles and even, white teeth which any American orthodontist would be proud of. She and Abdullah have been married for about thirty years and they have three grown-up daughters, Chaima, Fatima Zahra and Sara, and six grandchildren. Hayat and I quickly discovered that we had similar outlooks, values and senses of humour, even though our lives couldn't be more different.

A couple of weeks after I arrived to live in Essaouira, we hit the month of Ramadan, the ninth month in the Islamic calendar. Ramadan is the holy month for Muslims, when, as one of the five basic tenets of their faith, they are obligated to fast between the hours of sunrise and sunset for the whole span of that lunar month. Ramadan starts when the crescent moon is sighted, which of course is at different times for different countries, but always takes place within a 24-hour period. As the lunar year is shorter than the Gregorian calendar, Ramadan shifts forward by about eleven days every year. It is said that the Prophet Mohammed revealed that, during Ramadan, the gates of heaven are open and the gates of hell are closed.

In Morocco, I would say that almost everyone fasts, even if they are not particularly devout. The whole month is under-pinned not only by religious faith, but by deeply entrenched social customs. It is seen as a month of celebration and a time to be with your family. The fasting itself is difficult. Not only are you forbidden to eat during the hours between sunrise and sunset, which can average fifteen hours in summer, you are not allowed to drink or even swallow your own spit. One of the hardest things for some is that you can't smoke either, and, of course, no sex is allowed during the fasting hours. Pity the poor Muslims who find themselves in the land of the midnight sun – that small region north of the Arctic Circle where the sun remains visible all the time during a portion of the summer. They do have something worked out for just this situation, though: you can either follow the sunrise and sunset times of the nearest big city (Edmonton), or you can follow the times of Mecca, Islam's holiest city. Best place to be for Ramadan to my mind? Sweden in the winter with its measly four hours of daylight.

The breaking of the fast each day is called '*iftar*' ('break-fast'), and as I had just moved to the town, I was worried that I would not have any invitations on the first day of Ramadan, which would be a sure sign of catastrophic social failure. I need not have worried, as Hayat and Abdullah insisted I came to them that evening. I am not a Muslim, so I don't fast unless I have an invitation to *iftar*. Then I do, as I feel like I have to earn the right to feast, and it makes the whole experience a lot more meaningful.

I set my alarm the night before for 4.45 a.m. so I could wake up and glug down as much water as possible to see me through the day. Typically, I am a real thirsty Kirsty and drink about three litres a day in the summer. I couldn't face any food at that time and wasn't really worried about getting hungry, it was more the thirst. After gulping down a whole bottle of mineral water and listening to the last cries of the muezzin in my bedroom, I went back to sleep.

In Ramadan, everything is turned upside down, and day and night activities swap places. No one gets up early, unless you absolutely have to, and I was no exception. I decided that since I was fasting, I could do anything I liked that day and mooched around being exceptionally unproductive. The morning was fine and I didn't really miss my usual cup of coffee. Lunch passed and I was still fine, but around four o'clock a stonking headache took hold and my mouth felt as though it had been stuffed with cotton wool. I had that slightly nauseous feeling you get with jet lag, or when you wake up from sleeping too long in the afternoon, but multiplied by ten. By six o'clock, I was just watching the arms of my watch go around. I showered, being careful not to get any water in my mouth, and that felt better, and then I dressed in my nicest caftan ready for dinner at 7.40 p.m.

By 7.30 p.m., I was sitting on Hayat's sofa beside her mum and Abdullah. I say sofa, but it is actually a traditional Moroccan salon set-up, which is hard, low banquettes arranged in an 'L'-shape along the wall, covered in a yellow brocade with lots of matching cushions to prop yourself up on, and a round low table pulled to the middle of the 'L' where we would all eat. Hayat was still busy in the kitchen putting the finishing touches to the feast. *Iftar* has all sorts of special foods associated with it – Ramadan is a bit like a month of Christmases. At 7.40, the cannon went off, the call to prayer was sounded, and with a '*bismillah*' it was time to tuck in.

The first thing we all did was drink a glass of milk and eat some dates. In some places the dates and milk are mixed into a juice. Then it was time for the traditional soup, *harira*, which is made with lentils, chickpeas, parsley, celery, coriander, beef or lamb broth, tomatoes, thickened with flour and with little strands of vermicelli as the final flourish. I usually find it too gloopy, but after a day without liquid the combination of hot and salty was strangely thirst–quenching. You eat it with honey–drenched pastries called *shabakiyya*, which I love, even though (or possibly because) they are about 10,000 calories per mouthful. With the soup we drank our first glasses of water, but Abdullah warned me to go easy and not just gulp it down as that would upset my stomach.

Now that the first hunger and thirst was assuaged, it was time to relax and compare notes on our day of fasting. I had to confess that I had achieved absolutely nothing and Hayat and Abdullah laughed at my descriptions of headaches and thirst. 'You do get used to it,' Hayat told me. 'The first few days are difficult, but after that you just change your routine and it is fine. The hard week is the third week because you know that you are only halfway through and you are tired, but then soon it is the last week and you have extra energy for the end.' More food was brought out: mini pizzas, salad, fresh bread, olives, more sweet treats, fruit, a homemade smoothie, little pastries stuffed with meat and cheese, and lashings of mint tea. In the background, the TV was playing the special programmes for Ramadan: dramatisations of old stories like 'Elf Layla wa Layla' – 'A Thousand and One Nights'. After we had eaten as much as we possibly could, we all lay back on the banquettes and digested. By about 9 p.m. I stood up to go, thanking my hosts profusely for their kindness.

'We'll see you at 11 p.m.,' said Hayat. I looked puzzled. 'For tagine! I'm making lamb with artichokes,' she added helpfully.

'Tagine? Hayat, I am totally full, I can't imagine eating anything else.'

'Alice, don't be silly, you have to eat dinner, of course you'll come back and eat with us. The tagine is delicious and it's special.'

Although that early introduction to Essaouira was filled with feasting, normally I cook for myself as I would at home in the UK. What is not the same as the UK, however, is the shopping experience.

When I first arrived in the town, I was taken under the wing of Jane Folliot, who has lived in the country for fifteen years and in Essaouira for five and knows everything there is to know. I have decided the only talent I have is managing to attach myself to very knowledgeable people. She arrived at my flat with a map and a series of extremely useful instructions about all the day-to-day necessities, along with an old-fashioned shopping basket on wheels. When I explained that I had absolutely no sense of direction and needed everything to be explained to me in minute detail with landmarks, she girded her loins and gave me the idiot's guide.

'OK, Alice,' she said, casting aside the map with gay abandon and sketching out her instructions on a piece of paper. 'The medina is basically an 'H'. There are two main streets, which we call Tourist Street, where they sell all the tourist stuff like carpets and jewellery and scarves etc, and Haddada, which is where the food and local stuff is. You cross between one and the other here at the road opposite Le Glacier café, or slightly further up where the patisserie shop is. Other things you need to know are that there are two supermarkets outside the medina: Carrefour and Aswak Assalam for your cat stuff and a big open-air market just past Aswak Assalam every Sunday.'

I rewarded her efforts with a nice cup of tea and a biscuit and the next day sallied out with my piece of paper, my granny trolley and lots of small notes and change. Haddada is a broad avenue that is always busy but is absolutely packed at night. Coming from the Bab Sbaa end, heading up towards Bab Doukkala, you start off with the butchers. Meat on the right-hand side and chickens on the left. They are all spotlessly clean and fly-free and you can choose which part of the animal you want or go for ready chopped. The obligatory testicles dangle invitingly over the butchers' stalls, naturally. Past that are a series of stalls piled high with black, green and red olives flavoured with chilli, garlic, lemon or rosemary and mixed in with pickled turnips and carrots. Don't knock pickled turnip till you've tried it – it is surprisingly delicious.

Then you get to the fruit and vegetable stalls. Some do both, some specialise in fruit only. The goods are arranged in big open boxes and bags. The vegetable staples are tomatoes, courgettes, onions, potatoes, cauliflowers, aubergines and different kinds of marrow. You also get local avocados and artichokes in season. Less common are things like spinach or broccoli, and I have never seen kale – although that could be a blessing. It is a pick-and-mix system. The stall holder hands you a plastic basket and you fill it with what you want. He sorts it, weighs it and charges you accordingly. Because the vegetables are fresh, they go off quickly, so I would normally only shop for about three days at once. Salad stuff goes off within a day, as do strawberries, but they are full of taste. There is a separate set of stalls selling fresh herbs: different types of mint, coriander, thyme and parsley, which scent the air enticingly as you pass.

On the left are the newly renovated fish market and the small spice market. The fish market is an open tiled courtyard with a marble-slabbed centre. Fish caught that day are displayed on the counters. Sardines are what Essaouira is famous for and they are the cheapest things on sale. You can buy to take home, or you can buy for lunch and take your choice to the grillers at the back who will cook it up for you and serve it to you with extra salad and bread.

The last stop on the food hunt is the area where you can buy nuts and dates. These stalls also sell cookies, garlic, ginger and some spices. On that first expedition, having already loaded up my granny trolley with some lamb, a chicken, chilli olives and piles of fresh vegetables plus a large melon, all that remained unbought were some dates.

The usual greetings and compliments were exchanged and we got down to the nitty gritty.

Me: 'So, I would like to buy some dates. Which are the best ones?'

Ahmed: 'Ahhhhh, Lalla, that is a difficult question that can have many answers. What do you want to do with the dates? Are they for a tagine? Are they for eating? Are they for a juice?'

Me: 'For eating and maybe to cook in rice.'

Ahmed: 'It is according to what you like of course, but for me the very best dates are these ones from Saudi Arabia at 80 dirhams for a kilo (around £6). These are for eating. If you want something that is less good quality, I have them for 30 dirhams a kilo here. These are from Tunisia. Would you like to try?'

First I tried the Saudi date. It was soft and exploded on my tongue with datey sweetness. Then the Tunisian one; no exploding and about half the datey sweetness. There really was a significant difference.

Me: 'Wow. The Saudi ones are really good.'
Ahmed: 'Yes, they are definitely the best, then the UAE ones, then the Iraqi ones and finally the Tunisian ones.'
Me: 'Don't you have any Moroccan dates?'
Ahmed: 'No. It's not the right time of year, the Moroccan ones come after October and November. They are really good at that time.'

I decided that the Saudi dates were worth the extra money and splurged out on half a kilo. Then I turned for home, trundling my trolley behind me and psyching myself up for the three-storey climb.

One of the things that you notice the minute you get to Essaouira is the quantity of cats. They are everywhere – lounging fatly on a rug display; eyes eagerly following every mouthful eaten by a tourist at an outdoor café; or walking purposefully across the main square towards the port and boats full of newly caught sardines.

The Swiris (Essaouirans) tell us that Essaouira should be called E-*chat*-ouira and chortle uproariously at their little joke. The cats are treated relatively well and you will see cut-off bottoms of mineral water bottles filled with water left out for them, or cardboard boxes placed in strategic spots. But, being street cats, they do fall victim to all sorts of ailments, especially the kittens, and the Expats and Friends of Essaouira Facebook page is always filled with requests for people to foster or adopt street animals. Twice a year, a group of vets comes out from the UK to treat and sterilise as many cats and dogs as they can, clipping their ears to show they have done so, but there are still many more kittens than the streets can support and the mortality rate is high. People really do try to help, though, and none more so than Lavinia, my downstairs neighbour.

When I first met her, she was out at dawn and dusk every day treating two colonies of sick cats. The two most common ailments are cat flu and conjunctivitis and she was plying her patients with antibiotics and eye drops. It can be demoralising work as you lose kittens every day, but even if they do die, they at least have had more comfort in their short lives.

One of the groups of cats and kittens, in an alleyway near Bab Sbaa, was always clustered on a pile of old cardboard boxes. Vinny decided that one thing she could do was make them a cat house. An artist, she designed a five-star residence with an upstairs and downstairs and a flat area for snoozing, and I was brought in to translate for her to Mohammed the carpenter, whose shop is across the alley from us. Mohammed is an incredibly hard worker. He is in his shop from around 10 a.m. every morning till 10 at night, and he barely misses a day. He also has Mimi, the fattest cat in the whole city, who hangs out at his shop all day, helpfully testing out his workmanship by lying on every new piece of furniture he makes. His eyes lit up when he saw Vinny's design for the cat mansion, and I was very much surplus to requirements as they worked out measurements and wood thickness with sign language and a notebook.

A week later, the house was made and carried up to the roof where Vinny was to paint it. Hicham, Hayat's brother, was drafted in to help, and Hayat, Abdullah and I came out to the terrace regularly to exclaim, admire and offer glasses of water. Now the whole of our alley was involved in the project and excited to see the progress. The next step was to go to the medina to buy some sturdy chains to fix it to the wall somehow so it wouldn't be nicked. Finally it was ready, a thing of beauty, and a *carossa* was ordered to take it to its resting place. We all clustered round to wave Vinny goodbye and good luck.

Ten minutes later, I heard a ruckus on the stairs and poked my head out. There was Vinny, with the cat palace. What had happened? She told me that she had hit a snag. The riad in the part of the street where the cats lived had refused her permission to put the house against their wall. They said that they were worried it would be dirty and encourage vermin. This didn't make any sense as it was a massive step up from the cardboard boxes that were currently there, but it was their wall so another solution had to be found.

Vinny assumed a new role, Cat Ambassador, and spent the next week talking to all the businesses in the street to find out what could be done. In Morocco, it seems, nothing can be done too quickly and consensus is needed to make anything happen. Patience is not only a virtue here, it is an absolute necessity. After many cups of tea and chats, Pacha, who owns L'Atelier, a really cool, New York–style warehouse café with the best brownies in town and excellent WiFi, offered his wall for the cat house. Vinny brought the glad tidings back to our alleyway and Hayat, Abdullah, Hicham, Mohammed and I all applauded her tenacity and diplomacy and Pacha's generosity. The *carossa* was called back and loaded up, and this time the palace was successfully installed and can still be seen in all its glory beside L'Atelier, usually with a couple of cats snoozing inside.

Although Essaouira is rich in history, the thing that attracts most people to it is the beach. There are immense beaches lying both below and above the city and to my eye they all look similar, but to the locals there are distinct differences, as some are better for kitesurfing, some for regular surfing and some for paragliding. I must confess to not having tried any of these yet, although I do fancy kitesurfing, which whips people over the waves and makes them soar like seagulls when the wind is strong, and it often is.

That wind can definitely be your enemy when running, though, which, along with swimming, is the way I most often enjoy the beach. Even with the prospect of kilometres of empty sand ahead of you, it can be hard to get out of bed some (most!) mornings, so I was really pleased when Rachel Bonkink, a yogi who leads Vajra Yoga Retreats, said she would like to run with me. Over a few weeks we built up a great rapport, and some mileage.

While out trotting along our local beach route one day we decided that it would be fun to plan a mini adventure and run from the village of Moulay Bouzerktoun up the coast, following the beach back to Essaouira. Although Rachel had never run more than 5 kilometres before, her general fitness is excellent, so I put together a little three-week training plan (3 x 5–9 km runs every week back to back and two longer runs of 10 km and 13 km) and we set the date for a Monday three weeks later. We were a bit stymied by a week of rain and freezing cold in the lead-up, but the Monday dawned and we met at Bab Sbaa as planned at 8 a.m.

We'd arranged for Rachel's friend, Mohammed, to drive us up to Moulay Bouzerktoun and then to run back for three reasons: firstly, the prevailing winds, which can be extremely strong, are from north to south, so we would have the wind at our backs; secondly, psychologically, the thought of 'running home' is a powerful incentive; and, thirdly, there is very little in Moulay Bouzerktoun in terms of post-run celebration spots.

The beach lay ahead of us in all its virgin glory. It was a perfect day with a beautiful blue sky and great visibility and – hooray – a very mild wind. We set off over the first section of green seaweed and coral rocks where the Bouzerktounians gather mussels. Soon, we were hammering along on the sand feeling like goddesses and smiling like loons.

Those happy, smiling faces lasted about another three kilometres until we hit the quagmire. Deep, thick, wet, claggy sand, dragging down the legs and the spirits. We zigzagged up and down the beach looking for a harder surface 'Better up there?' 'Nope.' 'Harder up there?' 'No, just the same.' I got a weird pins-and-needles feeling in my feet but consoled myself with the thought, 'Nothing lasts forever.' True, but it lasted for the next 10 kilometres on and off, which seemed like forever.

Rachel and I talked our way along the side of the sea, enjoying the tiny seabirds pecking away diligently at the water's edge and the large flocks of gulls holding what looked like a very important board meeting further up the sands. At one stage the trail branched off the beach and into the scrubland, winding through sandy earth greened by the recent rain. To our left, dunes gleamed under the sun.

It's a mixed blessing when your destination finally appears in the distance, yet it is a long way to go. We were still in sand clag, and it seemed a lot further off than the total 16 kilometres I had banked on, but as we drew closer I realised that the back part of the city was jutting out further than our end point, which was at the other side. Rachel was right; we were nearly there, she wasn't just being ultra-yogi-positive. Leaving the sand was a relief and we trotted up the last few hundred metres to end, as all good trail runs do, in a car park outside the supermarket.

Ah! the pleasure of self-congratulation that ensued. We high-fived, hugged and declared our awesomeness to each other. Then, this being Morocco, we climbed into one of the horse-drawn buggies that act as a taxi along one of the big roads in the New Town, which is called the *autoroute*. Of course, we were greeted with great delight by the driver and the family of three already seated and were congratulated enthusiastically when we told them that we had run from Bouzerktoun. 'Blessings be upon you!' was the general consensus. We celebrated our triumph at Rachel's favourite juice bar with a reviving rehydration drink. Strawberries, pineapple, papaya and oranges all smooshed together. What a way to finish off a Monday morning – being an Adventurer is not a bad choice of job.

Beaches, cats and baby dreads. Essaouira is the home of the young Bob Marley wannabe. If you are a guy in Essaouira between the ages of eighteen and twenty-eight and you don't have dreadlocks, a straggly beard and a guitar, there is something very, very wrong with you. These are best accessorised, of course, with a pretty German girlfriend with a nose ring, a quasi-turban and baggy, stripy harem pants. Essaouira is famous for being a hippie hang-out and I'm told that now it is pretty tame compared to its heyday in the sixties and seventies. I posted a picture on Facebook of a river in flood that I was trying and failing to run through and got a message from a man called Jerry Bart: 'I bathed in this sandy river in 1968! Surrounded by hippies, those were the days. Some were naked, to the dismay of some locals!' Naked bathing? I can see why he would need all those exclamation marks.

Hippies may not be what they used to, but Essaouira does still attract musicians from all over the world for its huge open-air music festival which takes place in the summer. The town is always filled with music, from reggae covers to traditional trios performing outside cafés, but the main event is the Gnaoua Festival, which attracts up to 200,000 people.

Gnaoua is more than just music. It is a set of spiritual rituals, a healing ceremony, the name for an ethnic group and an intrinsic part of Morocco's history. The word *'gnaoua'* derives either from Ghana, which was used to denote a whole empire south of the Sahara encompassing Mauritania and Mali, rather than the modern country with that name, or from the Hausa-Fulani name 'Kanawa' for the people of Kano, which is in Nigeria and used to be the capital of a princedom.

Gnaoua was first used to describe those who had been captured, sold and transported from west Africa across the Sahara as slaves. In the traditional *gnaoua* songs they sing of their Bambara, Fulani and Hausa ancestors. The first large influx of slaves from the Niger river bend area of Mali and Niger goes back to Sultan Ahmed el-Mansour's conquest of the Songhai empire in 1591, when several thousand men and women were brought north. But the trade had been going since the eleventh century and was to continue right into the early 1900s.

I had believed that the first time I encountered *gnaoua* music was in Jemaa El Fnaa in Marrakech, where little bands play to entertain people in the evening. However, the music sounded extremely familiar and kept tugging at my consciousness. Later, I realised what it sounded like and where

I had actually heard it first. I lived in Ghana as a child and have vivid memories of Ghanaian women dressed in white with their bodies smeared in ash, dancing for days and nights at a time and transporting themselves into a religious trance as part of the Goat Festival. They had been dancing to music that was identical to what I had heard on the square.

Gnaoua is played on a three-stringed guitar (*gimbri*), big drums and *karakeb*, which are large, heavy castanets. It is sung, and what sounds like one song can be played for hours at a time. The best *gnaoua* practitioners are called '*maalem*' ('learned ones') and are highly acclaimed and respected. Although now it is played in short, radio-friendly bursts, traditionally *gnaoua* is a whole ritual of singing and dancing which takes place over a night of ceremony (*lila*).

Seven is a crucial number in *gnaoua*. It is the number of saints or spirits that the music is dedicated to. The music is designed around seven musical patterns, seven melodic rhythmic cells which make up the seven suites that form the repertoire of dance and music of the *gnaoua* ritual. During these seven suites, seven different types of incense are burned and the dancers are covered by veils of seven different colours. The *maalem* leads the music and dance and a woman, a clairvoyant, guides the dancing, the burning of the incense and the use of different garments and colours. The whole ceremony is meant to recreate or reflect the creation of the universe and to honour the saints and appease the spirits.

The festival, though, is a less intense affair. Serena, my flatmate, persuaded me to come to it when I was still living in Marrakech. 'But I don't like festivals and I don't know anything about music,' I cried as she turned a deaf ear. Two days later, I was established in a hostel dormitory with a shower that had hair and fungi in it that were not my own. That evening, on the roof of the hostel, sandwiched between a dope-smoking, sunburnt English girl and a Dutch boy pretending to be Jamaican, playing and singing his heart out with laudable enthusiasm, seeing Serena's happy, smiling face, I realised that at some point, and without me noticing, I had become the proverbial grumpy old woman.

That year there were two main sound stages: one in the middle of the big square and one on the beach. The streets were so packed that you had to queue to get round some of the corners, like Oxford Street at Christmas. Under the pressure of a temporary population explosion, everything stopped: water, electricity and mobile phone signal. Fortunately, no one cared. The crowd was completely mixed as all of Essaouira turned out to celebrate and enjoy the music. When I moved here Hayat was to invite me to go down to watch a couple of bands with her and her mother, who was in a wheelchair and in her eighties. The beach is always a mass of families with children ecstatically chasing the waves in the moonlight as their parents sit eating tagines on a picnic rug, listening to the music.

Everyday life is also filled with music. Music and art. There are more art galleries per head of population in Essaouira than any other place in Africa. On a Sunday, the local artists are 'at home' in their studios, which are mainly based in a long alleyway outside the city walls in a street off the main thoroughfare where the weekly market is held. There are also regular groups of visitors with paints and little easels clustered in Grain Square taking part in art holidays, sketching out their impressions of the archways and bright, patterned carpets. The art is great, but I have to confess to being over some of the music. I have got to the stage where I long to commit acts of violence when I hear the first few bars of 'No Woman, No Cry' starting up. Hayat laughs at me: 'Ah, Alice, how can you not like music when you live in Essaouira? Come to the square with me and we can listen to some *gnaoua*.'

It's an invitation I find easy to refuse, and because Hayat and I have developed a really nice relationship she finds it funny. Since we live in the same building, Hayat and I see each other numerous times a day. She huffs and puffs up to the roof to look askance at my cups of rooibos tea and home-made almond and banana brownies cooked in my oven the size of a toaster. I go downstairs to sit with her and Abdullah and her mum, the *Hajja* (which means a woman who has done the pilgrimage to Mecca and is a term of great respect), eat tagine and learn lots of new words and phrases in Darija, which amuses everyone. One of the first words she taught me she would only whisper when Abdullah wasn't in the room, because it was so naughty: '*sou'bazaar*', which as far as I can make out refers to a lady of the night who roams the streets looking for custom, and which is the nickname we have given to my younger cat. I'm not allowed to say it in front of men though.

Hayat is a great illustration to me of how things would be so different if I had been born in another place as well as how much binds us together as humans regardless of culture and upbringing. She is a real mixture of traditional and modern. She was educated to secondary school standard, got married in her early twenties to Abdullah, who is from a very similar level of family, and then raised her girls. She is a devout Muslim and prays daily and respects the con-straints of her faith. One day, I was in her house when a man arrived to deliver a mattress. She was wearing a T-shirt and leggings but immediately put on a large poncho-like cotton garment that went from the top of her head down over her shoulders, which she normally puts on when she is praying. Hayat is very polite and went through all the greetings and thanks as expected, but I noticed one thing that was very strange to me.

'Hayat, why didn't you look at that man when he arrived? You didn't look in his face once, all the time he was here?'

'Alice, that would not be respectable. I am a married woman. It is not our custom to look a man who is not our husband, or from the family, in the eyes. It would be too forward and somehow rude.'

Hayat has the spirit of an entrepreneur and is the driving force behind renovating the flats they own in the building and letting them out. She uses the money mainly for travel and for her daughters, all of whom have been well educated, but it is the youngest, Sara, who has gone the farthest. After completing her studies in textiles in Morocco, Hayat urged her on to go and study in France.

You know, Alice. It is very expensive to study there and I hate having Sara so far from home, but I really want her to have a great job and a great life and to be able to do everything she wants. I want her to be independent. Of course, marriage and children, but also other opportunities. I pushed her to go because that is the way to get a good job back here in Morocco or over there in France. She often gets homesick and cries when she talks to me. It's awful. She is lonely in France and misses her life here but she will have good work. I sometimes wish I could have studied and travelled more and done different things but . . . it's the will of God.

The hard work and sacrifices have paid off, however, as straight after her course, Sara succeeded in getting an internship with top fashion label Zadig & Voltaire.

Fashion is very much on my mind, as I want to get a piece of African fabric I bought in Timbuktu made up into a djellaba. Hayat gets on board with alacrity and we set a date to go to her tailor. He is on Baghdad Street on the way to Bab Marrakech. She arrives to collect me, dressed in a very smart djellaba of white linen with embroidered patterns at the hem, neck and sleeves and raffia slippers to match. The raffia slippers and shoes are a speciality of Essaouira. They make them in all different colours and styles and are allegedly extremely comfortable to wear. We set off arm in arm as Hayat detours to show me where she lived as a child (about five minutes away) and we stop to say hello to numerous acquaintances in the street.

The tailor is a small, neat man with a measuring tape around his neck in a small, neat shop with bolts of fabric behind him and an apprentice working on a foot-operated sewing machine beside the window. The whole street is given over to tailors and on the way up I had noticed long skeins of thread stretching down the lane and into the shops. When I looked more closely, I could see that they were being twisted into thicker cords and then hand-stitched onto the men's djellabas in rows of subtle decoration.

I take out my cloth, which I had pre-washed in cold water, and lay it out. It is a deep crimson with a print of golden leaves. Abd El Hakim measures it up and says there is more than enough for a djellaba, and Hayat and he enter into an impassioned discussion on suitable styles. We decide on a straight A-line, with no slits in the sides, so wider at the bottom. Because the print is already very vibrant, I pick out a dark green thread for the buttons and button holders down the front and strips of embroidery down the A-line and on the bottom of the sleeves. Then Abd El Hakim gets out his pattern book so I can choose exactly which pattern of embroidery I want. I am distracted by the giant paisley swirls, the tiny hearts and intricate ivy leaves and am tempted to go big but Hayat brings me firmly back into line by pointing out that there is already a lot going on in my print, and I reluctantly go plain, but make a silent promise to myself to come back with some less showy material so I can go big on the embroidery.

It's time to be measured, which is slightly awkward given all the constraints around male/female touching. However, Abd El Hakim is a master and holds the tape measure quite far away from me so that there is no touching at all and then deducts that from the numbers. Every bit of me is measured, even my wrists and the length between my neck and shoulder, as well as the distance between my neck and a third of the way down my back so that the djellaba hood can lie correctly. I fantasise about a large *shooshiyya* (tassel) to go on the hood, but Hayat is stern. 'No, it's too much.'

A week later and at a fantastic cost of just £15, my djellaba is ready and I go and get it then immediately put it on over my jeans and T-shirt. As I prance home in my finery, I collect dozens of compliments: 'Nice djellaba!' 'Wow!' 'May the blessings of God rain upon your head!' 'Gazelle!'

The Essaouira area is famous for its argan oil, beloved of cosmetic manufacturers. The argan tree grows in only two areas in the world: the south of Morocco/Algeria and Peru. The trees are quite small. They grow to about 8–10 metres high. But what they lack in height, they make up for in longevity and live up to approximately 200 years. The leaves are small and a longish oval shape. The branches are thorny and the trunk is gnarled, spreading out into a wide top. The tree flowers in April, producing small pale yellowy-green blooms. These then grow into the argan nut which is used to make the oil. The nut is about the size of a large almond and is covered in a thick, bitter, green outer layer. Inside the nut are the oil-rich seeds.

To get to the oil, you first have to remove the outer pulp, which is used to feed animals. After that, you get to the part that is shown in all the argan oil co-operatives. Many women's co-operatives have been set up to make the oil and earn a bit of cash to use for household expenses. It is a very labour-intensive process and the resulting oil is expensive by Moroccan standards.

First, the women crack the nut using a hard, flat rock. The seeds are then taken out and ground into a paste with a little water, using a stone rotary quern. The paste is left to settle and the pure oil is skimmed off the top. The paste is still oil rich and is made into the black soap that is used in the hammams as a scrub. The less good-quality paste is fed to the animals.

There are two basic kinds of oils produced: for cooking and for cosmetic use. The cooking oil comes from roasted nuts and tastes very nutty, a bit like sesame oil. The cosmetic oil is untouched. The reason it is meant to be so good for you, both as a food and as a skin product, is that it is rich in essential fatty acids and is more resistant to oxidation than olive oil. It is also extremely pure. Be wary, though – some unscrupulous spice shops, especially in Marrakech, will sell you product that has been liberally laced with olive oil. The safest way to buy is from a co-operative, and that way you also know that the money is going to local women.

One of the delicious side products from argan oil is *amlou* or Moroccan peanut butter. It is a dip made of argan oil, ground almonds and wild honey and spread on bread, pancakes (or *m'semen*) for breakfast. Nutritious and delicious.

There is a dark side to the argan trade and that has to do with tourism. The goats in Morocco love the argan nuts and have long been accustomed to climbing up the trees to eat them. In fact, it is said that the very best oil comes from nuts that the goats have eaten and then pooed out. I am not sure how that works and rather hope it is an urban myth. Of course, the spectacle of goats in a tree is an irresistible photo opportunity and I have taken my fair share of pictures, which never look quite as good on a screen as they do when you are out in the fresh air.

I was driving down the road to Marrakech one day when I saw a group of tour buses pulled up ahead of me on the opposite side. Incurably nosey, I stopped to see what was going on. A dozen or so tourists were outside snapping happily at a tree covered in goats. So far, so good, but when I got closer, I saw that the goats had been tied to the tree's branches and were standing there unable to move while the shepherd sat underneath waiting for tips. Without thinking about it, I stormed over to the bus driver.

Me: 'What do you think you are doing? These goats are tied to the trees. You should not encourage the tourists to take pictures and give money. This is torture. God made us all – humans and animals. Shame on you!'
Driver: 'Listen, lady. This is not my problem. They want to stop. Tell the shepherd not me.'

He had a fair point, but my experience in Jemaa El Fna with the squirrels had made me cautious, so I went for an easier target and stomped up the stairs into the bus.

Me [red-faced and furious]: 'Does anyone here speak English?'

(A few timid hands went up.)

'Do you realise that you are contributing to the torture of these animals by stopping to take pictures? Can't you see they are actually tied onto the tree? They are left there for hours. How would you feel if you were tied in what is basically a stress position for hours at a time just so that someone could come and take a picture of you? Please don't take pictures. Please don't give your driver or the shepherd a tip and tell them that you are not tipping them because tying the goats is wrong.'

Poor tourists. Accosted by a mad woman, flaming with impassioned wrath. The driver actually backed away as I left, probably fearing for his life.

The great thing about living in any place for a while is that you get to contribute a little to the society. I had done a bit of work for a great Australian initiative in Imlil in the mountains called Red Goes Faster, which fits wheelchairs to children who need them. The concept is really simple and effective. The wheelchairs come through Wheelchairs for Kids and are built by volunteers in Australia. Red Goes Faster ships them to Morocco and works with locals to find the children who need them and then delegates volunteers to go out and fit them. Every chair is built specifically for the child.

When I got to Essaouira, I put an advert on Facebook to see if anyone needed a chair and got an answer from a teacher called Bahija who knew of a boy called Abd El Raheem, aged seven. I met Bahija and we drove to the family's house.

When I first saw Abd El Raheem, I recoiled a little in shock. He has an enormous head, about three times the size of a normal head, and kind of triangular in shape. He can sit up unaided but it is obviously very heavy and after a while he needs to rest against something. His legs are immobile but he can crawl and scoot along using his arms. We sat and had tea with Zahira, his mother, and one of her other children, Miriam, a little girl of about five, and, of course, Abd El Raheem, who is the life and soul of any party. After five minutes with him you don't notice what he looks like, you just enjoy his company.

I told him what I was there for and showed him some pictures and videos of other children who had got wheelchairs. 'Wow,' he said. 'They are nice. *Quatre Quatre* (4x4). Mama, does this mean I can go to school? When can I get it? Have you got one now?' The pressure was on.

Two weeks later, I went up to Marrakech to collect the wheelchair and my friend Reda, who was coming down to fit it. Reda is a nurse specialising in prosthetic limbs. He works a six-day week and then gives a lot of his free time to union duties, as he is head of his chapter. On his only day off he was willing to come down and fit Abd El Raheem. When I told him how grateful I was and how much I appreciated the fact that this would mean he would effectively work fourteen days straight through, he said, 'Alice, it is my duty. How could I say no to this child?'

When we got to the house, the whole family was waiting for us, including the father, who I hadn't met before, and Abd El Raheem's older brothers. Zahira bakes the traditional round cookies of Essaouira, *kaka*, and sells them in the Sunday market and she had a big, freshly made plateful ready for us. Abd El Raheem was bouncing up and down in excitement and couldn't wait to see inside the big box. I got out my measuring tape to do his measurements so that we could fit the wheelchair to his size and Reda started unpacking all the various bits.

It was hot and it takes a long time to build a chair, around two to three hours. Reda was doing the bulk of the work, but I was helping turn screws and tighten nuts and bolts under his instruction and was soon dripping in sweat.

'Is it ready yet? Is it ready yet?' was the constant chorus from Abd El Raheem as he circled us, keeping an eagle eye on proceedings. 'Is it time to put the wheels on? Shall I get them for you?' Reda explained the process as we went along and I wielded the screwdriver and sweated, standing up occasionally to stretch out my back. At last we got the wheels on and were ready for the first fitting.

Abd El Raheem's father lifted him into the chair and rested his head against the headrest. Joy, in its purest form, spread across Abd El Raheem's face.

'Look at me, look at me!' He grabbed the wheels and started wheeling the chair. 'Get the cardboard box out of my way,' he yelled on his way down towards the door and freedom. 'Open the door, I'm going.' The whole family was clapping and Zahira was crying. Miriam ran round in circles shouting and trying to clamber onto the chair too. Abd El Raheem pounded his hands on the wheels and laughed and laughed.

A couple of weeks later I checked in with Zahira to see how she was doing. Abd El Raheem's dearest wish was to go to school and so, once she got the chair, she went along to the local school to talk to the teachers. At first they were reluctant as they didn't have any facilities to deal with a handicapped child, but after long discussions and working out how they could deal with the toilet issue (a nappy) and access issues (his brothers could help wheel him), they agreed. I was a little worried about how he would be treated by the other children, but Zahira told me it was no problem and that, although at first they were a bit wary, he had soon made friends and fitted right in.

Last time I visited, Abd El Raheem told me gleefully that he now had a girlfriend at school called Fozia.

Me: 'But, Abd El Raheem, I hope you still love your Aunty Alice the best?'
Abd El Raheem: 'Aunty, I do love you, but I love Fozia much more, she is really pretty!'

10

VALLEYS AND OASES

As soon as you cross the natural barrier of the Atlas Mountains, everything changes. The winds blow from across the Sahara and you leave the cool of Europe and the north behind for the warmth of Africa. In a country full of romance, the Valley of the Kasbahs is the Barbara Cartland of the genre. Red castles lord it over swathes of green, dotting the desert landscape. The colours are a violent cacophony of red earth, blue sky and green palm trees. They mirror the violent history of the region, which abounds in stories of murder and mayhem.

Kasbahs are actually fortified houses that were built for rich men to keep themselves and their possessions safe. They can stand alone or within a *ksar* (plural *ksour*), which comes from the word 'palace' in Arabic but means a group of buildings, including a kasbah, within a fortified wall – basically a fortified village. Sometimes the two terms are used interchangeably, and they are used slightly differently in other areas of the Arab world.

A kasbah looks like a proper castle, the kind you imagine when you are a child. It is made of compacted red mud and built large and square with very deep walls. It gets its distinctive sandcastle shape from four turrets which are built on each corner of the structure. These were for keeping lookout, or for firing from if you came under attack from rival tribes or ravaging bandits. Windows are kept small, both because of the weather, which is baking hot in the summer and freezing cold in the winter, and to provide cover under fire from enemies. The kasbah is the tallest building in the village, with the exception of the mosque, and is usually positioned to guard the entrance or exit to a place and to give the best vantage point.

A massive wooden door at the entrance gives out onto a courtyard with stables and stores for goods and animals leading off it. Ideally, there should be a water source such as a well in the kasbah itself in case of siege, as well as to make daily life a bit easier. On the upper floor there are sleeping and socialising areas and sometimes a prayer room. The kitchens and bread ovens are downstairs.

No kasbah is complete without its contingent of storks (the four turrets provide a very good spot for a hopeful stork family). The name for them in Tashlaheet is 'aswoo', and these ungainly, but somehow graceful, birds are everywhere in Morocco. They love the cities, where they are attracted by the easy food and scavenge all the rubbish tips. They build big, untidy nests of branches and twigs in high places, including on mobile phone masts. I've counted up to twenty-five nests on a really big pylon. Their favourite places seem to be the masts that have been cleverly disguised to look like palm trees, clearly a pretty good fake. They build their nests solidly and come back to them for many years. At sunset, you will see them circling on their wide wings in open spaces, making picturesque shapes against the darkening sky. It is against the law to disturb them, and if you do, you can get a prison sentence of up to three months.

Maybe this is because there is an old Amazigh belief that the storks are actually transformed humans and that they can cry human tears. That tale has been further embellished to become the history of the naughty imam (priest).

The story goes that one day, a Marrakchi imam got up out of bed as usual and dressed in his white djellaba with a black robe on the top and slipped his feet into a pair of soft, yellow *babouches*. He had his coffee and an omelette for breakfast and went about his day, tending to his flock. As usual, they were troublesome: there was a squabble between neighbours; the *qadi* demanded his attendance and his obsequiousness; and he heard reports that a rival imam has been bad-mouthing him in the coffee shop. At last, the day drew to a close and the sun went over the yardarm.

Then his mind turned not to higher things, but to the prospect of a nice glass of wine at sunset. Wine is forbidden, but man is weak and the temptation was irresistible. 'Just one glass,' he thought, 'the Lord is the all Merciful, the Compassionate.' Ahhh, the soothing feel of the red liquid, brewed in the vineyards near Essaouira, slipping down his dry throat and helping him forget the machinations of the rival imam. Soon one glass led to another and a warmth and comfort spread over him. But his day's duties were not done. He still had to do the evening call to prayer. He got up from his comfortable nest of cushions, downed a large gulp to make sure his throat was wet and his voice supple, and headed for the steps up the minaret. Oh, those steps were especially steep that night, round and round, up and up. Just as he reached the last one, he stumbled and stubbed his big toe on his left foot, catapulting into the open space at the top. A juicy epithet or two escaped and echoed around the city. Oh, foolish imam! He had clearly not learned the ninety-nine names of God, as one of those is the All Hearing.

Boom! The All Hearing was not, in this case, minded to be the Merciful, the Compassionate, and the imam was transformed into a stork, with his djellaba and robe made into black and white plumage and his *babouches* transformed into yellow legs. He was doomed to circle his minaret forever, no doubt repenting his sin and perhaps contemplating how to get his long beak into a glass of Merlot. Look up to a minaret at sunset, and you may spot him.

The most famous of the *ksours* in Morocco is probably Ait Ben Haddou, which is on the way to Ouarzazate, just south of the barrier of the Atlas Mountains and in the centre of the country – east to west – approximately four hours' drive away from Marrakech. Ait Ben Haddou owes its fame to films and programmes like *Gladiator* and *Game of Thrones*. In *Gladiator*, it was used for the fighting and training scenes. Look carefully in the scene where Maximus refuses to fight and you'll also see a whole group of storks. More recently, it was depicted in *Game of Thrones* as the slave city of Yunkai, the yellow city, which was conquered by Daenerys. According to *Game of Thrones* legend, Ait Ben Haddou was a place of learning in the ways of love. 'Yunkai is known for training bed slaves, not warriors. A slave in Yunkai learns the way of the seven sighs and the sixteen seats of pleasure. Yunkai can field an army of roughly 5,000 men, all slaves. In Yunkai, eunuchs are made by only cutting the testicles off, unlike the Unsullied of Astapor.'

A good place to ponder the life of a Yunkai slave and the potential geography of the sixteen seats of pleasure is the hill opposite Ait Ben Haddou, which is the exact spot that Daenerys stood to size up the city and was well chosen because it offers you the best view of the *ksar* and the valley beyond. A wide river winds through the valley at the base of Ait Ben Haddou, breaking up the rows of golden desert hills and supplying the green oases with their water. The *ksar* is built up a small hill and you can clearly see the fortified houses and the streets and alleys leading up to the very top. It is all built of the typical compacted red mud with soaring turrets and square fortresses, shadowed by tall palm trees. At sunset, it turns golden.

When you cross the river, you enter the *ksar* by a large gate, then you climb upwards through narrow alleys filled with merchants selling finely etched ink drawings, locally woven carpets and polished fossils. Sometimes you have to duck your head as you go into a tunnel, dug under a house or pathway. The contrast between the dark of the roofed alleys and the sun is blinding and you are constantly shuttling between the two. The town is barely inhabited now, only four families still live there, but they will show you round their houses for a small fee. It is a UNESCO World Heritage site and I definitely prefer to get there early in the morning or at sunset to miss the crowds. As you walk up the last few steps to the top, there is always a musician in traditional desert blue robes playing his *gimbri* in the shade of the wall and singing *gnaoua* songs. He has been there for years and will proudly tell you about all his TV and film appearances if you stop for a quick chat. He also sells CDs of his music.

From the top, it becomes apparent why this spot was

chosen to build the *ksour* on: you can see for miles in every direction. The valley stretches off to both right and left and you can clearly see the routes of the old trade caravans as there are *ksours* built at intervals all along the valley, like ancient petrol stations or motels but infinitely more glamorous. Encircling everything, and apparently endless, is the line of desert hills, bleached white at midday or glowing in the evening light.

Ait Ben Haddou was built to service the merchants who brought their goods along the ancient trade routes that I crossed from west Africa all the way up through Morocco and on to Europe. Trading across the Sahara desert has been going on for thousands of years, with artefacts being found dating back to 4000 BC. In a development as exciting as the invention of the wheel, the Amazigh revolutionised commerce by introducing the camel as a pack animal. These doughty beasts were, and still are, the perfect transport system for desert conditions.

A camel can carry up to 200 kilograms and average 35 kilometres a day. People here say that the camel was 'Designed by God with the desert in mind', and the word itself in Arabic, '*jamal*', comes from the same basic three letters as the word for beautiful, '*jameel*'. (If you ever want to pay someone a nice compliment, do be careful which of those two words you use.) Camels have a number of physical features which make them ideal for desert conditions. Their feet are designed for sand as the two toes and thick pads stop them sinking in. They have a good sense of smell, too. Allegedly the white ones have the best sense of smell and actually sniff out water, which is why they are always put at the front of the caravan. Their lips are rubbery enough to munch on the thorny little plants that are scattered across the desert without splitting

237

their skin and their lovely long eyelashes are not there just to look pretty; they seal the eye completely when it is shut so that the animal does not suffer during sandstorms. Most important is their ability to survive without water.

No one is quite sure how long a human can survive without water, but best guesses put it at three to four days, and that is not factoring in walking 35 kilometres a day in high temperatures across desert dunes. Camels can go without drinking for up to ten days. Contrary to popular myth, that is not because they store water in their hump, which is just fat, but because they can withstand very high temperatures and regulate their sweat so they don't dehydrate so quickly.

Standing overlooking the hill to Ait Ben Haddou, it is easy to conjure up a caravan 1,000 camels strong jostling through the gate and unloading its goods to be kept safe within the fortified walls. The oases valleys were the veins and arteries of ancient trade between Africa and Europe, but the heart and the liver were two towns: Sijilmassa, near Rissani, and Guelmim in the south.

Sijilmassa means 'a place where there is water' in Berber and was founded in the eighth century in the middle of the largest oasis in Morocco, the Tafilalt oasis, which is famous for its dates. Its fertile land and water supply meant that it was the ideal place to build a large-scale service station for the trade routes and, in its day, it was the most significant city in the whole south of Morocco and was wealthy and cosmopolitan.

The oasis is nearly 50 kilometres in length and the date palms cover the whole area right to the far hills, where there is an old Almoravid fortress built to protect the trade routes and to collect taxes from travelling merchants. The land was rich and there was water available, but the architects of the city actually built a 40-kilometre canal, called the Ziz, between Erfud and Merzouga to supply water to the oasis and industrialise its production to grow enough food to provision the caravans. The canal is the only structure of its kind in north Africa. There was a large local Jewish population who monopolised the minting of currency, and the coins minted in Sijilmassa were used all over Europe and have even been found as far away as China.

Nowadays, there is almost nothing to see, and finding it is actually rather difficult. It is a few kilometres out of the nearest town, Rissani, and there are no signs or information to help you. You have to stop and ask people. When I first got there, I didn't think I had got the place right because it just looked like a big building site, but as I climbed the slight hill that rises from the road, I started to see the outlines of a city. There are no full buildings, but what you can see clearly is the geography of it, and why it was so useful for traders.

The city covers 14 kilometres from end to end, with an entrance that you can still see to the east called Bab Riyyah (the windy gate). The outlines of the mosque, the madrassa and possibly the barracks, which are all in what must have been the main square, are still visible. Rich people lived on the slightly higher ground, while poorer folk stayed lower down where there were also the markets and storage areas. One of the things that proves this ruin was once a wealthy town is that when the architects first started excavating they found that many of the houses on the higher ground had indoor toilets – an unimaginable luxury.

One reason that so little of the city remains, and this is true of so much desert architecture in the country, is that the buildings themselves were made of mud blocks. This method of construction is still used today, although less so as people turn to concrete, which is much cheaper and quicker. Two wooden sheets are placed to form a gap, the mud is pushed in and then pressed down as hard as possible. It is left to dry and then oil or water is poured on top to make sure it is compressed enough. If the liquid soaks down, it isn't. If the liquid stays where it is, the next layer is added. Walls made this way are perfect for Morocco's climate because they retain the warmth in winter and the cool in summer.

Sijilmassa is an allegory for the decline and fall of any empire or civilisation. In the early days of its power in the 700s, it was grand enough to declare itself independent of the Abbasid Caliphate which then ruled the Islamic world from Baghdad. For centuries, it had a virtual monopoly on gold in the north and west of Africa, but then the trade routes shifted towards the sea and the Atlantic ports of Essaouira and Agadir, and Sijilmassa's power ebbed away. Finally it was sacked and destroyed by the Ait Atta, the same tribe that Zaid and his nomad family are from, and the dominant nomadic tribe in the region.

It would be wrong to say a phoenix has risen from the ashes, but the nearby town of Rissani has once again become an important trading post in that it has the biggest market in the region. Tuesdays, Thursdays and Sundays are the best days to visit, and it is, quite simply, the best market in Morocco.

The market is set out in a large covered or roofed square, which you can enter through a number of different *babs*. The livestock market is off to one side and parking is really easy. You just tie up your donkey in the enormous donkey park, pay your parking fee to the guardian and go off to do your business in the market, safe in the knowledge that Neddy will be there on your return. The donkey park is about the size of a football pitch and on a busy market day it houses a couple of hundred donkeys, dozing in the sun and flicking flies off their ears.

One of the first things that you notice in Rissani is that people here dress very differently. The men wear white robes and turbans, very similar to those worn in the Sudan, while the women wear the all-in-one wrap called the *milfah*, often with a tie-dye pattern in bright pink and white or blue and white. There are also many west African faces to be seen.

Inside, the market is arranged on a grid-like system with specific areas for the various goods. There is a mixture of open stalls piled high with olives and spices and little shops stuffed full of knock-off trainers and sports kit. The slatted roofs cast stripes of light and shade across the walls and floor and make you feel like you are walking into a constantly flickering black-and-white film from the thirties. Along one side of the boundary wall is the metal-working area. You can hear the *clang clang* of iron on iron before you can see it and then the sparks from the fires and basic blow torches come into view. I find the temptation to buy something here almost overwhelming. Mule shoes, fat-bottomed pots, picks, shovels, ornate grills for your windows, it's all here. It's not just new stuff for sale, though. In fact, a lot of the work seems to be in repairs, and you can watch, alongside the owner, as a wonky rake is fixed or a pan gets its handle resoldered.

I've never given in to that temptation, but I have bought some of the local pottery. As you can imagine in such a hot climate, Moroccans have come up with lots of ways to keep things cool. In Rissani, they make and sell the traditional clay pots where water is stored to keep it fresh and cold and the cups to dip in and drink from. These are painted with black designs round the rim and neck but are otherwise plain earthenware. I don't know what alchemy is used, but they do cool water down. They also give it a slightly smoky flavour which is acutely refreshing when the sun is hot.

Of course, I've also bought some of the local material and clothes. There is one part of the souk in the main clothes area where the garments are hung so closely together and in such abundance that you have to push your way through a technicolour cornucopia to continue on your path. It was here that I fell prey to an outfit which was meant for a man, but which I couldn't pass up. A short-sleeved shirt and baggy trousers, covered in elephants and palm trees in bright greens, made out of a linen-type fabric. Unfortunately, the first time I donned my new outfit, I was bending down to feed the cats when I heard an almighty rip. I had torn my trousers from waist to crotch and my bottom was protruding in a way that even frightened the moggies. 'Obviously not made for the female form,' I told myself consolingly, although I suspect the truth may be that I had been indulging in a few too many almond and honey pastries.

The oases and valleys of the kasbahs wend gently through this semi-arid region, but in two places they give way to dramatic, deep gorges: the Dades and the Todra. Millions of years ago, both lay at the bottom of the sea, and the sediment that got deposited around the coral reefs over the millennia was compacted and turned into the limestone and sandstone that make up the gorges today. The rivers of the same name, which cut out the gorges and wore away the rock, shrink and swell with the rainfall and snowmelt coming down from the Atlas.

It was this swelling that was to provide me with a mini

adventure in the Todra gorge. I had come to Morocco for the two-week cycling holiday with Saddle Skedaddle that was to introduce me to Charlie and finally end with me living in the country, but that was all way into the future. The trip was the Trans-Atlas Traverse and was a mountain-bike adventure across the mountains. The first day, when we offloaded the bikes from the van and set off across the rock and scrub of the mountains at an altitude of over 2,000 metres (6,561 feet), I thought my lungs might actually pop out of my chest, I was breathing so hard in the thin air, with my thighs pumping round the pedals as hard as they could to keep up with the others. The trip had been absolutely fantastic, with harsh climbs and super-sketchy descents across almost uninhabited country. Our group of cyclists had bonded through the challenge and as well as Charlie, who was leading the expedition, I made friends for life in two other riders: Angela Riddell and David Ward. David was to go on to design and build a bespoke bike for me when I undertook the Tour D'Afrique, an 8,000-mile bike race from Cairo to Cape Town, and Angela was to come and ride a stage of it with me.

The last day of cycling was to take us to the Dades Gorge, and it was to be a 100-kilometre day, which is a long way on a mountain bike. The night before it was cold and raining with ominous clouds banked up right the way to the horizon. Charlie gathered us together and told us that due to a combination of the weather, and the fact that some striking workers were blocking the route at Agoudau, he was going to change the route and take us to the Todra Gorge instead. One gorge sounded much like the other at that stage, and none of us demurred. The next day, we were up and out nice and early. Charlie had told us that a lot of the ride was downhill, and as the day progressed it proved to be true. We had pretty bad weather with rain and black skies, but apart from that everything was going well.

Entering the gorge, it felt fantastic to be on a bike rather than in one of the tourist coaches we passed, and I stopped to take pictures of the towering, sheer walls – they reach 500 metres in places. We rode on in great spirits, enjoying the fact we had made it to the end of our journey and drinking in the sheer immensity of the gorge itself. The Todra River, which is normally a gentle stream, was to our right and was foaming and brown, engorged by the recent rainstorms and greater than usual snowmelt.

We were on our way to meet Hassan Sukar (so-called because 'sukar' means 'sugar' and Hassan is a diabetic), the driver, and Abdallah, the general factotum, with the support vehicles to transfer us back to our hotel. Abdallah was a big favourite with the whole group. He had spent the trip trying to get the guys to wrestle with him, which they prudently refused to do because Abdallah is a giant – a gentle one, but nonetheless a giant. He looks like you imagine Hercules might, with shoulders knotted with muscle and a chest as wide as a car. We only ever saw his bearded face wreathed in smiles. Even though the whole cycle trip took place during Ramadan, Abdallah showed no sign of weakness, tossing cases and bikes and people up onto the van roof as though they were balls of cotton wool.

Charlie was chatting away to me at the back, when suddenly he stopped and said a couple of bad words. I looked to where his eyes had turned and saw our support vehicle with all our bags on the roof rack, stuck fast, in the middle of the raging river. It was tilting nastily to the left. What had happened was that the road had partially washed away but Hassan Sukar had thought he could make it across. However, the river was deeper than it seemed and he couldn't feel the road underneath. This double whammy meant he had hit some underwater boulders and stopped.

There was more to see. A coachload of Japanese tourists had parked up and were standing by the river, taking pictures and talking excitedly. We followed their gaze. There, legs akimbo in the middle of the torrent, was Abdallah – god-like, lifting up boulders the size of a small fridge and throwing them to the side, trying to clear a path. With every heave of his mighty sinews, a small chorus of gasps emanated from the Japanese. But, as fast as Abdallah was clearing a path, the minibus was tilting more and more and showing every sign of getting ready to either topple or float off downstream, or possibly both. Charlie had visions of the luggage and his entire tour's equipment being submerged and lost in the waters of the Todra. Several months disappeared off his lifespan.

Just then, Jocko appeared out of the mists in his truck, belching fumes out of its chimney, both built to withstand the apocalypse. Fag in mouth, he leapt out, thigh-deep into the water, and he, Charlie and Abdallah hooked the minibus up to his tow bar. Abdallah had to lift it physically out of the water. To the applause of the Japanese, the cheers of our group and the heartfelt relief of both Hassan Sukar and Charlie, the minibus and our luggage were saved and the minibus even started first time when it got across to dry land.

It was another car adventure that was to cement my love affair with the people of the oases and southern Morocco. I had been commissioned to update a couple of sections of the Fodor's guidebook and, as part of that, had decided to road-trip it through the oasis along the two classic routes. I set off from Essaouira and took the road out to Marrakech, over the mountains, down to Skoura and the Dades, then further down to Zagora and then back up to Agdz to cross by the lower desert road towards home. I was on the final leg, but had underestimated the distances and was eight hours in, with a few still to go, when I reached Taroudant, the busy metropolis that services that area south of Agadir.

It was about three o'clock in the afternoon and I was hungry and thirsty. I'd been driving since 8.30 a.m. and because of the big gaps between towns I had missed out on lunch. About 100 kilometres from Agdz I had spotted a farmer sitting on a low wall, near his mule, with a pile of fresh figs for sale. I screeched to a halt and bought a kilo for me and a kilo for Hayat. It wasn't really fig season yet but these were the very earliest bloomers, freshly picked off the tree and smelling of sweetness and earth. I am fatally addicted to Moroccan figs and ate six of them straight off the bat. However, that had been a long time ago and now I was starving. Low blood sugar and the stress of Moroccan driving are not the best combination.

Driving into the walled city of Taroudant, I was sure that I would get something to eat, but as I rolled into town, up ahead I saw the ubiquitous 'POLICE! Slow down! Stop!' sign placed at the edge of the road. Tummy rumbling, temper slightly frayed, and with that feeling of guilt that afflicts even the most innocent when confronted with a policeman, I pulled over and rolled down my window.

Policeman: 'Peace be upon you.'
Me: 'And upon you.'
Policeman: 'You speak Arabic? Oh peace! Welcome to my country. Where are you going?'
Me: 'I am going to Essaouira, God willing.'

Policeman: 'Ahh you still have some way on the road. Where did you come from?'
Me: 'From Agdz. I am very tired.'

I said this and looked up at him pathetically in the hope that he would take the hint and let me drive on. He was being very nice but my head was full of chicken and chips. It was a forlorn hope. Four years of Morocco should have taught me that there were never any shortcuts. The policeman was settling into his conversational stride and continued:

'As God wills! That is a long way, my sister. What is your job?'
Me: 'I am an Adventurer. I seek out adventures and then write or broadcast about them. Your country has blessed me greatly. I love Morocco.'

His smile got even bigger and he positively beamed at me.

Policeman: 'Thanks be to God! I am a literary man myself. I work as a policeman, but my passion is literature. I write poetry.'
Me: 'Oh peace! We are family then.'
Policeman: 'Yes, but I must still check your details. Wait here, my sister, while I go to the office.'

What? I had thought I was surely off scot-free as we were both literary lights, shining in our respective firmaments. I knew all my documents were in order, but I also knew that if he went to the office I was going nowhere fast. I pondered the wisdom of another couple of figs and decided that it wasn't worth the risk given the paucity of loo breaks. I fantasised again about chicken and chips and then started Googling pictures of doughnuts on my iPhone. Things were getting bad. Ten long minutes later, the policeman reappeared, striding purposefully towards the car, but he was not empty-handed; he was clutching a huge, ripe, yellow melon.

I rolled down the window and, with his beaming smile even bigger, he handed it in to me. 'My sister, this is for you,' he said, as he passed it over. 'And here is my number and my name. Next time you are in Taroudant, please, please come to have dinner with me and my wife and family and we can talk about books. I wish you a safe journey and a happy day.'

Ten months later, I was sitting in Essaouira on a cold February morning in that state of mild depression that comes after you realise you have already broken all your New Year's resolutions and the mince pies of Christmas are just a distant memory, when an advert popped up on Facebook. 'House sitters wanted for small home in desert oasis.' February blues forgotten, I sprang into action and emailed Peter and Annette, explaining why I was the house sitter of their dreams. They emailed me back to say that unfortunately they had found someone but that perhaps I could sublet the small studio house from Debbie, who had taken on the whole property. I stalked poor Debbie until she agreed and on 7 March I packed up the cats, Nellie and Squeaky, my bike, running kit and some luxury food essentials, including coconut milk and balsamic vinegar, handed my keys over to Amanda who had flown over from the UK to try out Essaouira life and set off for Tighmert, a tiny spot about 15 kilometres away from the town of Guelmim, eight hours' drive away inland and to the south.

The coastal road is spectacular, winding its way round the hillsides covered in argan and olive trees, overlooking the sea and occasionally passing through small towns and settlements, but I was glad I had driven it before because this time the whole world was covered in a thick, wet fog and all I could see was an infrequent mule or bicycle looming suddenly into view. I had to forget the scenery and content myself with listening to Hit Radio – *cent pourcent eets* (French accent needed). Hit Radio is my favourite radio station because it only ever plays twelve songs on rotation. These are played over and over again for about three months and then changed. This means that you can learn enough of the words to sing along with gusto and also play 'Guess the next song', which I did when my niece and nephew, Georgie and Jamie, and my brother Robbie came over to visit. I triumphed every time, due, perhaps, to my superior knowledge of the playlist. The other thing I like is the mixture of languages: Darija, French, Spanish and English are used interchangeably and a typical exchange goes something like this: '*Momo*, Morning Show, *qasama ou ma qasamash? Fatima. Kidira? Labas? Bisous!*'

By the last 50 kilometres, the fog had lifted and given way to the afternoon sun. Tighmert lies in a wide desert plain, bordered by high hills on each side. The car chugged up an escarpment and when I got to the top, I could see miles and miles of red desert earth ahead of me, with splodges of green oases, the landmark tall date palm trees just visible, and all of it bathed in that warm light you get at around 5 p.m.

Somewhat less picturesquely, I had arranged to meet Debbie at Marjane supermarket on the outskirts of town. I was quite surprised that Guelmim had anything as posh as a Marjane, but it is a handy landmark and also good for picking up groceries, so a perfect meeting spot. In the car park there were around a dozen campers parked up, ranging in size from van to palace. Lots of people bring them over from Europe to tour Morocco in the winter months when the weather is bad at home. One of them had two huskies tied up outside, looking longingly with their ice-blue eyes at my cats in the car. I did a bit of grocery shopping and then stood outside stretching my legs and looking out for a 4x4 or maybe a beat-up old Renault. What I did not expect was a black sports car to roar in, driven by a blonde in pink-framed sunglasses. Debbie had arrived.

I followed close behind her, feeling that my Toyota Yaris and manky jeans were letting down the side a little, and we headed for my new home. Soon we turned off the tarmac and into the palm trees, driving along clay roads wet from the recent rains. Hit Radio was turned off and I opened my window to hear the birds. Then, ahead of us was the blue gate and the high mud wall surrounding the compound. I pulled up and Debbie went on first to open the door.

After a couple of minutes, I could see that not all was going as planned, so I turned off the engine and got out of the car. 'The key won't turn,' said Debbie. She tried again a few times and then I had a go. 'You're right. It isn't turning.' This was not good news, as the wall around the garden is about three metres high. Nevertheless, we did a walk round to see if there were any places of ingress. There weren't, and what was worse was that when I climbed up onto a palm tree stump and stretched my hand onto the top of the wall to see if I could haul myself over, it started crumbling in my hand. The recent rains had soaked the clay and it was fragile.

At that moment, Richard and Andy arrived. They were caravaners who Debbie had met earlier and, in the spirit of oasis hospitality, had invited over for supper. I eyed up Andy, not for nefarious purposes, but because he was small and light, no extra fat on him and ideal for boosting up onto the wall. We found a spot where there was a palm tree quite close which he could use as the first two steps. I stood next to the wall with my shoulder as the next step and he stepped onto me and then up onto the wall. Hooray. Only problem was, it was a steep drop on the other side with no hope of breaking the fall. He was stuck on top of the wall.

Plan B. I set off out into the oasis in search of a ladder that we could pass up and then over. I struck lucky early. In the field of carrots and turnips about 100 metres from our gate, a woman was working.

Me: 'Peace be upon you, my sister.'
Jamila (as I later learned, Jamila means 'Beautiful One'): 'Upon you be peace. How are you?'
Me: 'Good, thank you. Excuse me but can you help us? The key to our gate doesn't work and we need to climb over the wall. Do you have a ladder?'

She did, so we walked round through the little street of clay houses and into her home, a big square courtyard opening onto a number of rooms. All the way over, she had been apologising because the ladder wasn't new. In fact, it was perfectly solid and handmade from wood. Heavy, but exactly what we needed. I carried it back, but it ended up not being necessary because in the meantime Andy had scrambled over the wall and we were in.

My first view of my new home. The evening sun was setting and the light was catching the tips of the tall palms at the far end of the garden. Two traditional houses faced each other across the large garden of soft succulents and spiky cacti. My overwhelming impression was of tranquillity and welcome. I could hear a pigeon cooing gently and two white butterflies danced ahead of me. My house is a long, low building built in the traditional style with red clay, poplar pillars on the terrace and turquoise shutters. It is a mini work of art, with geometric tiles and planters filled with pink and white geraniums and a tall, green, fleshy plant lining the terrace where there is a little seating area covered in faded turquoise mirrored cushions and a table with two chairs where I can write and eat.

Inside it is one long room, with a tiled floor and bamboo ceiling with poplar beams. At one end there is a bed built against the wall and at the other end a couch and table under two filigree brass wall lights that cast patterns on the ceiling. The kitchen area stretches along one wall, with tiled top and storage underneath hidden by curtains made of the local *shkka* cloth patterned in brown and orange with cream dots. At the far end, through an arch, is the bathroom with hot water powered by the boiler outside, which I was to find out does have a wee tendency to go out mid-shower and needs a knack to relight it. Everything is simple. There is just enough; not too much and not too little.

The garden is a delight and reaches right out round the back. There are trees and flowers and little seating areas. There is also a plunge pool for summertime when things get really hot and a fire pit for night-time barbeques. Everywhere you look, there are waving fronds of palm against the blue sky.

That first evening I released the cats from their travel cage prison and into the garden, wondering what they would make of all this nature after their rooftop terrace in Essaouira. The young one, Squeaky, spent the whole night rushing in and out of the house, up and down the trees, rolling in the dirt and chewing at bits of grass. She'd run back to me at intervals and *miaow* at me, as if to say, 'Wow! Amazing!' I agreed. The old lady, Nellie, surveyed the garden, then turned back to the turquoise cushions and settled herself down in the last patch of the day's sunlight.

The next day, I went off to give the ladder back to Jamila. She was baking her bread for the day, sitting cross-legged on the floor, kneading away, with her daughter, Ibtihal, and her niece, Noura. She told me that she lived here with her brother and her father and her two children. She had gone to Casablanca to get married but had been widowed and had come back. When I asked her why she didn't marry again because she was still young, she asked me where she would find a good man. I didn't have an answer for that one. She took me into the salon area off the main courtyard to meet her father, a venerable man dressed in a cream wool djellaba, who quizzed me about where I was staying and told me that Annette and Peter were much loved in the oasis. Her brother, who had just got back from twelve years working in Spain, was also there. She offered me *bessara*, the morning soup made from white beans, but I refused as I had just had breakfast.

'Jamila, what are you doing?' asked her brother. 'Is she sick, that you are asking her if she wants food? You only ask people when they are sick; you just bring it when they are healthy.' Sure enough, the *bessara* and mint tea arrived. I was already learning about oasis life.

Tighmert is about 17 kilometres long and gets its water from a place that is mysteriously just called 'the source'. There is a network of irrigation channels going through the date palms and patches of cultivated field. The irrigation channels are opened at different times for different homes and farms. Our irrigation channel is opened about once every ten days. When it is, we have to unblock the hole that leads from the channel outside to our well or water store in the garden. There are two blocks: the first is big rocks and some heavy-duty plastic in the irrigation channel, and then there is a pipe into our well with a big plastic cap that we unscrew. The well is about ten metres deep and takes a good hour to fill.

Carrots, turnips, potatoes and onions are all grown in the oasis fields as well as wheat and fassa, a green plant used as animal fodder. Of course, there are also the date palms and olive trees. There are plenty of sheep and goats grazing on the patches of grass and every house has a couple of chickens. There are lots of ruined walls around the oasis. The traditional houses soon decay if they are not maintained and lived in and heavy rainfall can be disastrous. Debbie reported that she had heard ominous booms when she first arrived. It had been raining hard solidly for five days and she was told that the noise was walls collapsing.

The big city of Guelmim is a mere 15 kilometres away and is the main town of the region with a population of around 120,000. It has been a centre of trade for centuries. The people of this region speak a slightly different language, Hassaniya, which is related to Arabic but also has many African language influences, including from Wolof, and is spoken as far afield as Mali and Senegal. It is an inheritance from the great trans-Saharan trade. The people are called Sahrawis, the desert people, and Guelmim is called the Gateway to the Desert, lying as it does on the fringes of the Sahara.

Guelmim rose to prominence as the main trading stop of the south in the eighteenth and nineteenth centuries when it took over from Sijilmassa as that city began to fade. Because of its location on the great plain of south-western Morocco, Wadi Nun (also called Wadi Nul), it was not only on the trans-Saharan route but also on the route to the Atlantic and the emergent trading port of Essaouira. Those links between this area and west Africa right down to Timbuktu cannot be underestimated. The leading tribe in Guelmim region were the Tiknas, and at one point a Tikna became mayor of Timbuktu. The trade network also became a family network, so cousins in Timbuktu would send their goods up to their cousins in Guelmim and vice versa. You can still see those family links in the faces of the people of Guelmim and the clothes that both the men and women wear.

One of the roads to Guelmim goes up a steep escarpment which needs considerable concentration while driving; the hairpin bends are blind corners and prone to sudden blockage from landslides. This makes it ideal territory for hold-ups and it used to be called the 'Valley of the Thieves' because bandits would lie in wait for the caravans and ambush them as they negotiated one of the thirteen hairpins that wind up to the top of the pass.

The heritage of the slave trade can be clearly seen in Guelmim, but being the descendant of a slave is now considered a kind of *baraka* or blessing. I was told this by Romain, a French anthropologist who I met in the town when I was making the BBC Two programme. He told me:

The descendants of the slaves make some rituals, you know, and music and everything. All the white families go to these rituals. If a white woman cannot have babies or has problems in the pregnancy, she goes there, to these rituals, and asks for the black population to give her a blessing to have a baby. And if and when she has a baby, the baby is considered part of the slave family, a descendant of the slaves. So, you see how a white man for example can become black, part of a black family, because of this blessing by the descendants of slavery.

In the glory days of the trade, the camel market at Guelmim was the biggest in all of north Africa, supplying the caravans crossing the Sahara which were often hundreds of camels strong. It still exists, and the best time to visit is very early on a Saturday morning.

It is held in a large square just inside the walls of the town. It is not primarily a camel market, but a general livestock market. When I visit, there are hundreds of sheep and goats *baaing* and *maaing*, a few dozen docile cows and a handful of camels who are now sold for their meat rather than for transport. There are almost no women in sight and the men are dressed against the dawn cold in black or stripy woollen djellabas. The animals all huddle in little groups, some lying down, others with their feet hobbled, and some of them protesting loudly against their current circumstances. Traders grab them and feel how meaty they are, then commence long and convoluted negotiations, ending in smiles and tea. It is a market for business of course, but it is also an opportunity to meet and talk and is clearly a social occasion.

I head for the few camels there are and spot my first women. They are deep in conversation with the merchant who is showing off a couple of fat specimens. They tell me they are buying for a wedding and the proud vendor tells me that his biggest camel will provide enough meat for 300 hungry guests. I like the look of the sole white one, which is called Ra'as ('head' in Arabic), because the white ones used to lead the caravans. Arabic is a very rich language and is estimated to have a vocabulary seven times as big as English. Although we have our special names for different stages of an animal's life and for different breeds – Belted Galloways (cows), Cheviots (sheep) – we are nowhere near being in the same league.

Al Fahal – a male camel who is very virile
Al Midifaa – a fat, woolly camel
Al Shamlal – a light, fast camel
Al Saood – a female who has given birth prematurely
Al Sharif – an old camel

Sharif is a really nice name as it is a term of respect and honour – the steward of Mecca, the holiest place in Islam, is called the Sharif of Mecca. Clearly, if you make it to a ripe old age as a camel, you deserve that respect.

As I was showing off my knowledge of camel names to the merchant, carefully memorised for just such an occasion, I spotted something weird going on. A big camel had been brought to its knees and was apparently being milked, except it wasn't a female and it wasn't its teats that were being pulled. In fact, it was a male camel and it was being made to pee into a bucket. Sitting on a stool close by was a tired, sick-looking woman, who was watching the proceedings. I went over to ask her what was happening. She told me that she had come to the market to buy camel pee because she was very sick; she had cancer. Camel pee, she said, is very good for you and helps cure lots of illnesses, including cancer and diabetes. She also told me that it could help clear the body of the *jinn*, the evil spirits that cause illness. When the steaming bucket was brought over, she gulped down a glass of the liquid and took the rest of it away in a bottle.

Part of the reason to move to the oasis was to explore the magnificent desert country around it, and on day two of my stay, I headed off to the mountains across the road with Debbie. We set off early, when the mountains were still shrouded in mist. The first section was easy, walking across the flat red earth. In the distance we could see a cultivated field and an industrial polytunnel.

We stopped to talk to the men who were loading up sacks onto their truck. The sacks were full of green broad beans, picked the day before and going off to the big market in Guelmim. They were quite shy with us but shook hands. We could hear the sound of guns going off and asked what it was.

'*Al jaysh!* ('the army') But don't worry, they are far away, they won't shoot you.' Phew. As we carried on, I could see little scurrying movements out of the corner of my eye. We stopped and stood very still and watched as field mice popped out of their holes to make their way towards the tasty beans. They were quite big, about the size of a gerbil, and there were lots of them.

A little further on, there was a dried river bed sunk down into the earth. In it we found clusters of white seashells that had been exposed years ago when the water flowed through. Hundreds of them, grouped in little clusters, and testament, I assume, to the fact that this area was once submerged under the sea. Geology is sometimes the most dramatic history and in this area you can see where the hills have been pushed up or the earth compressed into different layers of salty white granite and sparkling fool's gold. Although there was no obvious water, there were some tiny white flowers with yellow centres growing in the middle of the sand. Their leaves were long and triangular, dipping into the middle in order to collect the dew to give them the moisture they needed.

From the top of a small hill we looked down onto a little desert encampment comprising a squat building with tents scattered beside it and a couple of camels further up on the slopes beyond. I was hoping that we would get to meet whoever was living there, and sure enough Moroccan hospitality did not disappoint. As we walked down a woman came out of one of the tents and beckoned us over. The tent was boiling hot inside because she was making lunch: bread and goat stew. She had a hob powered by camping gas on the go for the stew and a small oven about the size of a crisp carton with two shelves, also powered by camping gas, for the bread. The bread was nearly ready and as we talked she flipped it over expertly. Her daughter had taken the hand cart to go and collect water from a nearby well where the water was sweeter and had left her looking after her granddaughter, who was sleeping but had a little rope tying her to the side of the tent so she couldn't toddle off. She woke up and when she saw us immediately started bawling her eyes out at these strange women.

'It's your hair,' said Ighiyya to Debbie, who has long blonde hair. 'She has never seen anything like it before.' Soon the bread was ready and we each tore off a chunk, tossing it up and down to cool it. Ighiyya had pulled out a little pot of the special preserved butter that is used here. It is boiled and keeps for weeks and tastes slightly rancid, but I have acquired a taste for it and tucked in. By the time we got up to go, the baby had got used to us and even produced a smile. Ighiyya told us to come back any time and we headed back, deciding to leave the further hills for another day.

For me, that meant two days later, as I had a real urge to get up to the top of the high ridge behind the encampment. As I was going on my own, I left details with Debbie about the route I was taking and said I would text her when I was down, in case I slipped and twisted something or something else befell me. I retraced my steps to the base of the ridge behind the encampment and started climbing. It took hands as well as feet and I passed a lone juniper tree jutting out which had found a tiny patch of water to nourish it. More flowers peeped out, a little bush of bright pink ones that looked like minute hibiscus and a tall, elegant, white star-shaped bloom on a base of thin, long leaves. The surrounding countryside is so hostile, it makes the finding of these little gems feel extra special. They would go unnoticed in an English country garden, but here they shine.

After another hot half-hour or so of clambering, I reached the top to be buffeted by the winds on top of the ridge. In one direction, I could see all the way across the fields and green-houses to our oasis and the mountains behind it. In the other direction, Guelmim shimmered faintly, and behind me there was an endless swell of hilltops. Tantalising, but for another day. I'd reached my ridge top and I wanted to go back down and say hello to Ighiyya.

Back near the encampment, I was met with the sheep dogs barking and warning me off. The noise brought out a young woman dressed in purple who chucked a stone at the dogs and beckoned me in. Her face was full of life and she gestured animatedly to me to come into the tent and sit down. Her name, it transpired later, is Fatimatsu, and she is deaf and barely speaks, having had mumps as a child. In the tent was Khwayddin, a woman in her seventies with no teeth but a welcoming smile nonetheless, and Khadija, a plump, pretty girl of twenty, as she told me proudly. 'Too young to get married; I'm looking for a good one.'

I sat down and tea was brewed and we chatted away. Fatimatsu followed our faces eagerly and when I mouthed my name to her slowly was able to say it back to me and tell me her name, to our mutual delight. Khwayddin asked me to take her picture but drew her veil across the lower part of her face – 'no teeth!' she said. Her photo shows just her eyes, nose and cheekbones, swathed in a brown–purple veil. Her skin is weathered with lines at her eyes and on her forehead. Her eyes are outlined in black kohl and a greyish hazel. High, defined cheekbones and a noble, straight nose make her beautiful. When I showed the women the photos of themselves and then revealed the photos I had taken of Ighiyya and the baby, they were delighted. 'Ahhh. You are clever! You didn't tell us you were here before. By God. You are one of us now. You are a Sahrawi.'

Khwayddin asked me if I would like to see her goats, to which there is only one polite answer. We went outside and she showed me the nanny with her three kids. She'd given birth a few days before. One of the kids was very weak and could barely stand. 'Three is too many,' said Khwayddin. 'This one will die.' I left in a flurry of kisses and headed back home.

When I had imagined living in the oasis, I had imagined a rather solitary life. I should have known better. My social calendar here is packed with generous invitations. Friday is couscous day and Debbie and I have been invited to eat with Ali and Mbarka and their family. Ali comes to collect us at 12.30 and we walk through the oasis to his family's house. He lives in a large compound with his three brothers and their families. We are met with kisses by the two children, Mubarak (eight) and Ibtisam, which means 'smile', (ten) and Mbarka's brother, Salih, and ushered into the salon and onto the comfortable cushions. There is a clay brazier, blazing with hot coals and a teapot bubbling happily on top. The table is laden with bowls of dates, almonds, walnuts, little sweeties a bit like smarties and crunchy, sugar-coated seeds. We settle in and watch Ali as he performs the tea ritual, pouring the tea in and out of the glasses.

'This,' he says, 'is Sahrawi tea. I have to make sure that the *rza* is exactly the same for everyone, and when you drink it, you drink down to the *rza*.' The *rza* is the foam that is created by air bubbles going into the tea when you pour it from glass to glass – in the north of Morocco it's called '*kaskoosha*'. 'When you come to a Sahrawi's house to drink tea, you have to drink three glasses,' he explains. 'Often we will come in and drink three glasses, go out the door, then come back and drink another three.'

While we are drinking tea and I am fending off constant offers of walnuts and other goodies because I know that an enormous couscous is about to appear, we ask how Ali and Mbaraka met. I'm especially interested because Ali is a Sahrawi and Mbarka is an Amazigh, a Shluh. It is Salih, Mbarka's brother, who responds.

'What you have to know is that the Sahrawis like to marry the Shluh. They are very good women and the family does not put conditions on the bridegroom like a Sahrawi family does. If you want to marry a Sahrawi, it will cost you the same as a house, around twenty million.' I try to work out what counting of the dirham this is in, I think the *ryal*, which means divide everything by twenty to get dirhams. 'You have to give the family of the bride one or two camels, fifty each of the three kinds of materials to make *milfahs* (the women's robe), and at least two million in gold. It costs the same as a house,' he ends triumphantly.

Inspired by the tales of weddings, Mbarka leaves the room and comes back clutching two bags filled with *milfahs* and jewellery and it is dress-up time. Debbie, who is not a show-off, shrinks, and I, who is, dive into the bags. Mbarka shows me the three kinds of *milfah* material: the *kantor*, which is often made in Turkey, the *gaz* and the *shkka*, which is west

African and a kind of loosely woven linen in dark purples and greens with a geometric pattern. She tells me that you never wash a *shkka* because the material is too fragile, so you only wear it for special occasions. Then we start wrapping me in a lilac and dark blue *kandor*. It is a piece of material around 2.5 metres long and half a metre wide. There are two holes, one for your head and one for your arm, and then you wrap the rest about yourself from head to foot. It is surprisingly easy to wear and to walk around and do things in, and I wonder if I can get away with wearing one out and about.

'Now I am going to show you our Shluh wedding jewellery and dress,' Mbarka tells us, and pulls treasure out of the second bag. There is a band for the head with two large hoops of silver which go over your ears, a red and orange striped cloth ('It's real silk,' interjects Salih), which goes over the head, then a band of cloth with red embroidery, a large silver medallion in the middle and rows of dangling silver squares, which goes on the forehead to just above the eyes. On top of this you wear the *piece de resistance*, a crown of five conical silver spikes interposed with large amber beads. Mbarka looks like a princess, with her round face, soft brown skin and big eyes a perfect balance to all that fierce spikiness.

Then it's my turn – but first I have to have my lips blackened. Mbarka shows me how to rub the cloth of the special *milfah* onto my lips to transfer the dye onto them (the cloth is imbued with a black dye). 'When we go to the hammam, we sometimes wear this for the whole day so we can get the black onto our bodies, and then, when we scrub it off, our skin is white and clean,' she tells me. Then I outline my eyes in natural kohl powder with a wooden stick and I start to feel glamorous. The clothes are a big tiered white skirt and the dark brownish-purple *milfah*, which is slightly less glamorous on me, especially since I am already wearing leggings and a T-shirt with a djellaba on top. I feel like one of those fat-bottomed dolls that you can't knock over because they keep bouncing back. The jewellery is fabulous, though, and the really great thing about it all is the fun we are having. Ibtisam and Mubarak are capering around me giggling and taking selfies, Salih and Ali are paying the obligatory compliments and discussing where they can find me a husband, and Mbarka is fussing, smiling, tucking and folding to make sure it looks just right.

We've had two of our obligatory three cups of tea, and the table is cleared ready for the couscous. First we wash our hands, then we all exclaim in delight as the toppling tower of food is place in front of us. I opt for the eating by hand option and Ali joins me. Soon, I have spread couscous far and wide. Ali, on the other hand, is as pristine as if he had been using a spoon. 'I'm a Sahrawi,' he says smugly. The couscous is lamb and delicious, and we all dedicate ourselves to the feast.

Afterwards we lay back on the cushions, praising our hostess and listen to Ali as he recites some poetry for us. I film the kids with my effects app that superimposes monsters and dancing reindeer onto them, which is an enormous hit, and a couple of hours pass. I feel completely at home. Debbie turns to me and says, 'Could they do anything to make us feel more welcome? Could they be any more hospitable?', and she is so right. I say how glad we are to be here and how grateful we are and Salih answers, 'You know, for us, the big days, the happy days are when we have guests. You have your family in Scotland but we also are your family now. We are your family here in Tighmert.'

When we leave, Mbarka presses a gift of *milfahs* on us in

spite of our protestations and we exchange kisses and compliments. But we are not just seen off at the door; the whole family walks us home. Mubarak and Ibtisam grab one of my hands each, letting go only to bring me a flower or show me where their dad's olive trees grow. There is a slight breeze whisking the clouds across the blue sky and rustling the leaves of the date palms. I am walking on the damp red earth and listening to the sound of the birds. My heart is full. I'm in Morocco.

Index

Index

camping
  Atlas Mountains 96
  Marathon des Sables 44, 47, 48, 53, 57
cannabis cultivation 151–5
Capote, Truman 135
carossas (carts) 205
Carthaginians 174, 201
Casablanca 105, 107, 160–70
  half-marathon 164–5
  history of 161, 162–3
  industrial and commercial hub 163
  population 161
  Rick's Café 169–70
  shopping mall 169
Casablanca (film) 126, 169
Catroux, General 175
cats 203, 213–15, 222, 252–3
Cervantes, Miguel de 132
Ceuta 149
Charles II of England 127
Chefchaouen 140, 141, 144, 148–51, 159
  blue-painted houses 148, 149
  cannabis cultivation 151–5
  history of 148–9
  Jewish community 148–9
  Spanish Mosque 149
children
  handicapped 228–31
  share of work 82–3, 179
  street children 46
Cleopatra Selene II 146, 147
clothes, traditional 129, 241, 262–4
  see also djellabas
co-operatives 226
Colquhoun, John 64, 65
Cooper, Tommy 124
Cordoba Caliphate 128
Cornul, Théodore 202
couscous 119, 151, 193–4, 264

cows 99
Crimean War 162–3
crops 91, 254

Dadda Atta 173
Dades Gorge 242, 243
dates 212–13, 238
Daughter of the Desert
  see Marrakech
Dead Sea 141
Debbie (landlady) 248, 250, 254, 257–9, 261, 262, 264
deforestation 156
desert
  fascination of 38–9
  night camping 41
  see also Agafay Desert; Marathon des Sables; Sahara Desert
desert foxes 38
divorce 168
djellabas 108, 111, 166, 188, 224–5
dogs 17–18, 181, 190–1, 260
Douar Samra 79
doughnuts 8–9
dowries 262
dreadlocks 218
dress code, female 166–7
drought 187
drug laws 151, 154
  see also cannabis cultivation
dunes 41, 61, 62
  running on 50–1
dung beetles 39

Eid 194
Eighty Years' War 130
El Hakim, Abd 224, 225
El Inglizi, Ahmed 202
El Kabir, Mohammed 180, 182
El Kalaa 155–6
El Raheem, Abd 228–9, 230–1